Secrecy, Sophistry and Gay Sex In The Catholic Church

The Systematic Destruction Of An Oblate Priest

First Edition

Published by The Nazca Plains Corporation
Las Vegas, Nevada
2011

ISBN: 978-1-61098-212-2
E-book: 978-1-61098-213-9

Published by

The Nazca Plains Corporation ®
4640 Paradise Rd, Suite 141
Las Vegas NV 89109-8000

Cover Photo
Ben Mobley

Author Photo
Les Sterling

Art Director
Blake Stephens

Dedicated to Steven E. Webb

Secrecy, Sophistry and Gay Sex In The Catholic Church

The Systematic Destruction Of An Oblate Priest

First Edition

Rev. Richard Wagner Ph.D., ACS

CONTENTS

FOREWORD

There was a murder, you know.

I have a story to tell. It's a true story that provides an intimate and sometimes disturbing look into the unseemly inner-workings of the Catholic Church. It is primarily a story about how this institution deals with dissent in its midst, but it also shows to what lengths the Church will go to silence a whistle-blower. What I am about to recount happened between 1981 and 1994. It involves the highest levels of the Vatican bureaucracy—The Sacred Congregation for Doctrine and Faith and The Sacred Congregation for Institutes of Consecrated Life, secret documents, corporate incompetence, canonical corruption, and institutionalized homophobia on an epic scale. This is my story; a retelling of my 13-year battle I had with my religious community, The Missionary Oblates of Mary Immaculate, following the publication of my doctoral thesis, *Gay Catholic Priests; A Study of Cognitive and Affective Dissonance*. (NOTE: The complete dissertation is included below as Part 2.)

My name is Richard Wagner. I am a Catholic priest, albeit without formal faculties to act as a public minister. I was ordained in Oakland California in 1975. And I am the only Catholic priest in the world with a doctorate in Clinical Sexology. My research into the sexual attitudes and behaviors of gay Catholic priests in the active ministry is unprecedented and is as fresh and timely today as it was the day it was completed. Following the publication of my dissertation there was a firestorm of international publicity. The press dubbed me "The Gay Priest," but my research and what it implies made patently clear that I wasn't the only gay priest. In fact, there is a sizable segment of the clergy population that is gay and these men are forced to live duplicitous lives of repression in secret. This often creates an atmosphere of extreme isolation and loneliness that can and does drive these men to desperate measures to find emotional and moral support they should be receiving from their Church. These men love their Church, but hate what is it doing to them. And as bad as the situation was back in the early 80's, it's even worse today.

My groundbreaking research broke the code of silence surrounding this delicate topic. The Church's single-minded effort to quash the emerging story and silence me showed that I needed to be "dealt with" in the most severe fashion; an example had to be made of me. If other priests started coming out of the closet and demanding to be treated with dignity and respect it would certainly undercut the entirety of Catholic sexual moral theology—there is no place for non-reproductive sexuality within that paradigm. Needless to say, this notoriety (some say infamy) effectively ended my public ministry.

The irony is that at the same time my story was unfolding an unimaginable scandal, involving hundreds of Catholic priests across the globe, was also brewing. Cardinals, bishops and provincials worldwide were, and still are, furtively shuffling pedophile priest from one crime scene to another. They were, and still are, involved in a massive corporate cover up of their own crimes and those of their brother clergy.

While I was singled out for 13 years of Church vitriol, public character assassination, spiritual depravation and communal shunning, my superiors claimed that they were simply trying to protect the Church from scandal. These same Church leaders and others like them were lying, prevaricating and sabotaging any effort to uncover the burgeoning clergy sexual abuse scandal that would soon rock the front pages of newspapers all over the world. And here again they claimed they were only trying to protect the good name of the Church. But in shielding the identities of the perpetrators, covering up their crimes, blaming the victims and ignoring the severity of the problem, they were actually perpetuating the abuse.

The public panic among Church officials toward me—a single up-front gay priest in their midst—is in stark contrast to their apathetic and anemic response to the systemic clergy sexual abuse that now engulfs them. And there's a reason for that. The Church, then as well as now, uses the specter of gay priests as a scapegoat for their ecclesiastical malfeasance. The faithful are being manipulated by cynical Church leaders, including the Pope, who whip up bogus scandals involving homosexuality, both inside the Church and in society at large. They make it a practice to conflate the notion of a happy, healthy, integrated same-sex attraction with pedophilia, which is an outrageous lie. But the deception continues and it poisons the minds of pious people of faith. It also provides the necessary smokescreen for the thousands upon thousands of childhoods they've actually destroyed while bankrupting their dioceses and rupturing the trust of millions of believers.

I am confident in making the comparison between my struggle and the clergy sex abuse scandal, because I have first-hand knowledge of this criminality. I was sexually molested as a 14-year-old boy in an Oblate seminary in southern Illinois. And not one of the religious superiors I told about these incidents, while I was in formation, did anything about it. Any wonder why I would then seem to have an "attitude" problem especially when it involved my religious superiors?

My story is the story of a Church that will go to any length, even violating its core principles—Gospel values that form the fundamental tenets of faith—to protect its public image. In other words, this is a story of a Church out of control.

I've scrupulously included numerous internal documents below, some of them very sensitive in nature, that pertain to my story exclusively. But despite the very specific nature of these documents, they illuminate how Church leaders respond to a crisis. As in the clergy abuse scandal, no one in the Oblate chain of command can or will accept responsibility for any wrongdoing. And since the cast of characters is constantly changing, everyone can avoid accountability. Each individual hides behind the corporate persona; this in effect provides an effective means of deniability.

The Church, which is generally a stickler for precision and accuracy, can and does claim collective amnesia when the historical record points directly back to it. There is a pattern of evasion and sidestepping, of innuendo and disinformation, lying and public shaming, all in an effort to shift blame and avoid accountability.

As any clergy abuse survivor advocate will tell you, establishing an accurate historical record is essential for making his case; it's also a painstakingly arduous task. However, Church internal documents are often "sub rosa"—put under the seal of ecclesiastical secrecy. The penalty for divulging these documents, or even alluding to them, is excommunication, the same penalty for breaking the seal of confession.

Nor can anyone in a leadership position in the Church truly apologize for injuries inflected, either personally or collectively. When there is a statement of regret it is always halfhearted and presented in the most passive and innocuous way. Such statements may actually concede that an injury happened, but it is never because of anything Church leaders have done or failed to do. And their preferred remedy for this inconvenience is that we all should pray for healing. However, when these same Church leaders are pressed to address the issue of restitution for their egregious deeds, they stonewall. When amends are finally wrestled from them, they claim it is due to their charity and good will, never from their moral obligation. In other words, their deep "regret" is for hardships *endured*, but never remorse for hardships *inflicted*.

When I pressed the Oblate leadership for accountability in my case, as so many advocates for rights of those effected by the clergy abuse scandal have done in their dealing with the Church, the leadership reflexively inverts the blame; they villainize the victim. We victims of ecclesiastical crimes as well as our advocates are immediately recast as malicious persecutors of the Church. Our quest for justice is generally reduced to a grubbing after money. Money, they say, that belongs to God's people. They accuse us of bullying them, the defenseless long-suffering Church leadership. They claim our true objective is to destroy or demean God's Church and to undermine the integrity of Church teaching.

My story begins at its end. On July 28, 1993 I received a formal obedience from my legitimate Provincial superior, Fr. Paul Nourie, OMI. Under my vow of obedience I am obligated to do his bidding. However, both he and I knew that this was a sham obedience, one I actually helped him concoct. This final kabuki-like dance we were doing was purely for show. It was to overcome the only remaining canonical impediment to sealing my fate as an Oblate of Mary Immaculate.

When I refuse*d* the obedience, as I had to, my 25-year membership in the community would soon come to an end. While this was a very sad time in my life, the truth of the matter is that everything that could be lost in terms of my religious affiliation and my priesthood had already been taken from me. I had already been in an ecclesiastical limbo for 13 years. Every possible punishment had already been meted out.

To be clear; Fr. Nourie's contrived obedience was a face-saving effort for the Oblate leadership. Once I'm out of the way no one would ever know what really happened. No one, least of all my brother Oblates, would know that my sacred vows were subverted by our community's leadership to cleanse themselves of any responsibility for the destruction of my priesthood and ministry and the massive breakdown in canonical due process.

It was indeed a sad time for me, but it also set a dangerous precedent, which has the gravest implications for every Oblate, and indeed every Catholic religious, as a bearer of rights. What follows is my last gift to the Church. It is a letter I sent to every member of the Provincial Council, the men who were soon to decide my fate. It is as thorough a presentation of the facts as possible of all the events that lead up to this imminent ecclesiastical fratricide.

CHAPTER 1

Introduction

February 23, 1994

My fellow Oblates,

      Fr. Nourie's obedience of six months ago, ordering me to dissolve all my personal, professional, and financial affairs in San Francisco within 15 days and to move to an Oblate house in Seattle, is not a morally binding or even a coherent requirement. By the leadership's own fault I have not been an Oblate except in name for many years, and until this obedience I have had no official dealings with Fr. Nourie during his entire tenure as Provincial Superior. This obedience is an attempt by the General leadership, under whose direct instructions Fr. Nourie is acting, to bring about my *de jure* dismissal from the Congregation without having to face inquiry into my *de facto* dismissal.

      As an Oblate I was killed off long ago; and now the leadership is attempting to exhume my Oblate corpse and administer to it the appearance of a legal hanging—hoping all the while that no one notices. You owe it to one another if not to me to stop this grotesque deception and to insist conclusively upon the right of every Oblate to just and equitable treatment. If any of you has the least regard for the kind of society you live in, and hence for the kind of men you are, you will at long last *hear* me.

Before I lay out the extraordinary details of this case, I shall devote the rest of this section to a brief survey.

In 1981, following my public self-identification as a gay priest, the Superior General stirred the provincial leadership to initiate dismissal proceedings against me. The latter pressed these proceedings even though I tendered apologies for any scandal I may have caused, provided explanations of my actions and beliefs, and offered a full retraction of any statements that my superiors deemed contrary to Church teachings. Even before the local leadership forwarded the acts of dismissal to Rome, they dissolved all financial and spiritual bonds uniting me with the Congregation and set me adrift. But once the acts were in Rome the formal process stalled, and the general leadership adopted an indecisive and irregular course of action whose overall effect was my dismissal in practice. This aberrant state of affairs, with one illusory interruption in 1988, has gone on for nearly 13 years. During all this time, with no semblance of due process having been applied, I have had no canonical standing in the Congregation, enjoyed no part in the spiritual life of the community, and received no contributions to my livelihood.

The first part of my ordeal consisted of a protracted and diffuse process that no one party to it could define. My requests that the leadership arrange an impartial hearing to examine the history of the case and to clarify my status went unheeded, and the process degenerated into an intermittent, open-ended interrogation into my beliefs and dispositions that the leadership allowed to drag on for seven years. No matter how often or how thoroughly I answered their questions, the representatives and leaders with whom I had to deal—and they were many—resorted to further insinuations of misconduct as the only way to explain a state of affairs that they did not know how to resolve without acknowledging their own egregious errors. The more I protested the lack of due process and observed that my uncanonical separation was becoming more final with every month, the more the leadership judged me to be negative, uncooperative, and unfit to be an Oblate.

Those years involved great personal suffering for me, not only because of the process itself, which was a torment, but also because of the practical termination of my religious and priestly vocations and the consequent need to reshape my life entirely as a layman. The effect of those years was that all viable membership in the Congregation, and indeed its very worth in my eyes, expired. Realizing as well that the leadership was determined that I should leave, my sole concern then was to save my priesthood.

Therefore in 1987 I reached an understanding with representatives of the General Leadership to leave the Congregation voluntarily by finding a bishop who would incardinate me into his diocese. I agreed to this solution, with three conditions: 1) That the leadership publicly affirm me an Oblate in good standing; 2) That they acknowledge at a minimum the doubtfulness of the process to which they had subjected me; 3) That they assure me of a good faith effort to help me in my transition to secular priesthood. The Superior General, Fr. Marcello Zago, OMI, appeared to have met the first two conditions in his letter to me of June 1988, in which he expressed his regrets for the hardships I had sustained since 1981 and embraced me as a brother Oblate. The worth of his gesture, however, depended crucially upon whether the leadership was prepared to follow through with positive efforts to facilitate my transition.

Considering the ruin that the leadership had visited upon my vocation, the personal injuries that I had needlessly and uncanonically sustained, and my willingness to forgive these and leave the Congregation so long as I received help in saving my priesthood, the leadership had the deepest obligation to accord me gracious and unstinting help. Their verbal solicitude and mutual character-witnessing over the years notwithstanding, that obligation was never met, nor was even the semblance of normal standing in the Congregation achieved. Quite the contrary. The local leadership, guided by the General Administration, constantly played interference with my efforts to incardinate in the Archdiocese of San Francisco, while simultaneously refusing to normalize my status by assigning me to the ministry that I had developed after Fr. Zago's apparent exoneration of me in 1988. Two years of hard work toward establishing myself in the Archdiocese of San Francisco—which had every promise of succeeding with a minimum of patience and creative effort by the leadership— were consequently made to fail. That was when my hope of surviving as a priest failed as well.

In 1990 I wrote to Fr. Zago to request information about the appeal process and to lay before him a summary of my grievance, citing the General Administration itself as the party ultimately responsible for all that had happened to me. I wanted the leadership to acknowledge that whatever may have been their individual motives regarding me; their *collective* behavior was unacceptable and wrong. Following the pattern of his predecessor never to allude to the specifics of what I might say in defense of myself, the most Fr. Zago had to say in reply was that my grievance was "most negative". He patronizingly waved it away and instructed me to begin a dialogue with yet a third provincial about other options.

Since I had already lost a quarter of my life in futile effort along those lines, not to mention all the years I had spent preparing for my vocation, I resolved to lose no more. Therefore I have refused to let the case revert again to the provincial level and I have clung to Fr. Zago as the person finally responsible to provide remedy. The history of this case proves beyond question that the leadership has accumulated an enormous moral and material debt to me, and I maintain that a due sense of equity toward a fellow Oblate calls for voluntary and full restitution. This call is the immediate cause of Fr. Zago's instruction to Fr. Nourie to place me under obedience. It is precisely to evade accountability for my degraded condition as an Oblate and as a priest and to elide the Congregation's outstanding debt toward me that now leads the General Administration to contrive this *second* dismissal process.

Key to the leadership's success in this endeavor is simplicity to the point of deception. This simplicity is manifested in Fr. Zago's mock-bewildered summation of my case in his last note to me of June 25, 1993: "I cannot see how you can pretend to have a financial claim towards the Congregation from whom you received your formation without giving back the promised missionary commitment." And again it is shown in Fr. Nourie's laconic remark in August 1993 when he states that my moving into an Oblate residence was necessary "... if being an Oblate is to have any significance whatsoever."

The leadership hopes that such vague insinuations of misconduct—couched always in protestations of their unflagging good will—will justify this obedience and my eventual dismissal. In a letter written to me after I declined his obedience, Fr. Nourie wrote: "...your absence from the community is considered illegitimate. As you know, such absence, if protracted, can constitute cause for your dismissal from the Congregation." But three years before this, at the time of my appeal to the General Administration, Fr. Zago remarked: "When I wrote to you in June of 1988, I did not sanction in any way the continuation of your absence from community."

The innuendo centered on the word 'absence' is crucial to the leadership's effort to obtain my *de jure* dismissal, and I shall examine it closely toward the end of this history. For now I shall simply note that the term entered the process in the summer of 1987, when certain Oblate representatives surreptitiously defined my situation as "tolerated absence." Afterward, the leadership deliberately planted this harmless-sounding label in virtually all their official documentation of my case. The meaning of the term and the reason for its concerted repetition are unmistakable in hindsight: it is propaganda designed to create the false impression that my peripheral standing in the Congregation is the result of my unlawfully absenting myself at some indeterminate point in the past rather than the result of the leadership unlawfully banishing me.

In short, it is an attempt to sweep the history of this 13-year legal aberration under the rug of Canon 665 §2, simply by *declaring* me guilty of unlawful absence. This attempt to transfer culpability through the repetition of a word, however, cannot survive an impartial reading of the dossier. Thus the leadership hopes that the present obedience and the ensuing six-month "absence" will be sufficient to procure my dismissal without having to look any deeper into the history that explains the emergence and persistence of the much longer "absence."

My defense—as always—is to bring that history to the fore.

CHAPTER 2

1980 - 1983

On November 21, 1980, I published an article in *The National Catholic Reporter* entitled *Being Gay and Celibate—Another View*, written in response to an anonymous article published earlier in the same paper. The anonymous author began his article by stating, "Right now, I do not have the courage to sign this with my name. I stand alone in faith. Perhaps I shall write again and take that risk." He went on to explain: "I am writing to share my reflections with the many gay priests and religious who are suffering while coming to grips with their identity—those who are alienated, isolated, confused, afraid and hurting."

The author was concerned with the repressive, even phobic atmosphere that surrounds this subject in the Church and with the consequent hiddenness that typifies the lives of homosexual priests and religious. He wanted to spread the good news of his experience that one can be gay and celibate and acceptable to God. I fully sympathized with the unknown author's sense of isolation and with his wish to be open about his sexual identity without fear of reprisals, and I agreed with his opinion that sexual orientation does not condemn a person in the eyes of God or disqualify him or her for a celibate vocation.

On the other hand, I was struck by his simplistic and judgmental attitude toward gay priests or religious who, for whatever reason, engage in sexual activity. His running toward epithets such as 'cheaters,' 'hypocrites,' and 'exploiters' to characterize such priests seemed to me an evasion of the human depth and seriousness of the problem. Such condemnation, I wrote, "can only serve to reinforce the feeling of isolation and anguish which so many gay priests and religious experience in today's church."

At the time I wrote this reply, I was also completing my doctoral dissertation, *Gay Catholic Priests: A Study of Cognitive and Affective Dissonance*, based on three years of extensive study of gay Catholic priests, in the active ministry, across the United States. This research had made me sensitive to the thoughts and emotions with which homosexual priests were grappling with their dual identities and practices, and I had little patience for dismissive platitudes, especially coming from one who was himself a gay priest.

My article did contain some provocative-sounding statements, such as the one quoted by the *New York Times*: "One should not underestimate the severe psychological conflict and self-preoccupation, which total sexual self-denial, can engender in some people." But my object was not to condone, much less to encourage, sexual activity by anyone. My sole aim was to bring a critical perspective to bear on a subject that was all too easily locked away with the key labeled "bad priest." Being gay myself and "out" to my superiors, I had long felt that homosexuality in the Church eventually had to be brought into the open and discussed with candor and maturity. That is why I requested permission from my superiors to develop an up-front gay ministry in the first place and why they had sent me to graduate school to obtain credentials qualifying me for such work.

During my personal development I gradually came to believe that the first step toward bringing this subject into the open was for gay priests and religious to make ourselves known—in much the same way as gay people were coming out in society at large—and that was the prime motive for adopting gay Catholic priests as the subject of my dissertation and for submitting my article. Together they were my own coming out, and my encouragement of others to do the same. I took the risk, in other words, that the anonymous author had the prudent good sense not to take. I ended my article with the following remark (eliminated by the editor of *The National Catholic Reporter*, along with much else unfortunately, from the published version):

> The anonymous author concludes with a call to courage, the courage to believe that we are acceptable to God regardless of our sexual identity. I agree wholeheartedly that we must have that courage. But we must have the courage for more than that. We must have the courage also to break out of our anonymity and isolation, and the courage to ask openly, honestly, and deeply the questions, which press upon us so urgently.

I would repeat this coming out in a disastrous television interview taped on February 6, 1981, on which I shall have much more to say below.

These acts of public self-identification are the "crimes" that ultimately would bring ruin to my religious and priestly vocations and have brought us, 13 years later, to our present deliberation.

Superior General Fernand Jetté, OMI, after reading my article in Rome, wrote to Provincial Superior Paul Waldie, OMI, on February 8, 1981, with the following instructions:

> [Fr. Wagner's] declaration: "I, too, am a gay priest..." and the principles he expresses in that article are incompatible with the teachings of the Church and with the vows he has pronounced.
>
> If there isn't in [Fr. Wagner] a sincere disposition to change his way of life and to fully accept the requisites of the commitments he has taken, the simplest solution would be that he personally ask to leave the priesthood and religious life. Otherwise—even though the solution would be a still more sorrowful one—he will be dismissed from the Congregation.
>
> ...By doing nothing, we are not helping this confrere who has installed himself in a false life, nor are we helping the People of God who are scandalized by such attitudes, nor are we helping the Religious Institute which loses all credibility.

Attached to Fr. Jetté's letter was an even more explicit document entitled *How to Proceed?* written by the Procurator General of the Institute, Fr. Michael O'Reilly, OMI. It began:

> Father Wagner should be made to face up to the incompatibility of is life-style with the commitment he made by Religious Profession and the reception of Sacred Orders.
>
> If he is not prepared to make an honest effort to abstain from homosexual activity, he should be helped to come to a decision to seek release from his obligations as a priest and religious.

From my public self-identification as a gay priest, Frs. Jetté and O'Reilly concluded that I had adopted patterns of belief and conduct amounting to an active abandonment of my religious commitments. This was a completely false assumption on their part. But neither official so much as suggested the need for further inquiry to ascertain the facts. Guilt was presumed from the beginning, and despite my vigorous protests in the months to come of this mode of administering justice, the process Frs. Jetté and O'Reilly set in motion moved inexorably forward.

Fr. Waldie received Fr. Jetté's letter on February 20 and called me to the Provincial House the following day to read it. I was stunned. Since its publication in late November, the *National Catholic Reporter* article had generated no fallout at all, of which I was aware. No letters to the editor were published condemning the piece; I received no negative mail or phone calls; the response of friends and acquaintances was mostly bland; and Fr. Waldie, who read the article when it was published, responded mildly, certainly not with alarm.

My coming out in the press was a non-event on the local scene and virtually forgotten by early February. Of greater concern at that time were the alarming events associated with an interview taped for the local television program, *Bay Scene 7*. From the perspective predating Fr. Jetté's letter this interview was the first sign that I was on the wrong track.

On February 6, 1981, the date the TV interview was taped, I was an Oblate in good standing, not accused of misconduct, under no ban, and certainly not figured as a renegade priest intent upon scandalizing the Christian community. I was an Oblate scholar whose research was regarded as an illuminating contribution to the understanding of a long-hidden aspect of Church life and was being received with a sobriety appropriate to the theme. I was also an out and proud gay priest. I was out to my provincial and most of the men I lived with before I was ordained and I was now out publicly thanks to the *National Catholic Reporter* article.

Looking back, one easily sees the danger lurking in my success. It was all but inevitable that identifying myself as a gay priest while discussing a large sample of gay priests who were at once sexually active and critical of the vow of mandatory celibacy would lead many viewers to infer that I myself must be one of the sample.

I should point out that when I designed my research project, with the help of my advisor, Wardell Pomeroy, Alfred Kinsey's associate, I proposed to find a sample of 50 self-identifying gay priests, not 50 sexually active gay priests. Although I expected that there would be some sexual activity in my sample, I could not have anticipated that 48 of them would be currently involved in partnered sex, a surprising and remarkable result. In hindsight it is difficult to see how I could have expected that my own public coming out, a risky endeavor all by itself, could possibly be combined with a public discussion of the results of my research without disaster resulting. "Pride goeth before a fall," as scripture says. But in this case the pride was not rebellion but simply the satisfaction of knowing that I had done my job well and the conviction with which I publicly "stood up" for gay priests and religious.

In neither the NCR article or the taped television interview was I condoning the behaviors of my sample, much less intending a public exhibition to my private life. At that time I had no sense of danger, much less that I had placed my vocation in mortal peril. In short, I believed—deluded as I no doubt was—that as a self-identified gay priest I could give an interview on my research, that I was qualified to do it, and that the result, though inevitably controversial, would be overall constructive. I could not have anticipated the ghastly impression that the media's craving for sensation on the one hand and the Church's dread of scandal on the other would together generate.

How did the *Bay Scene* fiasco come about? In mid-January the program's director approached the president of my graduate institute (The Institute for the Advanced Study of Human Sexuality) about the possibility of doing a segment on the Institute. The president told the director of my dissertation and suggested that I would be a good representative of the Institute. Within days I was introduced to the director. I assure you that before doing the interview I asked for guarantees about the type of questions that they would ask, and I pointedly stressed the seriousness of the matter, the importance of keeping attention focused on the dissertation, and the need to avoid any hint of sensationalism. Moreover, I inquired with others about how much I could rely upon the director and the host of the program to keep their focus on my research, and I was told I could trust them.

The interview was taped during a two-hour session. Several times I interrupted the interviewer to insist that certain questions not be asked. I objected in particular to his repeated attempt to turn the conversation to my private life. I have also recorded my conviction that I did not answer what I take to be the most provocative question from the point of view of Fr. Waldie's subsequent allegations, but that that question was provided with an answer from a different part of the interview after taping. I was completely inexperienced at this sort of thing and had no idea of the editorial liberties that television programmers take with taped interviews. On the whole, however, despite some misgivings, I felt that the taping had gone well, and I signed the release before leaving the studio. As it turned out, the station reduced and rearranged two hours of tape to a bare 15 minutes of airtime, and the result was as far removed as it could possibility be from what I had expected.

From my point of view, it is what happened to the tapes after I signed the release that constitutes the real scandal of the *Bay Scene* interview. While I am not saying that two wrongs make a right, a second wrong can make the first look very much worse than it actually was. In this case the first wrong—I have never denied this and virtually begged to be forgiven for it—was that I gave myself to such an enterprise to begin with. The second wrong was that the program was hijacked and turned into an opportunity to discredit my work and me. The story of how the tapes on February 6 passed into other people's hands and became theirs to tamper with at will is fantastic; and were it not that it all happened to me and the proof for it all exists, I would myself not believe that members of the local church could stoop to such tactics. Here, however, I shall keep the details to a minimum.

Fr. Robert Sunderland, SJ, a Jesuit working on the editorial board at KGO-TV heard that a program involving a homosexual Catholic priest had been taped and was scheduled for airing on February 14. The Jesuit apparently found the very idea preposterous and concluded that Richard Wagner must surely be a priest impostor. He contacted the Archdiocese with this information, and the Archdiocese then contacted Fr. Waldie. Fr. Waldie informed the Archdiocese that, yes, Fr. Wagner is a Catholic priest and an Oblate in good standing. Having learned that Fr. Wagner was not only a legitimate priest but enjoyed the good opinion of his superior, Archdiocesan representatives contacted the management of KGO-TV, arranged a private viewing of the tapes, and persuaded the management to cancel the original program date.

These representatives made no further attempt to contact Fr. Waldie to determine what was at issue or to arrange a happier solution. Nor did they contact me to see if I would not agree to changes that they would find more acceptable or even to cancel the program altogether, an alternative I certainly would have preferred under the circumstances. Instead the solution, from their point of view, was to re-edit the tape and end it with a five-minute "rebuttal" by Fr. Gerald Coleman, SS, an instructor of moral theology at St. Patrick's Seminary in Menlo Park, California. Fr. Coleman's remarks decisively shaped the subsequent perception of my character and views and more than anything else explains the uncritical acquiescence and haste with which Fr. Waldie set about to expedite Fr. Jetté's instructions. Fr. Coleman's remarks were a frame-up, a conscious and deliberate attempt to defame me. And in the tumultuous and panicked aftermath of the program, Fr. Waldie, despite having no reservations about me, or my work up until this point, discards everything he knows about me after years of living together and accepts Fr. Coleman's every word as the truth.

Fr. Coleman's contributions were nothing more than a string of *ad hominem* statements. This is so clear that it is difficult to understand how intelligent people, especially those responsible for assuring that I was treated fairly, were unable to see through them.

Fr. Coleman attempted to do three things: to discredit my research, which to him meant denying that homosexuals exist in the priesthood; to attribute to me the preposterous view that the dictionary definition of celibacy somehow exempts homosexual priests from the requirement to live a sexually abstinent life; and to insinuate, to the extent of directly asserting, that everyone must assume that I personally am sexually active.

It was Fr. Coleman's remarks, not mine, that finally condemned me. His reasoning was essentially the same as Fr. Jetté's and it provides an excellent illustration of what gay priests and religious mean when they talk about their sense of repression, fear, and isolation in the Church. Here is a sampling of the logic with which any gay priest who dares to speak his sexual identity in public can expect to be confronted.

Fr. Coleman begins his part of the interview with an admission that he has "never read or seen" my dissertation, and then he sets out to show that its conclusions cannot possibly be true. One might wonder how he could challenge the study's conclusions without having read the study, and the answer is, with a syllogism. He observes that a study published by sociologists Alan Bell and Martin Weinberg entitled *Homosexualities* had been "critiqued" because "homosexuals studied homosexuals". He then generalizes: "Whenever that happens you will automatically get a bit of prejudice and bias [in favor of homosexuals]. Inevitably that is so in this situation as well." Since Richard Wagner has admitted being homosexual, Fr. Coleman reasons, there is no need to review his research to know that its conclusions—whatever they might be—are "automatically" and "inevitably" unreliable. (NOTE: Coleman is wrong; both Alan Bell and Martin Weinberg are heterosexual men.)

After disposing of my research, Fr. Coleman then turns to the idea that my work and remarks were an attempt to rationalize or justify homosexual activity on the part of homosexual priests. "I think," he says "it is very important to redefine what Fr. Wagner was indicating; that [to the contrary] celibacy is really a very positive commitment on the part of priests to serve the church in a chaste sort of way, which rules out any kind of genital activity. And thus…I do not see how anyone can justify the two positions simultaneously."

The interviewer's next line of questioning has to do with the dictionary definition of celibacy, and it is here that Fr. Coleman insinuates that I was attempting to justify homosexual activity by citing the dictionary definition. Fr. Coleman reminds the audience that the concept of celibacy "is taken over into an ecclesial, theological context" and thus is made to include homosexual activity. On the whole, the viewer is left with the impression that Fr. Wagner prefers the "secular" definition over the "ecclesial" definition, that he does not think of celibacy as a positive commitment, and that he personally is trying to have it both ways.

Fr. Coleman is simply repeating in a vague, pedantic way an idea that I had stated more precisely: "The church presumes that there is no [licit] sexual activity outside heterosexual marriage, and thus she feels that a renunciation of heterosexual marriage is enough to satisfy a commitment to sexual abstinence." Again, the overwhelming impression Fr. Coleman leaves with the viewer is that not only is Fr. Wagner automatically and inevitably biased in his research and personally trying to have it both ways but he is theologically stupid as well.

Fr. Coleman's closing remark—the remark that also ends the program and informs the passive viewer as to the meaning of what he or she has just seen—is the noose around Fr. Wagner's neck: "…when one says that term 'homosexual priest,' the assumption is that they are acting out their homosexuality; as we wouldn't normally use the term 'heterosexual priest' because if we say that we are acting it out." Since Fr. Wagner applied "that term" to himself, he must be assumed to be acting out his sexuality. So declares Fr. Coleman. (NOTE: Coleman is wrong again, because no heterosexual priest would hesitate to identify himself as straight. And no one would think less of him if he did.)

Now if Fr. Coleman had not been on a mission to destroy my reputation, he might have said that while many uninformed or careless people resort to this *ad hominem* argument, it is wrong for them to do so considering Church teaching, which has distinguished between the morally neutral homosexual condition and overt homosexual conduct since 1976. He might also have pointed out that the distinction between orientation and behavior has been a virtual cliché in the scientific, legal, and moral literature on homosexuality for more than a century.

Interestingly, shortly after the *Bay Scene* controversy died down, Fr. Coleman himself, in a series of articles on homosexuality in the archdiocesan newspaper, stressed the importance of the distinction between the homosexual condition and homosexual behavior. In his commission to rebut Fr. Wagner, however, Fr. Coleman did not mention the distinction and elevated the *ad hominem* fallacy of inferring overt conduct from psycho-sexual identity to a rule of thumb that everyone ought to apply in the case of self-identified gay priests and religious.

Of course it is simply false to say, as Fr. Coleman does in the quotation above, that if a heterosexual priest were to discuss his sexuality "we" would assume that he is involved in sexual activity. From St. Augustine right down to our own day there is a vast body of literature by celibate men discussing the difficulties of the celibate life given the power of the sexual urge and the attractions of the female sex. A strikingly pertinent example of this was provided when the public furor over the Bay Scene program was in full swing. Fr. Miles O'Brien Riley, a spokesman for the San Francisco Archdiocese and a Bay Area television and radio personality, when asked by the *New York Times* (February 27, 1981) to respond to the controversy, remarked: "I'm heterosexual and it's damned hard to be celibate and heterosexual with the pressures we face and to go home to an empty room at night. I'm lonely for a woman—he [Richard Wager] is lonely for a man."

None of my public remarks about my same-sex orientation come close to this type of graphic language, and that Fr. Riley or any other self-identifying heterosexual priest can talk about his sexual desires in the context of his celibate commitment with impunity is a remarkable illustration of the double standard that applies to homosexual persons. You can be sure that if Fr. Coleman were to suggest in public that Fr. Miles, given his statement, must be acting out his sexuality, it would not be Fr. Miles who would find himself in trouble.

Of course Fr. Coleman was right when he said that heterosexual priests do not normally refer to themselves as heterosexuals. But the explanation of that is the same as the explanation of why Fr. Miles was not silenced for confessing his longings for a woman. The prevailing assumption has always been that *all* priests are "good" heterosexual men. Moreover, there are those who feel duty bound to deny and conceal that the church has in her service a significant population of men and women who happen to be homosexual. Again, the very reason I spent three long years compiling the data for my dissertation.

After the take-over of the *Bay Scene* program, the producer, who had been taken off the assignment, kept me informed of developments. Because he had persuaded me to do the program in the first place, he was effusively apologetic, explaining that the events then taking place were "the craziest thing I have ever seen." On February 19, he brought VCR equipment and a copy of the final version of the program to my apartment. I felt sick when I saw what a shambles it had become and what a devastating impression it was bound to make.

Two days later, on February 21, Fr. Waldie showed me Fr. Jetté's letter. The following evening of February 22, with no prior announcement, the *Bay Scene* program aired—and from that point forward my voice was drowned out.

During our meeting the previous day, with the TV interview still pending, Fr. Waldie asked me to write a letter explaining my two-month-old article in the light of Fr. Jetté's reaction. The following day the program was broadcast. Within two days "scandal" was breaking all over the Bay Area, and shortly thereafter it was picked up by the wire services. The coincidence of the arrival of Fr. Jetté's letter just as the *Bay Scene* scandal was breaking made my situation extremely precarious. The only plan of action I could come up with was to go ahead with the letter Fr. Waldie had asked me to write. If I could provide a satisfactory explanation and apology for my November article, hopefully the television imbroglio could be dealt with on its own later.

At the same time, I realized that the Superior General's assertions were essentially of the same *ad hominem* variety as Fr. Coleman's and that to answer the one was largely to answer the other, and I wrote my letter with that in mind. Nevertheless, it was imperative to keep the two events distinct; for if they were allowed to merge into a single blurred impression of misconduct, then truly all hope for justice would be lost.

In the first five days of pandemonium following the TV interview, I composed the letter Fr. Waldie requested, completed it on February 26, and hand-delivered it to the Provincial House the same day. In the letter I clarified the distinction between being gay and being sexually active; reaffirmed my commitment to religious life by denying the presumption that I had "installed" myself in any other life; offered to repudiate any views my superiors deemed offensive or unorthodox; and forswore further public discussion of homosexuality in the press or media. Above all, I expressed my apologies, because despite my deep commitment to the issue of gay identity in religious life, membership in my religious community and survival as a priest were my paramount values. From the day I delivered this letter to its final acceptance by the Oblate leadership seven years later, I consistently argued that it provided the only authentic basis for reconciliation. Given its extremely important role in the controversy, I shall here present the full text.

Dear Father Waldie:

Please forgive this letter's formality, but as Emily Dickenson once wrote, "With death a formal feeling comes." Truly I feel threatened with a kind of death, for priesthood within the Catholic Communion has been my life's blood.

Father, this has been the most agonizing time in my life. When I first entered into this ministry to gay people I knew I would have to face hardships and that these would include suspicion, rumor, and open hostility. But what have I said or done to deserve *this*?

It is one thing for a man to be *accused* of wrong doing, for then he knows he can defend his honor; but it is another to have it *asserted* against him that he is a wrongdoer, for then there can be no question of inquiry and justice. That persons in authority should wish to make serious inquiry into statements I have made or am alleged to have made or into positions I have taken or am alleged to have taken is clearly within their right. But no sound system of jurisprudence begins with a conviction of guilt.

I deny, unequivocally and in good conscience, what has been asserted against me. It has never been my practice to make public profession of my sins; that is a matter strictly between me and my confessor; and no one has the right to demand to know or to presume to know that sacred confidentiality.

As for what I have said in the public forum, my statements must be taken on their own merits and within their proper context. *I have never in any public forum intentionally or knowingly affirmed or denied sexual activity on my part subsequent to my vows of celibacy and chastity.* If in the judgment of my superiors I have made statements, which can be so construed, I am more than willing to deny that in my writing of those statements I intended that they should be so construed.

Father, have I not from the beginning of this pursuit sought your advice and kept you informed? Have I ever practiced deceit or withheld information? Have I not always proceeded in complete openness and good faith?

Prior to you receiving a letter from the Superior General, I had no indication that the path I was pursuing might result in such a calamity. Time and again did you not approve and commend my efforts in this direction? Indeed, just one day before you received that letter was I not greeted with open arms by you and other members of our community for having fulfilled so thoroughly and so well the obligation, which I contracted with you three years before? I now look back on that evening with great sorrow, that our embracing and joy should have become over night such mockery.

From the beginning, as you know, I have made no secret of my being gay. From the first I have tirelessly repeated the difference between being gay and being genitally active. And by no means is this distinction peculiar to me; psychologists and sexologists universally acknowledge the truth and usefulness of this distinction. So that there may be no mistake, I will quote in full my dissertation on this subject:

"Also something should be said about the use of the term 'gay.' The choice of this term over the more pervasively used 'homosexual' or 'homophile' is more than a personal preference. It is used to indicate a higher degree of homoerotic self-awareness. Though an individual might experience homoerotic feelings, and even give them physical expression, the term 'gay' would not be used to describe him unless his homoeroticism was part of his self-identification. In other words, the term 'gay' is used to denote a person's conscious effort to integrate his homosexual orientation with the rest of his personality. This conscious effort presupposes a conceptual framework in terms of which the person tries to understand himself and interact with others. It is important to point out that this definition does not necessarily denote a sexually active lifestyle. It is possible for an individual to self-identify as gay without having a single overt same-sex experience."

Father, when I reached the stage in my course of study of choosing a dissertation topic, I discussed with you on many occasions what the nature of this study would be. Again you approved and supported my efforts. You know and can confirm that I obeyed you and your council's recommendations and prescriptions to the letter, that I did not shirk your advice or resist your instructions and that in every respect I acted honorably and in good faith.

You were among the first people to read my dissertation. Again you commended and encouraged my work. Again you offered no caution or warning, either with respect to its contents or the proper vehicles for making it public. You also read my article in NCR, to which Father Jetté has taken such exception. And it is clear that you thought the article was within the limits of legitimate inquiry, that the issues raised were important ones deserving a rational Christian response and that I neither implicated myself nor in any way degraded or put at risk the clerical dignity.

I mention these things to encourage you to come forward, should it be necessary, to defend my good name.

Father, as you know, special circumstances surrounded my article's publication in NCR, and it is *imperative* that Father Jetté be made aware of these. Let me say without further ado, however, that *it was never my intention to advocate or defend sexual activity on the part of priests and religious, or in any way to challenge the teaching authority of the church in such matters.*

As you know, the article, which appeared in NCR was a serious abridgment of the original manuscript, which I submitted. I had never published before and had no idea of the liberties an editor might take with a manuscript, especially one, which treated subjects as complex and controversial as these. As you know, I was shocked to discover how my original manuscript had been edited and immediately wrote the man responsible, expressing my astonishment and disappointment. I have a copy of my letter as well as this man's reply in defense of his actions; and he himself, if he is an honorable man, will confirm these facts.

Then what were my intentions in writing this article? As you know, it was written in response to an article by another gay priest. And let me point out from the start, with respect to both his article and my own, that the difference between being gay and genitally active, is unambiguously clear.

My article was a response to what I perceived to be three troublesome aspects of his.

First, that the author felt constrained to remain anonymous, that he was *fearful* to disclose his identity, despite his being faithful to his vows. I wanted to assure this person that he need not fear disclosing his identity, and to encourage him to enter into fraternal relationship and dialogue with others who share his plight of hiddenness, isolation and anguish.

Second, I was responding to what I perceived to be the illogic of *his* arguments and the semantic confusion of *his* distinctions, which (in my opinion) tempted him to judge carelessly and harshly those who, for diverse and complex reasons, might engage in sexual activity. In no sense did I state or imply that this person represented persons in authority or that his arguments represented authoritative church teachings on these matters. The arguments presented in my article were addressed solely to him and what I perceived to be his confusion. The arguments in my article are arguments which persons—"those who would still ask"—might and actually do bring against arguments such as *his* —*not* those adduced by the church in support of her doctrines and rules.

In no sense did I intend the teachings of the church as the frame of reference for my article. And let there be no mistake, even if this man's positions happen to be consistent with those of the church, the church's positions are ill-served by the unsound reasons he adduces in their defense. I am persuaded that the church has greatly more cogent and compelling reasons for requiring and enforcing mandatory celibacy for priests and religious than the faulty arguments he adduces. I am convinced that responsible theologians would agree that his arguments are not *the* arguments for a proper and thorough defense of mandatory celibacy. The issue, in other words, was not whether this man was correct in his positions, but whether he was correct in his *defense* of those positions. As for the teachings of the church, they are not for me to judge; they are the province of the duly appointed teachers of the church.

Third, I was responding to what I perceived to be a tendency by this author to assume a facile and dangerous attitude of judgment contrary to Jesus' teaching that we judge not. I wanted to remind this author that as Christians we are under a constant obligation to make every effort to understand, love, and forgive those who fall short in their moral lives. Part of any such effort to understand would be a clear delineation of the questions and reasons such people might pose to explain or justify their behavior. In no sense did I wish to imply that it is not within the clear *right* and *competence* of church teachers to answer such questions and reasons.

In the writing of my article, I made a strenuous effort to put a distance between "those who would still ask" and Richard Wagner, and to avoid assuming a position of advocacy that might be construed as contrary to church teaching. I sincerely thought that I had put the whole complex of issues in a sufficiently clear framework of *inquiry*. For example, crucial arguments are concluded with questions, not declarative sentences; in the presentation of arguments I avoid the first person singular; and in those places where the first person singular is used, I employ locutions such as "I *suggest* that *perhaps*" before the statement that follows. Perhaps I do not know the proper formulas for avoiding advocacy, but I sincerely thought these were adequate. In any case, in the original manuscript I explicitly denied that I was advocating sexual adventuring.

The last paragraph of my original manuscript was a call to Christian courage, understanding and love. This emphasis is at the heart of my ministry to gay people, in or out of religion. The persistent attitude that sums up and dismisses out of hand a whole people as simply degraded and leprous and not worth the time of day is patently contrary to the attitude of the Gospels. In a very real sense, the moral shortcomings of gay people are as a mote compared to the swollen logjam of fear, prejudice, hatred, oppression and complacency in men and women who otherwise strive for righteousness.

Father, anyone who does not understand, or refuses to see, the extraordinary hardships under which these people labor will never appreciate my ministry or the spirit of my article. As you know I personally have had to face the most fanatic intemperance because of being gay and trying to serve gay people. There are those who have condemned my dissertation while openly admitting that they have never read it, those who have shunned my letters apprising them of my work and inviting them to enter into dialogue, and those who have sought to discredit me and my work without ever seeking council with me to determine my true motives and positions. I am convinced that their reactions against me are in fact not against *me* at all, but against some enormity of their own imaginations. The very identification "gay" provokes an almost panic fear in persons who know nothing about my work, and, apparently, do not want to know.

Father, it is pointless for me to further defend my article or my motives for writing it, for, as I have already said, the bottom line is this: *If in the best judgment of my superiors they consider the article or any part of it to be advocating principles contrary to the teachings of the church, then I will freely renounce that article or any part of it that has given offense.*

I would like to say something about my consistent policy with regard to divulging the intimate aspects of my personal moral life. My remarks can be confirmed by numerous individuals both in and out of the church.

From the years of our acquaintance, you yourself can witness to my consistently taking pains to make clear the difference between being gay and being sexually active, and my consistent refusal to discuss the details of my personal moral struggle. Father John Mulligan, SM, of the Institute of Spirituality and Worship in Berkeley, who on several occasions has invited me to speak to groups of priests and religious on sexual topics, will also witness to my carefulness in this regard.

I shall cite only one more salient example. At the Institute for the Advanced Study of Human Sexuality, where I studied for my doctorate and am now an [unsalaried] assistant professor, I have consistently refused inquiries into my personal moral life. In this respect I have been quite unique, for explicit discussion of personal sexual attitudes and behaviors is the rule at this institute, where squeamishness about such topics does not exist. Throughout my three years there I have practiced the utmost guardedness and discretion with respect to my personal moral life, and this in deference and honor to my primary vocation. This can be corroborated by scores of individuals at the Institute, both teachers and students. I might also mention in this context that three of the highest respected professors at the Institute were given copies of the NCR article and asked to comment. They each individually remarked that they could not tell from the article whether I personally was sexually active. To each of them I replied, "That was what I intended, and that is as it should be."

At the beginning of my course of study, my systematic reticence was considered an eccentricity, but by the end, and at present, all understand my position and respect my independence. Throughout my course of study I said nothing, I did nothing, to dishonor my vows. Never has my sojourn at this Institute been an occasion to take my profession lightly or to tolerate tactlessness or insensitivity with regard to my higher calling.

I am persuaded that my life in this highly visible ministry will bear scrutiny. I am not claiming to be free of error but I am convinced that any reasonable person who looks at the evidence and considers the extraordinarily difficult position I occupy will find in me a more than usual disposition and effort to keep within the limits of propriety.

Father, one thing cannot be stressed enough in the process to come, if it must come: *the work into which I entered with the full knowledge and approval of my community is without precedent.* Naturally mistakes were bound to be made. I am the first to admit this. You know that in the past I have sought consultation with authorities in the church to help me formulate legitimate and concrete means of pursuing this ministry. You know that I have been refused such consultations. You know my present willingness and eagerness to enter into dialogue.

As for the trials and errors of these last weeks, I openly confess my share of the responsibility. As you know, prior to you receiving the Superior General's letter, I voluntarily assured you that I would never again use the popular press or media to pursue my ministry. Not even the Holy Father in Rome can remark on sexual topics without his remarks being distorted beyond recognition. How did I imagine that I might be able to do so? In light of this, I am sorry for any injury I may have done the local Church, my community, or my own ministry.

Father, you know that I have never denied the teaching authority of the church. You know that no teaching authority worthy of the name discourages or inhibits free inquiry. The questions and arguments with which I am routinely and inevitably confronted in my work—to which my piece in NCR witnesses—require calm, deliberate, and reasoned answers. For they are not posed in a spirit of defiance; they are an invitation for open, honest, direct dialogue. Our church is preeminently the church of reason; she never shirks dealing with the most complex issues in a dispassionate, detailed, and reasoned way. If I reproduce arguments, which are presented to me, I do so to make clear that those who argue in this vein are more that errant fools to be dismissed or foul sinners to be cursed with epithets. They are human beings endowed with *minds*, who, if they are wrong in their reasoning, must be brought to the truth, not with silence or condemnation (they know these only too well), but with patient reason inspired by love.

Father, you of all people embody and represent this patient reasoning love for me, and I have faith that Father Jetté, too, is a man of patience, reason, and love. In the difficult time to come, if it must come, I pray that we turn a deaf ear to those who slander others; who traffic in hearsay and innuendo; who arrogate to themselves the judgment of God; who make hateful caricatures of those they should strive to understand and love; who systematically seek to discredit rather than reason with those with whom they disagree; who deny that any need exists rather than meet the need with courage, charity, and love.

Finally, I must express my gratefulness for your assurance that during the process to come, if it must come, everything will be done according to law. Never in my life have I had so vivid an insight into the value of the rule of law as against the rule of men. I invite you to begin the process which—I have faith—will justify me in the eyes of the law. As for the eyes of men, let us ceaselessly pray that they may be opened, so that we may at last see face to face and be reconciled in Christ.

Father Waldie, you are always in my prayers.

———————

This letter was as clean an act of abjuration as my superiors could have asked for, and I fully expected Fr. Waldie to forward it to Rome and help me allay Fr. Jetté's misapprehensions. Fr. Waldie, besides being my superior, was a close personal friend, and our relationship was confiding and even confessional in nature. We trusted each other completely, and while hearing his confessions I shared with him more about my personal life and struggles than most religious would share with their peers, much less their major superior. Open-minded, sensitive, prayerful, deeply committed to his religious calling, Fr. Waldie was a role model for me, not least because of the humanity and lack of prejudice with which he befriended me as a brother.

As my major superior, he more than anyone else, encouraged and supported my efforts to develop an up-front gay ministry. When I offered discussion groups on homosexuality to priests and religious at the Graduate Theological Union in Berkeley, he defended me against detractors in the Congregation. He assured me that the community would stand beside me when the going got tough, as we both knew it inevitably would. He sanctioned and arranged community financing for my graduate studies in San Francisco, and I met and talked with him regularly throughout my years of study. I told him of my dissertation topic and arranged with him for payment of my travel expenses when my research required travel to other cities. He read my article in the *National Catholic Reporter* when it was published and he found nothing objectionable in it. I called to tell him about the television interview the day after I taped it. He advised caution and recommended I write an advisory to the bishops of San Francisco and Oakland, which I did. He was among the first to read my dissertation when it was finished in early February and he congratulated me on a job well done. Only two days before the Superior

General's letter arrived from Rome, I was greeted with embraces and pats on the back at Mount Mary Immaculate. On the day we met to discuss the General's letter, Fr. Waldie agreed with me that the General was overreacting, and he urged me to write an explanation with that in mind.

But when the TV interview aired and the heat was on, everything changed between Fr. Waldie and me. In a startling turnabout that I shall never forget as long as I live, he abruptly pushed me away from him and immediately began to pursue the alternatives Fr. Jetté had posed to him: to urge my voluntary departure from the Congregation, or failing that, to begin dismissal proceedings.

On March 2, 1981, Fr. Waldie published an issue of the provincial newsletter devoted entirely to putting as much distance as possible between the Oblates of Mary Immaculate and the impressions created by my television appearance. It was of course imperative under the circumstances for Fr. Waldie to apprise the community of the situation and to try to introduce calm so that the community could make a more dispassionate inquiry. But his letter went far beyond that. In his anxiety to protect himself and the community from any hint of blame, Fr. Waldie uncritically, and probably unconsciously, adopted *in toto* Fr. Coleman's caricature of my views and proceeded to paint a picture of me as a just-discovered anomaly in the Congregation's midst. This letter is fascinating for a number of other reasons, and I would like to examine its two most important paragraphs:

> Without prejudice to the history of our efforts to understand, support, and encourage Father WAGNER in his professed desire to live within the framework of the Roman Catholic Priesthood and the guidelines of religious life upon the disclosure of his "homosexual orientation" to us after his ordination, it can be stated without qualification that the views of Father WAGNER presently expressed via the media on the subject of homosexuality and particularly as they bear on the question of priestly celibacy and chastity are singularly and uniquely his own personal views and they in no way represent or should be implied to represent the thinking, the attitude, the viewpoint or the understanding let alone the practice of the Missionary Oblates of Mary Immaculate. At this point it is clear that Richard WAGNER has given a different definition to priestly celibacy than is commonly understood within the Catholic ecclesiastical and theological community and as understood by us as Missionary Oblates.

...At the present moment, Father Richard WAGNER has been asked to answer in writing his explanation [sic] of his public statements. The official process has begun. We are following the procedure of due process in order to protect both Father WAGNER's rights as well as the rights of the Congregation. Again, our community has attempted to support and stand by Richard WAGNER during these last few years after he had identified himself to us as having a homosexual orientation. This was not improper behavior on our part given the fact that he wanted to remain a priest and religious and we had the duty and our religious commitment to each other to help him do that. Homosexual orientation of itself does not preclude the possibility of faithfully living out priestly celibacy any more than a heterosexual orientation does. Our conduct during this period has been responsible and accountable and so have Richard WAGNER's up to the present moment. His statements via the media have changed this. Therefore, although we do not disassociate ourselves from Richard WAGNER as a person or as a religious brother, we categorically stand apart from him in his views of homosexuality and priestly celibacy.

In the course of his repudiation of my supposed views Fr. Waldie begins to introduce the very conflation of events that I had relied upon him to help prevent. Note in particular his curious pretense that he had not already received and read my letter of February 26 and his equally curious description of his request for an explanation of my newspaper article as though it were a request for an explanation of the TV flap (which I would not be given a chance to explain until mid-May). I had hand-delivered my letter to the Provincial House the same day I completed it, on February 26, and Fr. Waldie read it the next day upon his return from a weeklong retreat (see Fr. Waldie's *For the record*, May 14, 1981, item #5).

Fr. Waldie's avoidance of any mention either of my newspaper article or of Fr. Jetté's reaction to it was remarkable and was probably the result of his uneasiness at having not objected to a writing whose author *his* superior was prepared to do nothing less than kick out of the Congregation. In his newsletter, Fr. Waldie went so far as to say that my conduct as a self-identified homosexual within the Congregation "has been responsible and accountable up to the present moment" of my media (i.e., television) statements. This was the beginning of his attempt to shift the blame for my trouble from my newspaper article to my

TV appearance. One might also note that Fr. Waldie clearly understood the distinction between orientation and behavior, a matter on which I personally had tutored him. However, he did not use the distinction to any effect. He might have introduced it at the beginning of his newsletter by way of cautioning the Province not to jump to conclusions about my personal life or even my opinions, despite the compromising impressions left by the television program. Instead he deliberately left the question of my conduct vague and used the distinction between orientation and behavior only to explain why such a person as Richard Wagner, once known to be a homosexual, was permitted to remain in religious life at all. I also had to take issue with his statement: "…upon the disclosure of his "homosexual orientation" to us after his ordination,". The truth of the matter was that I had "come-out" to him and his predecessor as Provincial, Fr. Carignan, before I was ordained.

When I first saw Fr. Waldie's newsletter, the ominous code words, "The official process has begun" leapt out at me, and I asked myself—as I would go on asking for the next seven years—What is this process exactly? The supposedly reassuring phrase, "We are following the procedure of due process…" was nonsensical coming at the conclusion of a newsletter that had just pronounced me "in clear and evident opposition to the Church's official teaching."

The first meeting between Fr. Waldie and me after the television interview was on March 11, and it marked the almost total breakdown of communication and comprehension between us. Fr. Waldie expressed his understanding of the meeting the following day in his official reply to the Superior General, and again two months later in a letter and attached document entitled *For the record*. The March 12 letter to Fr. Jetté represents Fr. Waldie at his best and at his worst.

Without a doubt he was the most sensitive and articulate of all the Oblate officials with whom I have had to deal during this controversy, and I am certain that he experienced his part in having to arrange my dismissal with genuine anguish and heartache. Despite his numerous mistakes in judgment and even perception, he ardently wanted a quick and painless solution and he tried sincerely to be above board and honest in all his dealings with me. Moreover, the sureness of his personal commitment to the celibate ideal and the correctness with which he strove to embody it in his life and to encourage his fellow religious to do the same, was matched by a compassion that enabled him sincerely to comprehended and sympathized with people whose struggles were markedly different from his own, both in kind and in degree.

It has often occurred to me that if I had been gifted with any of Fr. Waldie's delicacy of feeling and expression the worst aspects of my own public expressions, especially their bluntness, might have been averted. But these positive aspects of Fr. Waldie's character were not what I noticed about his letter to Fr. Jetté. Before I discuss the negatives, however, let me present the letter itself.

It is with great personal sadness and yet with the firm assurance that the right course of action has been chosen that I write to you concerning the Reverend Richard Wagner, OMI.

After a period of two weeks for personal reflection on the questions you raised within your letter to me regarding his "sincere disposition to change his way of life and to fully accept the requisites of the commitments has taken", Richard has decided that he cannot honestly do that and be true to himself and true to us. Yesterday, we had a long but rather intense talk together. It is my firm conviction that Richard cannot at this moment at least affirm his vowed life as we within the Church and within the Congregation understand and affirm it. We came to the conclusion [that] to get involved in a process of denial and subtle distinctions about what he may or may not have said or written would not be honest. Therefore, although he does not choose personally to resign, he understands that the next procedure for us would be to go the route of canonical dismissal from the Congregation.

As provincial and as I have come to know Richard Wagner even more clearly during the past few weeks, I concur with his decision and judgment. To act otherwise would be patently dishonest and not authentic for him. Our course of action given the facts facing us is clear. Although Richard does not disavow the value and validity of priestly celibacy and chastity as understood within the catholic tradition, he presently holds views contrary to this teaching and cannot bring himself to change his thinking.

This whole experience has been a learning one for me both as a priest, religious, and provincial. It is clear to me that we need to look carefully at this question of human sexuality in both a frank and honest manner within our formation process. In dealing with other provincials I know that Richard Wagner is not unique but most remain in the closet as the expression goes. We need a climate and atmosphere within our ranks that this question of sexuality can be raised and looked at honestly. To make a statement to formators of what ought not to be and then proceed to think that all buy into it will not do. I am grieved and deeply saddened by what appears to be an unspoken problem among us. Although formation is a life long process, we need to face the issue of sexuality as this is integrated into our life as vowed celibates.

How do we help and support our members to deepen the value and meaning of their vow of chastity? It appears that just the negative aspects of not marrying and not having the right to have genital expression of their sexuality is what most are aware of when a discussion ever occurs on this issue. Unless we really grow in our appreciation on the personal level of the meaning and value of this commitment, it should not surprise us that some members will find rationalizations to live contrary to the vow. If celibacy and chastity does not produce within us dispositions and qualities of sensitivity, availability, gentleness, kindness, in a word—that we truly become loving persons, then there will be strong temptations to look for other ways to become loving persons. I strongly believe in our vow of chastity and our oath of celibacy. I think that it can produce these qualities and dispositions. I affirm it even though I too struggle with it within my life.

There will be a formation meeting in April 1981 at Kingshouse in Belleville, Illinois. Formation personnel and provincials will be in attendance. One of the main issues is human sexuality and how we are facing it within our formation houses. I pray that it will be a fruitful discussion and sharing among us. Charles Breault will be in attendance, too. I ask your prayers for this meeting. The present case in point might give a clearer focus and concern to the topic we will discuss. We can learn from this and good can come from it. I believe that.

I am sorry that you have to contend with this, Father Jetté. You have so many concerns and problems to face and deal with each day. I don't know what the exact procedure is and therefore would wait to hear from you. You can be assured that due process has been followed. My concern is that both the rights of the Congregation and Richard Wagner be honored. I feel that so far this has been the case.

Thank you for your attention to this matter.

I detected in these remarks an obsequious unwillingness to contradict Fr. Jetté's "false lifestyle" assertions about me. Fr. Waldie did not even mention my letter of February 26, except to claim that we had agreed in our meeting that it would be dishonest of me "to get involved in a process of denial and subtle distinctions".

The principle "subtle distinction," of course, was the distinction between orientation and behavior, the very ignorance or disregard of which resulted in Fr. Jetté's false inference about my personal life and his instructions to Fr. Waldie that I be persuaded to leave the priesthood voluntarily or face dismissal. In his apparent anxiety to ingratiate himself to Fr. Jetté—reflected also in his anxiety to reassure Fr. Jetté of his own commitment to the celibate ideal—Fr. Waldie was reluctant to suggest any possibility that the Superior General might have acted hastily or inappropriately. Instead he immediately busied himself with trying to confirm Fr. Jetté's presumption of guilt.

Fr. Waldie expressed this two months later in his document *For the record*, which was supposed to be a review of "due process" up to that moment. "Although the General did not make his judgment on solid facts," the document reads, "his assumptions were correct and on target. The problem was method and procedure not truth or honesty." Without alluding to the newspaper article or TV interview, Fr. Waldie based his defense of Fr. Jetté's "truth and honesty" regarding me entirely on his, Fr. Waldie's, personal knowledge and convictions about me.

This was a very dangerous path for him to stray on to. His claim that he had learned things about me in the weeks since the TV interview that he had not know in the previous ten years of our acquaintance was simply false. Fr. Waldie and I, as I have mentioned, had a relationship that was confessional, in the formal sense of that word, for two years up to the time I am discussing. It was our custom during these sacramental occasions to speak without inhibition about our personal moral struggles, our understandings of our vowed lives, and a wide range of related issues of Church doctrine and practice. Our "intense" meeting of March 11 was necessarily an extension of our habit of mutual candor, and neither of us could pretend not to know what he knew of the other. The difference, of course, was that now Fr. Waldie had assumed the role of a prosecutor. In this role he began to toy with information divulged under the most protected circumstances as though it were public evidence to confirm Fr. Jetté's otherwise unfounded judgment of guilt and to justify recommending my dismissal. In other words, he was making no attempt to keep clear in his own mind information that he might know about me as a confidant and confessor and objective information that he might use to support Fr. Jetté's conviction of me.

His entire approach was repeatedly to exhort me to be "honest," that is, to admit that my personal weaknesses and doubts, as well as my convictions, were of such a nature and such a degree as to disqualify me as an Oblate and priest. In short, to forgo defending myself and to give up trying to save my religious vocation.

Fr. Waldie was taking the "If" clause of Fr. Jetté's instruction to him literally: "If there isn't in [Fr. Wagner] a sincere disposition to change his way of life ...." He imagined that in his pursuit of Fr. Jetté's "simplest solution" he was oblige to penetrate behind my written explanation of February 26—which he himself would later describe as "very fine"—to the hidden wellsprings of my thoughts and feelings. My every attempt to bring Fr. Waldie back to objective events and to my written statements addressing Fr. Jetté's concerns elicited only further hectoring to the effect that I wasn't being honest with myself. Because *he* knew that I really didn't believe in celibacy as the Church understands it and that I really didn't want to conform my life according to that understanding. But I threw such exhortations right back at him. What about you? What about your innermost thoughts and emotions, or those of any other Oblate for that matter? The Church does not purge priests and religious for their private genital functions or for their private pondering on Church doctrine and practice or even for their conversations with fellow priests or religious on these issues.

The only suitable objects of inquiry—when inquiry is called for—are publicly expressed opinions and/or publicly known behaviors; and these become dismissible offenses only when repeated, habitual, or pertinacious violations are proven and when the miscreant, even after such proof, cannot be persuaded to renounce his false opinions or sincerely strive to amend his behavior.

Nothing in my public statements and behaviors approaches such a profile of offense and obduracy. Just the opposite is true. In my written reply of February 26 I had offered to abjure any opinions that my superiors deemed contrary to Church teachings, I reaffirmed my commitment to religious life by denying the presumption of being otherwise committed despite my shortcomings, and I agreed to keep out of the public eye. That formal statement was all that Fr. Waldie or anyone else had any right to demand of me by way of answer to the specific "charges" put forth by him and Fr. Jetté.

For Fr. Waldie to claim that he had knowledge about my private life and opinions that rendered my formal defense unacceptable and that justified his setting it aside was not only canonically wrong but morally suspect as well.

But Fr. Waldie had another reason for disregarding my defense. Somehow he persuaded himself that "about the same time" as I was writing my defense I was also going on television in a blatant act of bad faith that rendered my defense "dishonest." He expressed this chronological error most clearly in his letter to me of May 14:

> In his letter [of February 8] the General evidently judged that you were de facto living a life style not in alignment with your vowed commitment and asked me to bring you to acceptability. ...I did not send your explanation of the NCR article to the Superior General because in the meantime you appeared on public television and expressed ideas and values seemingly in contradiction to what you wrote in your explanation of the NCR article. I, as your provincial, had made the judgment that your written response would place you in a bad light, in a dishonest position, because of what you subsequently had said on television that seemingly countermanded your written explanation. Therefore I did not send your letter on to the General.

Fr. Waldie's confusion was no doubt partly due to his having seen the television program for the first time on videotape after his return from retreat on February 27 and after he had read my letter. That, combined with the public furor caused by the program, gave him neither the time nor the calm to reconstruct the actual relationship between events. But it remains a mystery to me how he could have completely forgotten that I had informed him of the program immediately after its taping on February 6th.

It was at that time that he had instructed me to write an advisory to the bishops. He had spoken with the Archdiocese to confirm my standing as a priest and Oblate, and that my letter of February 26 itself alludes to the interview. Fr. Waldie carried his imagined picture of the relationship between my written defense and my TV appearance right into our meeting of March 11 and held to it even in the face of my vigorous head-shaking and protests, "No, Paul, that's *not* how it happened! Why do you keep saying that?" Try as I might to bring him back to objective events and to my written defense of February 26, he would not let go of what he considered to be his main proof of my dishonesty. And he would persist with this picture until June 5, when I finally put before him a written account of the TV interview, its relationship to earlier events, and his disastrous and probably irreparable misrepresentations of me to the Congregation and to our superiors in Rome.

Apart from wishful thinking or self-deception, what could account for Fr. Waldie's remark, in his March 12 letter to Fr. Jetté, which convinced him that during our meeting of March 11 I had somehow agreed to give up my written defense? The stressed wording of Fr. Waldie's letter—"Although Richard does not disavow the value and validity of priestly celibacy and chastity ... he presently holds views contrary to this teaching..."—indicates that something is not as it was being represented.

Let me back up to give an idea of where I stood with the Oblates before the roof fell in. I had been assigned to postgraduate study to obtain credentials that would qualify me for an up-front gay ministry and I completed that assignment in early February.

Under normal circumstances the natural next step would be for Fr. Waldie and me to discuss the specific shape of the new ministry for which my education had prepared me. Obviously Fr. Jetté's reaction to the newspaper article and the uproar produced by the TV interview put a serious crimp in my dealings with my community. From my point of view, however, the situation was by no means hopeless. My sincere desire to make amends as reflected in my apology of February 26, combined with a little patience to let the storm pass—and public outrage, however intense, does move swiftly—should have brought my superiors and me to a calmer moment. We could then discuss my future ministry and the ground rules for preventing a recurrence of unwanted events. But this would never be allowed to happen.

During my fateful meeting with Fr. Waldie on March 11, when it became clear that he was not going to accept my written statement and that he wanted me to leave the congregation voluntarily, I told him emphatically that I would not do so. There simply was no reason for me to leave. I then asked, "What would it take to bring about reconciliation?" Fr. Waldie replied that I would have to accept official church teaching concerning homosexuality and celibacy and to affirm that I was willing to live my life accordingly. Since I had already given those assurances in my letter of February 26, I said, "I have no problem with that. What comes next?"

This was the decisive moment of our meeting, the parting of the ways, which would never again converge—and it is precisely this moment that goes unmentioned in Fr. Waldie's official recollections of what took place between us.

In effect Fr. Waldie answered *Punishment*. Of course he did not use the word 'punishment' but that was exactly what he meant. If I insisted on staying, he told me, I would be required to end all contacts and associations with the gay community, the object of my ministry; be required to undergo a psychiatric evaluation; be forbidden to identify myself as a gay person; and be barred from ever again writing, speaking, or teaching on the subject of sexuality. He may as well have proposed to put me in a straightjacket and lock me away. My response at that point was, "No, I won't accept that!" Such a punishment would be professionally and personally disastrous to me, not to mention absurdly out of proportion to the "crime" of public self-identification as gay.

When I consider why Fr. Waldie thought such a harsh expedient necessary, I could only see it as a wish to make amends with his superiors by impressing them with his toughness. He too, after all, was in the hot seat and was working to tidy his own name at roughly the same speed he was sullying mine.

So naturally I "agreed" not to pursue my defense further. The writing was on the wall. My defense was discarded, Fr. Jetté's conviction of me was allowed to stand unaddressed, and the only hope of my remaining in the Congregation was to accept whatever punishment my superiors might capriciously wish to mete out. Furthermore, it was suddenly clear to me that by not accepting the proposed punishment I was going to be dismissed—not for my supposed false lifestyle and/ or heterodox principles, but simply and solely on the grounds of disobedience.

Fr. Waldie ended his March 12 letter to Fr. Jetté with a request for information on the dismissal process. He could not have known when he confronted me with the outline of his punitive obedience that he had also inadvertently stumbled onto the dismissal process itself, namely, to *engineer* a truly dismissible offense by means of my vow of obedience. For in fact no one had any intention of following up on Fr. Jetté's assertions about false lifestyle and contrary principles, Fr. Waldie's assiduous digging in those directions notwithstanding. No evidence other than Fr. Waldie's belated convictions concerning my dishonesty and unworthiness to be a priest was ever produced to prove my supposed false lifestyle, and in all the hoopla no one bothered to cite a single statement by me that needed retraction.

In early April Fr. Waldie attended the formation conference in Illinois. Also attending was Vicar General Francis George, OMI, (NOTE: He, Francis George, is now Cardinal Archbishop of Chicago) who brought with him from Rome the guidelines about the dismissal process that Fr. Waldie had requested. The document's typographical quirks, which I reproduce to some extent here, indicate that it was hastily thrown together. Considering that my very priesthood was at stake, the document's slapdash appearance and its use of a monogram to refer to me were profoundly disturbing. I actually wept to see how completely I had already been "dismissed" in the minds of those who had an obligation to see that I was treated fairly.

(NOTE: The only reason I have a copy of the following documents is Fr. Waldie gave them to me. During our March 11th meeting he promised me that the dismissal process would be totally above board, that there would be complete transparency. He gave me these documents in the spirit of that commitment. This proved to be a huge mistake. These were sub rosa documents sent him from Rome for his eyes only. It's clear that Fr. Waldie was duly chastised for this blunder, because he would never share another internal document with me. His commitment to transparency was as fickle as his original commitment to stand by me when things got rough when he launched me on my up-front gay ministry.)

DISMISSAL

BEFORE THE DISMISSAL PROCESS IS BEGUN

1) There must be a serious external fault, imputable to the individual. This fault can be either against the common law or against the particular constitutions of the Institute.

2) To establish this, an ENQUIRY should be made and all the relevant EVIDENCE collected.

   The existence of the crime should be established with MORAL CERTAINTY. This can be done [if]:

   (a) the crime and its imputability are NOTORIOUS;

   (b) the accused has CONFESSED to the CRIME, either during the ENQUIRY or OUTSIDE THE ENQUIRY.

   (c) the existence of the Crime is proven v.g. i) documentary proof, ii) evidence of witnesses, iii) expert evidence.

3) In the case of R.W.... great care is needed to proceed in such a way so that we are fair to him and to the Congregation and Church. Justice must not only be done but be seen to be done.

4) [sic] In this case, probably the best, if not the only way, would be for the PROVINCIAL to give R.W. A FORMAL OBEDIENCE UNDER VOW & in writing:

   i) to return to live in a determined Oblate House or Residence on or before a given date ... everything very precise;

   ii) (possibly) to abstain altogether from his present ministry regarding homosexuals and to refrain altogether from any public pronouncements (press, radio, television) in the matter.

SHOULD R.W. fail to do that which has been formally demanded of him, then the FORMAL PROCESS OF DISMISSAL could be begun by the Provincial.

[Here the document outlines the first canonical steps.]

It is essential that all the documentation be kept. Also, any defense, which the accused makes must be faithfully forwarded for presentation in the final stages of the case to the Holy See. AT EACH STAGE ... before each warning ... the accused should be afforded an opportunity to defend himself.

[Further information on canonical steps.]

[In all of this] perhaps it is better to heed the adage: festina lente!

[Concluding canonical steps culminating in confirmation by the Holy See.]

The document's author virtually admits—even without benefit of having read my defense—that Fr. Jetté's assertions concerning my lifestyle and beliefs were not a credible basis on which to press for my dismissal. Instead "the best, if not the only way" to achieve that end would be simply to set aside Fr. Jetté's (and Fr. Waldie's) convictions of me and start all over by manufacturing an altogether new "crime" more likely to pass the scrutiny of the review authorities in the Holy See.

Let there be no mistake: the document addressed the method for achieving my *dismissal*; it contained no suggestion that the obedience, whatever its content, might facilitate reconciliation. The leadership was to manipulate my vow of obedience into a coercive device to bring about an end that they were unable to achieve in any other way. Fr. Waldie, as I have stated, had already given me a pretty good idea of the punitive content of any future obedience. He never withdrew those depressing prospects or tried to reassure me that after a period of healing I might be able to take up, with appropriate guidelines and precautions naturally, the ministry that I had worked so hard to develop. My work up to that time—and the Congregation's considerable investment—was simply to be discarded, and there would be no two ways about it. Likewise the leadership would not accept my original defense and thus they would not move to retract the judgments handed down concerning me, nor would they inform the Congregation of my efforts to explain myself and to apologize to them.

If I stayed in the Congregation it would be as someone branded guilty of crimes that no one had any intention of proving, or clearly defining for that matter, and I would apparently spend the rest of my life marking amends for those assumed misdeeds.

Overall the cynicism of the document *Dismissal* is simply incredible. Considering its depersonalized way of referring to me and its startling recommendation that Fr. Jetté's precipitate judgments be allowed to drift into the background unanswered while a new and provable "crime" is hewn out of my vow of obedience, the document's professed concern for my just treatment and its almost cheery "Festina lente!" were to my ears little more than mockery.

Following the advice from Rome to proceed cautiously, Fr. Waldie told me in a meeting on May 3 that he saw this as a possible opening to reconciliation. He made no positive suggestions, however, about how we could achieve such an outcome and he continued to press for Fr. Jetté's "simplest solution" (my resignation from the priesthood) as the only "honest" option open to me. Moreover, he clung even more doggedly to the three parts of his own "indictment" of me, as reflected in his May 14 cover letter and attached document *For the record*.

The first part was his claim that I had rendered unacceptable my "very fine" defense February 26 because my "subsequent" act of going on television was blatantly dishonest and self-refuting. The second part was that during the interview I had (now quoting Fr. Waldie) "...attempted to give a definition to the promise of celibacy that suggested that one who had taken this promise could still legitimately involve himself in homosexual activity". And the third part was his insinuation, always expressed hypothetically, that my private life was inconsistent with my vowed life. "*If* you are in fact living in a life and life style that is incompatible with our Oblate life style and commitment ... then you should make a definite decision to choose which life and life style you will live in and by. You cannot have it both ways." (My emphasis.)

The assertions about promoting a redefinition of celibacy to accommodate homosexual behavior and trying personally to have it both ways obviously came straight from Fr. Coleman's remarks at the end of the television interview. As for Fr. Waldie's original contribution—based supposedly on his quite recent insights into my private life and thinking—that I had adopted a lifestyle in contradiction to my religious commitments and thus had placed myself in a dilemma that I could resolve only by leaving the Congregation and the priesthood, I rejected that repeatedly. Whatever my personal shortcomings, I told Fr. Waldie, I did not see myself as being in any such dilemma. I resented his badgering presumption that he knew me better than I knew myself and his insistence that if only I would see myself as he now saw me—and ultimately that was what he meant by my being honest—then naturally I would fold my tent and migrate elsewhere.

Fr. Waldie summarized our meeting of May 2, and his understanding of the events and conversations preceding it, in his communications to me of May 14. At the end of his cover letter, he announced the immanent end of all financial support of me (and he did terminate it that month, without so much as a second thought as to how I was going to survive). Then, in the next paragraph, he expressed his and his council's concern that due process had been followed and he made the following request: "...I have specifically asked you whether you judged that I had been following due process to your satisfaction. I would appreciate in writing from you your estimation or acceptance of this fact or not."

This was the first time he had asked me to give a written account of his perceptions and activities during the two months since he rejected my defense of February 26. While I was drafting my response, Fr. Waldie arranged still another meeting for June 7, 1981, to review again the matters we had discussed on March 11 and May 2. However, in attendance this time would be Jesuit canonist Fr. Richard Hill, SJ, to serve as witness to the discussion. Since I was unable to finish my response until June 5, I decided to take it with me to the meeting. When the three of us took our seats, I produced copies and asked that we read them together, since it presented my position in a methodical way that would probably get lost in a free-for-all conversation.

The letter rejected outright any suggestion that the community followed due process in my case. I carefully reviewed Fr. Waldie's attempt to use his confused chronology to dismiss my defense of February 26, thus allowing Fr. Jetté's original assertions about my newspaper article to be set aside in favor of pushing an identical set of assertions based on the television interview. I went on to show that Fr. Waldie based his claim that I attempted to redefine celibacy on Fr. Coleman's remarks, not on mine, and that my supposed admission of sexual misconduct was the result of creative editing after the taping of the program. In any case, my letter of February 26 was an honest and thorough offer to make amends, and I announced clearly that I had always stood by and continued to stand by that letter. I concluded by turning directly and pointedly to Fr. Waldie's repeated insinuations based on his personal knowledge of me and related this to his wanting me to confirm in writing that due process had been followed in my case. Here I quote the relevant paragraphs from my letter:

Paul, for some time now you seem to have taken
the position that any defense I might offer would necessarily

be a subterfuge. You have used your own unsubstantiated convictions about me as if they were decisive, when in fact, apart from evidence, they have no weight at all. Need I remind you that judges are as subject to law as anyone else, that that is why there are laws and due process, that that is the only thing that distinguishes the rule of law from the rule of men? Judges are obliged to judge on specific and precise charges, holding strictly to the evidence pertaining to the case, according to predefined criteria of what constitutes proper evidence, and following step-by-step procedures established by law and tradition. Now if a judge were to convict someone in lieu of evidence simply because he really *believes* the accused to be guilty, he would, in any system of justice worthy of the name, be subject to impeachment.

Now you consistently indicate in your remarks that no evidence is relevant because you personally are not convinced of my innocence, that is, you imply that the General's presumption of guilt has somehow assumed the status of something other than a presumption simply because you have come to share it. You further state in your *For the Record*: "Although the General did not make his judgment on solid facts, his assumptions were correct and on target. The problem was method and procedure not truth or honesty." What a piece of legal sophistry that is. Surely you know that in a legal proceeding truth and honesty are not separate from method and procedure; that they are inextricably bound together.

You say that though the General had no solid evidence for his allegation, he is nonetheless right. And why? Because you, you say, know the truth. But how do you know the truth in these matters? In other words, (1) do you have independent solid evidence to substantiate this presumption of guilt; and (2) if you do, is this evidence of such a kind as would be appropriate, given the principles of our church, to present in this case? Specifically, in what one respect has my alleged notorious lifestyle changed from more than one and a half years prior to the NCR article to this present day? What fragment of information do you have now that you did not have then? And what is it about this information now that makes you suddenly unable or unwilling to do your level best to ensure that I am protected according to law in these fantastically convoluted proceedings? More specifically, do you have pictures of me in compromising embraces? Do you have depositions from those who may have collaborated in my presumed lifestyle? Have you gained the confidence of my confessor and acquired information from him, which he is vowed never to divulge? Or are you, as my superior and friend, in possession of certain confidences, which I may have shared with you? And are these hypothetical confidences different in kind or degree from the confidences you possess of other Oblates but under no circumstances would think appropriate to make public? To put it bluntly, were you to be in possession of such hypothetical confidences would you be prepared to set a precedent as ugly and repressive as all this implies?

You have asked me to declare directly whether due process has been followed. I have told you before, and I repeat now, I haven't the vaguest idea what due process might be in a case such as this.

I have not been afforded competent and reliable counsel, and my only recourse has been to seek your advice— only to have my conversations with you misreported and thrown back in my face as if they were a signed confession of guilt. When you ask me if due process has been followed, I can only reply not according to the common understanding of due process in a humane system of justice.

According to such a system of justice, or any approximation to it, the proceedings of these last months have been nothing less than a farce, though the consequences have been anything but funny. I refer not only to the realities discussed above, but also to the following. You continue to talk as if, were I to remain a priest, certain exactions would be demanded of me. But you know full well that practically all the punishment that can be meted out already has been, and this, I should add, out all proportion to any reasonable charge, which might be brought against me.

I have been effectively silenced (I'm still holding to my promise), I have been ostracized from my community, I have been stripped of my faculties, and I have been denied all financial support, and have had my medical insurance revoked (these last two things prior to any ruling by the council). Since practically all the punishments that can be inflicted already have been, all that remains is the one, last act of humiliation, namely, to strip me of my *de jure* title, the *de facto* priesthood having long ago been scrapped.

I can only conclude that you have a most unusual understanding of due process. To you it seems to mean two things only: (1) moving at a snail's pace, perhaps on the outside chance that the accused may incriminate himself further; and (2) presenting a chronology of the given sequence of events and asking the accused to confirm its correctness. (Whatever else it might mean vis-a-vis your obligations to your superiors is hardly a question for me to judge.)

Now neither of these understandings of due process is correct. Due process, in this country at least, has always denoted a *speedy* trial, and this for the purpose of removing the onus of guilt from the innocent as quickly as possible. More than this, due process means, to resort to the dictionary, "a course of legal proceedings carried out regularly and in accordance with established rules and principles." I think that I have shown sufficiently that the proceedings of these last months have been at best irregular and *ad hoc*, the very opposite of what is meant my due process. In fact, they have been so irregular that punishments have been inflicted out of all proportion to any reasonable allegation, which might be brought against me on the prior assumption that I am guilty, period.

Being *a priori* guilty, I was given three recourses: (1) to admit my guilt by leaving the priesthood voluntarily; (2) to seek reconciliation, which in this situation clearly means to accept any exaction which might be imposed on me given the presumption of guilt; or (3) to stand my ground and be dismissed. Can any question remain why I have consistently chosen the last alternative?

Now given your limited understanding of due process, I have shown that you have not followed it on the second point, namely in your chronology of events. How you can present these errors in typescript and ask me to confirm them as if they were the simple truths in this matter is incredible to me. I cannot believe my eyes. These are not subtleties; they are errors so gross that they sting like a slap to the face. If you wish to have me dismissed on the tonality of what I am alleged to have said, or on what I am recorded to have said despite all the mitigating circumstances, or on your own unsubstantiated, quite late-to-develop convictions about my personal moral struggle, go ahead. Do what you must do. Do it, and accept the consequences. But in the name of God, please, Paul, at least get the facts right and in proper order. I prize my priesthood too dearly; it has been so much my identity and lifestyle, to see it thrown away so cavalierly. I cried to see how unworthy it had become of peoples' most careful attention.

When the reading ended, Fr. Waldie was the first to break the silence. His exact words were, "Oh my God, I think I've made a terrible mistake." After a pause, Fr. Hill spoke. It is noteworthy that he did not ask, "In what way?" He said simply, "Let us assume you did make a mistake. Where does that leave us?"

I do not exaggerate when I say that from that moment the objective grounds for having me removed from the Congregation had completely evaporated; in any event the leadership had so mishandled the process up to then that it was an embarrassment to consider it further.

What, then, were we to do? Setting aside my letter without further discussion, Fr. Hill turned the conversation in an entirely different direction. For whatever reasons, Fr. Hill argued, the situation between the Oblates and me had developed to the point where, justly or unjustly, I had been thoroughly discredited as an Oblate and priest. Matters had evolved to the point where the community regarded the situation as beyond mending, the truth or falseness of the original conviction being by now wholly beside the point. Given the Oblate leadership's strong preference for my departure, it was impossible to see what future I might have as an Oblate. However, since I interpreted a voluntary departure as tantamount to an admission of guilt for crimes that no one was prepared to support with a shred of evidence, the only remaining option to resolve the impasse was dismissal. But dismissal is a difficult thing to procure, and the Holy See does not endorse such moves for light and transient reasons. Therefore, the community must provide objective grounds for dismissal, and one need look no further for those than the vow of obedience.

Fr. Waldie agreed entirely with Fr. Hill's recommendation, which of course was the route Oblate officials in Rome had already proposed to him. Thus my awareness as early as March 11, 1981 that the leadership would shift my supposed guilt for unorthodox views and/or false lifestyle *in toto* to my vow of obedience came true.

My position at that point was surrender. If the Congregation was resolved to sever its relations with me no matter what I might have to say in defense of myself, and if the only remaining question was the means to achieve that end, then a contrived obedience it would have to be.

So on June 7—strange as it may sound—I entered into a "gentlemen's agreement" with Fr. Waldie. While the whole scenario, like the document it was predicated on, struck me as unbelievably cynical, I agreed to give the leadership the objective grounds it needed to have my *de facto* dismissal formalized. Fr. Waldie and I agreed, with Fr. Hill as our guide and witness, that: (a) I would be given a peremptory order under vow to take up residence at St. Mary's parish in Oakland (an indifferent choice); (b) that I would refuse in writing to obey that order; (c) that Fr. Waldie would send to me the two required canonical warnings; (d) that I would not respond to these warnings; (e) that Fr. Waldie would forward the relevant documents to Rome with the recommendation that I be dismissed from the Congregation on the proven grounds of disobedience.

Fr. Waldie issued his obedience on June 22, 1981. I replied as rehearsed on June 27. Since this act was to mark the death of my religious vocation, however, I felt compelled to register my outrage at the deliberate abuse of my vow of obedience as a device to dispose of me when all other reasons for such action had disappeared. While I was willing to give my superiors the disobedience they needed to remove me, I wanted them to know that what they were doing was wrong. I wrote

> This absolute, unilateral obedience, is an affront to what I have always appreciated the vow of obedience to mean, namely, the collegial responsibility binding you and me to seek together the will of God in our lives. I know that as my duly appointed superior you have the authority to do what you will, but I believe such a demand does not reflect the fundamental theology of this evangelical council to which I pledged myself in perpetual commitment. Therefore I reject any assumption that this obedience is or could ever be a true test of my fidelity.
>
> ...I believe that any true community must acknowledge and respect the uniqueness and integrity of its individual members. And this not only for the wellbeing of its members, but for its own wellbeing, the two in the final analysis being one. Certainly never should an individual member be sacrificed to maintain an appearance, an illusion, that the community enjoys unanimity; or to free itself of the continual need for self-examination; or to exempt itself from the obligation to seek out and purify the meaning and spirit of fidelity. Without a constant

wariness of itself *any* community can become faceless, rigid, and without compassion. It can crush individual creativity within its ranks and thus undermine its very own resources for maintaining itself and building its future.

Community cannot designate conformity for conformity's sake, discipline for discipline's sake, obedience for obedience's sake, nor any narrow and arbitrary "tests" for the purpose of proving a member's loyalty. Community is the result of individual persons freely joining in diverse ways toward a common good—in trust—each bringing the fruits of his individual work to the common work of all. But whenever the solemn intonations of power and command are invoked against a loyal member in order to save face, community has already cracked at its foundation. It has ever been the case, in all times and places, for the sake of community, that responsible men have *had* to say "No".

Despite the Oblate leadership's talk about observing due process and respecting my rights as an individual, by June 1981 the provincial leadership had severed all financial support of me and every vital tie with the community. Two months later they forwarded the acts of dismissal to Rome for review by the General Administration and eventually the Holy See. From that moment on I was suspended in a non-canonical state; and even though, as it happened, the General Administration never forwarded the acts to the Holy See for confirmation, I have remained in that state to the present day. The only right I retained, as I shall presently narrate, was the "right" to diffuse and redundant interrogations whose putative aim was reconciliation but whose net result was to reinforce the estrangement between me and the community and to further erode my priestly vocation. Though in principle I was a fully entitled Oblate, for all practical purposes the leadership had dismissed me from the Congregation, and I immediately had to arrange my life accordingly.

On November 10, 1981, Fr. Waldie and Fr. Leo Dummer, OMI, came to my apartment in San Francisco to take back my Oblate car, the last remaining material link I had with the Congregation. During his visit Fr. Waldie told me that the Procurator General, Fr. Michael O'Reilly, had recently asked him for more information about my case. I had a right to defend myself, he told Fr. Waldie, and he encouraged me to write the Superior General directly and, in Fr. Waldie's words, "...let him ask you precise questions so that he can come to understand what you are saying." I assumed that the acts of dismissal forwarded to Rome in August included my correspondence to Fr. Waldie, and I could see nothing I might add to what I had already said there. Besides I was anxious and depressed much of the time, shifting back and forth between anger at what I experienced as betrayal and grief at the sudden and permanent loss of religious fellowship. Also, except for odd jobs, I was unemployed and looking for work and had no leisure for difficult correspondence. Consequently I did not view the general leadership's solicitation of a defense as a hopeful sign. To me it indicated nothing more than a wish to put the last procedural touches on my dismissal.

I do not know if canon law prescribes a time limit beyond which deliberation on a proposed dismissal becomes unreasonable and injurious to the person concerned, but by March 29, 1982, more than a year after Fr. Jetté convicted me on grave matters and eight months after the acts of my case were forward to Rome, I was astonished to read in a letter from Fr. Waldie: "The Superior General wrote to me recently indicating that the General Administration does not want to proceed too rapidly on this important matter." Suddenly there was talk of dialogue, even though, as I have mentioned, anything that might signify practical and spiritual membership in the Congregation had already vanished.

My only contacts with the Oblates since August 1981 were a few brief telephone exchanges with Fr. Waldie. He acknowledged the deterioration of my standing in the community in the first paragraph of his letter: "I surely grant you that you have been in limbo as far as our response to you as individuals and as a province goes. ...Given the relationships that did exist before, this remains difficult and painful for you and those of us who were in relationship with you." With everything in the past tense, the natural question I had was: Dialogue about *what*?

In his correspondence to me of March 29, 1982, Fr. Waldie quotes Superior General Jetté, who, interestingly, now rephrases the two items of his original conviction of me as questions that he wants Fr. Waldie to put to me:

...in dialogue with Father Wagner, I think it is necessary to always come back to two essential points:

1) concerning doctrine, does he integrally accept the Church's and the Congregation's position regarding the nature and the obligations of the vow of chastity?

2) in practice, does he sincerely want to conform his life to it and help other priests and religious to do likewise? It is

a question of honesty with himself and with the religious institute to which he has committed himself.

In a meeting with Fr. Waldie on April 30, I answered "Yes" to both questions. As I had already satisfactorily replied to these points in my letter of February 26, 1981, I saw no reason to repeat myself. Yes, I accepted the Church's and the Congregation's understanding of the nature and obligations of the vow of chastity. Yes, I sincerely strove to live accordingly—and I rejected any insinuation that I influenced priests and religious to do otherwise. As for the *sincerity* or *honesty* of my replies—the *deep* questions that got Fr. Waldie into such a muddle—what could possibly satisfy them besides my direct answers? Yes meant Yes! Those answers, combined with my previous discussions of my opinions and practices, ought to have been enough. In a letter to me the day after our meeting, Fr. Waldie announced: "I will write to the General and tell him that you would answer 'yes' to both questions and I would invite him to write you directly to begin a direct dialogue with you." But as events would prove, Fr. Jetté, like Fr. Waldie before him, was very reluctant to take 'yes' for an answer. In fact, he was unavailable for any answer at all.

CHAPTER 3

1984 - 1986

Two years later, Fr. Charles Breault, OMI, General Councillor for the United States, invited me to meet with him at the Provincial House to discuss my case. The meeting was held on March 26, 1984. There Fr. Breault presented me with a letter from Fr. Jetté dated February 8, 1984, and he requested that I read and respond to it in his company, with Fr. Seamus Finn, OMI, my good friend and classmate, attending as a witness.

Before I discuss this letter, I must emphasize that in all the intervening time between my last meeting with Fr. Waldie in April 1982 and my meeting with Fr. Breault in March 1984, the sum of my contacts with the Oblates was a few bewildered telephone conversations with Fr. Waldie. Fr. Waldie's explanation for the extraordinary hiatus—though he too thought it excessive—was that Fr. Jetté had many pressing responsibilities and that I should not presume that my case had any special priority with him.

It had been three years—very long years I might add—since Fr. Jetté had declared me guilty of grave offenses and steered Fr. Waldie toward arranging my removal from the Congregation. At the time of Fr. Breault's contact, I was in every respect living the life of an independent agent. I had begun to get on my own feet financially with a small house-cleaning business, and in my off hours I nursed along a private practice of psychotherapy. Though I was far from emotionally reconciled to losing my religious vocation and all my former friends and associates, I entertained no hope—given the abruptness and completeness with which the leadership had thrust me from community—that the formal severance would not eventually be forthcoming. I interpreted the faint murmuring of "dialogue" and "reconciliation" as an indication that the dismissal based on a trumped up obedience had no merit. And what was left was little more than bureaucratic prudence and a needless prolonging of the pain of separation.

Consequently I was surprised to read Fr. Jetté's first paragraph to me: "For the past three years, this situation has been quite uncertain...." What was uncertain? I had refused a direct obedience from my major superior; that was established beyond a doubt. Was Fr. Jetté acknowledging that the reasons for my refusal might have merit? Was he perhaps prepared to accept my Yes answers to the two questions he posed to Fr. Waldie two years earlier? Needless to say, it was a crucial letter and deserved the closest scrutiny.

Fr. Jetté acknowledged that he had finally read my defense of February 26, 1981, and quoted a passage from it that denied that I advocated sexual activity by priests and religious or challenged Church teachings. But then Fr. Jetté simply dropped the letter and the passage without further comment and turned immediately to a series of new accusations, the most important being that I disobeyed my Provincial two and a half years earlier when he ordered me to take up residence in an Oblate house.

In another unexpected turn, Fr. Jetté then held out the possibility of reconciliation, but he quickly followed this with a clear signal that my dismissal—despite his personal reluctance to follow through on it—was still very much a live option. Of course, this made no sense at all. Because in all of this he made no allusion to the reasons I had previously tendered for refusing Fr. Waldie's obedience: namely, that the obedience and the resultant dismissal process originated when Fr. Jetté pronounced me guilty without inquiry; that Fr. Waldie dismissed out of hand my letter of defense; and that Fr. Waldie, following the General Administration's guidelines, engineered the obedience precisely to side-step these uncomfortable facts.

By ignoring entirely the direct relationship between his own unjust assertions, Fr. Waldie's refusal to tender my response to them, the resort to a punitive obedience as the only way to procure my dismissal, and my obliging refusal of that obedience, Fr. Jetté was free to awaken a new suspicion. Abstracting my specific act of disobedience from its defining context, he now proposed to treat it as indicative of a more general indisposition to obey.

In short, despite the solicitous word 'reconciliation,' Fr. Jetté's letter represented no movement at all. On the contrary, matters had become considerably more obscure if only because of the three-year gulf that had opened up between my *de facto* removal from the Congregation and this belated, diffuse inquiry into my disposition to obey. What did the leadership, really, want of me that I had not provided several times already?

Three years into my banishment, the leadership could have taken obvious procedural steps that could have broken down the ever-building wall of suspicion behind which they were isolating me. Those steps were: accept my letter of February 26, 1981 on its merits. Retract the false judgments that lead to the unacceptable obedience and bring explicit closure to the two-and-a-half-year dismissal process. Cleanse the atmosphere of the rhetoric of guilt and punishment and pave the way for a good faith dialogue concerning appropriate reassurances to the community and an honorable assignment for me. We would then *see* if I acquit myself according to my professed vows.

This direct procedural approach was exactly what the leadership failed to adopt because to do so would require that it acknowledge gross procedural errors on its part up to that point. Instead the leadership opted for what amounted to an *ad hoc* psychological inquiry while doing nothing to remedy the non-canonical state to which they themselves had consigned me since 1981. The putative aim of this inquiry was reconciliation but its context was the unresolved dismissal process. It disregarded my written defenses of myself in the face of baseless assertions of guilt. The *illegitimate* obedience that grew out of that disregard now eclipsed my defenses with an open-ended suspicion of my disposition to obey the *legitimate* requests of my superiors *under normal circumstances*.

Aside from sketching his understanding of the situation, the specific purpose of Fr. Jetté letter was to introduce Fr. Breault, who, on Fr. Jetté's behalf, would ask me to respond to five questions. Here is how Fr. Jetté itemized the questions:

(1) Do you accept the teachings of the Church concerning consecrated chastity and ecclesiastical celibacy? What, in your opinion, is the content of this teaching?

(2) Do you agree to maintain an external behavior which is in conformity with this teaching and which does not contradict it either in word, in writing or in act?

(3) Do you agree to live in an Oblate community and to accept, from your Provincial, an apostolate which would not be that of ministry to homosexuals?

(4) Do you agree not to give any talk, nor to publish anything, on the question of sexuality, without the explicit permission from your Provincial?

(5) Do you agree not to present yourself publicly as "gay"?

The meeting was held at the Provincial House on March 26, 1984. I repeat—and I cannot stress this enough—no one gave me a copy of this letter until the beginning of the interrogation by Fr. Breault on that day. Obviously it was impossible for me on the spur of the moment to clearly apprehend its contents, although I was able to divine during my "witnessed" reading that all was not right with it.

The worst for me was not the contents of the letter, which I was far from clearly assimilating, but the manner in which Fr. Breault confronted me with it. To spring such a difficult document on me out of the blue—even though it had been available to others for almost two months—and to expect me to respond to it without preparation and before witnesses was unconscionable.

I shall not review here Fr. Breault's notes on the "jeremiad" I delivered during that grueling three-hour session. I remember little of it myself. The heat of anger, the sweat running down my back, an earthquake occurring almost on cue—those I recall. And my pathetic appeals: "Is there anyone who can help me with my rights? Can anyone help me?" "My friends! It's tremendously hurtful to me."

Fr. Breault invited me to write directly to the Superior General.

On June 11, 1984, I sent Fr. Jetté a 17-page, single-spaced account of my case up to the time the local leadership forwarded the acts of dismissal to him. I included answers to his five questions, and I outlined the procedural route by which the general leadership might resolve the situation. Needless to say, I was disgusted with the process and quite pessimistic about its outcome. I had so few expectations for it that I wound up mailing Fr. Jetté the next-to-last draft, replete with typos and misspellings. Producing the final typescript seemed like the labors of Sisyphus—and how I longed to be out from under that accursed stone. This was 1984, the strangely apropos Orwellian allusions aside, and before I caught my second wind.

I do not wish to quote from this letter extensively, but if my readers are willing to pick their way through the poor typescript, they will see that it did successfully restore the historical context and proposed the general terms of the solution that the general leadership would adopt more than four years later.

There are three things to notice in the following excerpts: (1) my insistence on hewing to the history of the case, (2) my insistence that the leadership openly acknowledge its procedural errors and set them right, (3) and my objection to the renewed effort to make obedience the issue upon which everything would turn:

> While I appreciate the conciliatory spirit of your letter, I am amazed to find no reference to the historical context, which has brought us to this day. Excuse me if I speak with candor, but from my point of view any attempt at reconciliation without such a context is doomed to the fate of every previous attempt. I contend that a careful analysis of the facts and sequence of events show that I have been the victim of a grave injustice.
>
> [My review of the history of the case.]
>
> ...This is the context of the 'situation' without which we cannot possibly discern what would constitute an authentic reconciliation, if such is really wanted. While no one has ever asked me to air my view of what actions would have to be taken to resolve this impasse, perhaps it is high time I volunteered to give it. Let me stress, however, that this is not a demand on my part, nor even a request. After all the frustration, disappointment, and anguish I have been through these past years, I would be foolish to allow myself the hope of a happy ending.
>
> Bearing all the foregoing in mind, I tell you with the utmost sincerity and without the least hesitation or doubt that the only way to rectify the situation is to restore forthwith the *status quo ante* Fr. Waldie's misguided rejection of my defense of February 26, 1981. His decision, based as it was on his quite erroneous reading of the situation, set this case fatefully on a course of confrontation, which found its issue in the manufactured disobedience of June 27, 1981. My letter of February 26, 1981 provided the grounds for a speedy and, above all, *clean* resolution of the problem. In it I abjectly begged forgiveness for my blunder; I answered the Superior General's misunderstanding with regard to my lifestyle vis-à-vis my self-identification as gay; I provided abundant reassurances with regard to repudiating statements my superiors objected to; I forswore resorting to the press or media in the future; I reaffirmed my vow of celibacy and chastity by rejecting any insinuation that I was living in any other way. I think that any reasonable person who took it upon himself to understand the actual sequence of events and the extraordinary circumstances

surrounding them would find in my letter of February 26 more than enough to allay the need for more radical measures.

Restoring the *status quo ante* of February 26, 1981 would require two courageous moves.

First, the obedience of June 22, 1981—or *any latter-day, disguised version of it* —would have to be revoked without qualification. One would have to forthrightly acknowledge that the orchestrated attempt to use my vow of obedience as the best, indeed the only way of fixing the outcome of my dismissal was itself a violation of the spirit of that solemn vow. At this point, there is no way I can accept any peremptory command, no matter how innocuously phrased, to return to community, because given the context, such an order can only be interpreted as a repeat of Fr. Waldie's obedience of June 22, 1981. I have made it abundantly clear why I can never go back on my refusal of that obedience. I remind you that these unhappy events have left me with nothing except my honor, and I would have to be a very perverted character indeed to throw that away. Apart from living in community, I have to live with myself. While to ignore the history of that obedience and my reasons for rejecting it might in fact restore me to community, I would return a worthless person deserving of no one's respect, least of all my own.

The second move would have to be an acceptance of my apology and reassurances of February 26, 1981. Moreover, the last three years of being an outcast, of receiving no support, of being without faculties, and of being kept in ignorance of my fate (although certain of eventual dismissal) would have to be acknowledged as *punishment enough*. That being acknowledged, and my apology and assurances accepted, I would then be restored as an Oblate who has made good on his past mistakes and who is worthy of being embraced again by the Congregation. After a reasonable period of time, when all are adjusted to my restored membership, I would then be able to enter into fraternal dialogue in an atmosphere of mutual trust to determine how I might best serve the church—either within the Congregation or in another community or diocese.

At the end of my letter, I proceeded to answer the five questions put to me by Fr. Breault the previous March 26.

Father, at last we are brought up even with the questions you put to me in your letter of February 8, 1984. I shall now answer them in serial order.

1) The teaching of the church concerning chastity and celibacy is that all persons who take these vows shall not engage in genital activity. I have never maintained that these vows meant anything other than this, nor have I ever disavowed their positive content. In the case of homosexuals, however, I have pointed out the *INARTICULATENESS* of what it means to be a vowed celibate. For one thing, I believe that the homosexual's vow is binding indirectly in this specific sense: "Since the church recognizes no licit sex outside the institution of marriage she feels that a renunciation of heterosexual marriage is enough to satisfy a commitment to sexual abstinence and that nothing more needs to be said." For another thing, I have observed that the homosexual's vow of celibacy has a highly ironic quality. Unlike a heterosexual man, when the homosexual man takes this vow he is pledging to forgo sexual relations, which he is morally required to forego even if he does not take it.

Obviously pointing out the indirectness and irony of the homosexual's vow of celibacy can never be construed as somehow condoning sexual activity on his part. Similarly, it would be nonsensical to suggest that the dictionary definition of celibacy might be used as some kind of loophole, which would justify sexual activity on the part of a homosexual priest.

Why even mention the indirectness and irony of the homosexual's vow? Simply to emphasize that homosexual priests and religious come to take their vows from a quite different social and psychological direction than their heterosexual counterparts. Not only does the church require them to live celibately even when they do not vow to do so, but the special quality of their situation is never dealt with directly and explicitly. On the contrary, the secrecy that surrounds the subject is so great that a homosexual usually feels compelled to conceal the fact of his orientation for fear of reprisals.

It is the fear and anxiety engendered by the hiddenness that is the real issue in all of this. With respect to homosexuals, the formation process is a complete failure, because there is no attempt to deal frankly and forthrightly with their unique situation. So we should hardly be surprised to discover that persons who live in extreme isolation and loneliness might seek other avenues of human contact. And while it is true that sexual activity is incompatible with celibacy, surely there is nothing gained by calling such persons hypocrites.

Everyone acknowledges the difficulty of living a life of sexual abstinence. What surprises me is how little compassion and understanding there is when we discover that not all are equally close to fulfilling the ideal. Certainly it is my firm conviction that the crisis in today's church regarding the issues of homosexuality and celibacy is not going to be resolved by redoubling the repression and hiddenness in the hope that homosexual men and women in religion will remain "our little secret." Homosexual men and women are not morally culpable for being such and it is wrong and wrong and wrong to treat them as if they were.

2) Yes.

3) This is the obedience of June 22, 1981 restated. I can honestly say that I do not reject the idea of living in community; in fact I look forward to the opportunity when I can once again enter into dialogue with my superiors to discern the Spirit of how I may best serve the church. However, if reconciliation is possible only if I blindly agree to this demand without my superiors first attending the task of clearing my good name, as outlined in my case above, then you have no choice but to issue the decree of dismissal.

4) Yes.

5) Even though I find this last request most disquieting and believe it only adds to the atmosphere of repression and

secretiveness that pervades religious life, I would, in the spirit of reconciliation, pledge not to disclose my sexual orientation in any *PUBLIC* manner.

Considering the length of this letter I will close here. There remains so much to be said, but I am so very tired. I hope to hear from you soon and pray that together we might find our way out of this dark thicket. If, however, our paths must part, I hope that we both can say we have learned much that will help us further God's kingdom.

In mid-July Fr. Jetté acknowledged receipt of my letter and assured me that he would respond more fully in due course. Then another interruption ensued. In early January I suffered an attack of appendicitis which all by itself very nearly brought about my dismissal from the Congregation.

As I was without medical insurance, I was at a loss what to do and languished more than 36 hours in extreme pain. When my condition grew intolerable, I, with great difficulty, dressed in my clerical shirt, called a taxi, and used my expired insurance card to get through Emergency Receiving at St. Mary's Hospital in San Francisco. I was placed on a gurney, and the small reserve of my consciousness not devoted to pain was siphoned off into a humiliated dread that it would be discovered that I was uninsured.

My condition was so serious, however, that they rolled me into surgery before checking on my insurance. The hospital staff did not confront me with the issue until after I recovered consciousness post-surgery.

I feigned surprise that my insurance card was no good. And then did the only thing I could do; referred the hospital staff to the Provincial House for an explanation. (NOTE: As it turned out, the Province was obliged to pay over $15,000 out-of-pocket to cover the cost of their negligence. As I discovered later, they had no right to deny me insurance coverage for all of this time. Once restored to the insurance roles; I remained insured by the Oblates till 1993, when my story ends.)

I had a long and difficult recovery that required the doctors to reopen the incision and leave it open for regular irrigation until it closed on its own. Nevertheless I resolved to get off Oblate "dole," and I insisted on permission to leave the hospital and perform the irrigations and dressings myself at home without nursing assistance. This cut down considerably on the final medical bill. I also returned a $100 gift ("for cigarettes") from Fr. Andrew Harris, OMI, the new Provincial, to help defray expenses and to emphasize the inappropriateness of my situation.

I am not sure he understood the gesture. My illness and recovery consumed nearly two months, during which I was unable to earn any income at all. Not a single Oblate inquired how I was going to manage during that difficult time. Fr. Harris notified me in mid-February that I would be re-enrolled in the Oblate insurance plan "until such time as we have clarity around your relationship with the congregation", but not once did I avail myself of this policy until after my exoneration in 1988. I mention all this to explain this remaining material link with the community and to register my opinion that had the leadership not been financially burned by this emergency, I would still not be covered by insurance to this day.

On February 15, 1985, Fr. Jetté replied to my letter of eight months earlier. After spending the first part of his letter fine-tuning the positive definition of chastity, he seemed to turn away from his inquiry into the depth of my acceptance of Church teachings on chastity and my commitment to practice the same. In their place he now proposed to focus exclusively on the newly emergent question of my disposition to obey. "In substance," Fr. Jetté wrote, "what is being asked of you here is what is asked of every Oblate who wishes to be a member of the Congregation: to live in an Oblate community or be disposed to do so, if possible; to be ready to do the apostolic work required of him by his legitimate Superior."

Again, there was no reference to the fact that my absence from community was imposed on me by the community itself following an unfounded judgment of guilt handed down by the General Administration; that my defense in the face of this unjust conviction remained unacknowledged; that Fr. Waldie's subsequent obedience was a hasty attempt to oblige the General Administration despite these procedural gaffs; that my defense of myself in the face of this illegitimate obedience was also ignored; and that the four-year-old dismissal process itself was still not brought to formal closure but allowed to linger pending still further inquiry into my disposition to obey.

With the background of the controversy entirely suppressed, all that remained was a freestanding suspicion that I was somehow being refractory on a matter "asked of every Oblate who wishes to be a member of the Congregation." On balance the rhetoric would seem to have shifted toward reconciliation, but the way the General Administration held this prospect out was anything but promising.

In blunt language, the leadership's "solicitude" toward me came down to: "Never mind the past. Will you *obey*?" And it was becoming clear to me that the more I insisted that the past be remembered, the more the leadership would press the insinuation that I had difficulties with my vow of obedience.

Fr. Jetté concluded his letter with an "emphatic" request that I take up this point with my new Provincial Superior, Fr. Harris, who had already been in office about a year. With the case once again returned to the Provincial level that was the last direct contact I would have with Superior General Jetté.

In early May 1985, I had my first official meeting with Fr. Harris and Fr. Paul Nourie, OMI, a member of his Provincial Council. Fr. Harris conveyed the general sense of this meeting in his summary to Fr. Jetté of May 17, 1985. Three times my confreres raised the question of obedience, and three times I answered that the question made no sense, or only a very misleading sense, in abstraction from my four-year *de facto* dismissal. Reconciliation, I repeated, depended entirely on acknowledgment of that history and had to include an explicit exoneration and clarification of my status before the details of reentry could be discussed.

Amorphous, quasi-psychological talk about my dispositions—especially with all the past procedural issues still outstanding and my direct answers to the previous questions simply spurned—was in my opinion quite beside the point. And I made it clear that given the indefiniteness of the process up to that time, my current livelihood and household were not on the table for discussion.

The fruitlessness of my conversation with Frs. Harris and Nourie reflected the complete uncertainty by all the parties concerned as to the nature of the process we were involved in. What canonical procedure were we following, if any? Obviously many things had gone wrong with the handling of my case, and I experienced this latest phase as simply the perpetuation, by way of avoidance, of the leadership's original errors. Despite talk of reconciliation, the process had degenerated into a type of corporate dithering. This was caused in part by poor communication between the General and Provincial leadership, even though the latter always deferred to the former for instructions.

In our first meeting, for example, Frs. Harris and Nourie seemed unacquainted with the long letter I had sent to Fr. Jetté the previous June, with its historical diagnosis of the case and my recommendations for a procedural resolution. Consequently, with them I seemed to be beginning all over again. As his addendum to his May 17 letter to Fr. Jetté makes clear, Fr. Harris was as perplexed as I about the nature of the process or even who was responsible for it:

> It seems to me we need some clarifications, comments, responses
> from the person in the General Administration handling this
> case. Some questions I would have:

- Does the General Administration wish us to follow specific guidelines? If so what are they?

- Does the General Administration expect a written statement from Richard or the Provincial? If so what areas should these statements cover?

- Does the General Administration have recommendations regarding the re-entry program? If so what are they?

- Can the Provincial at this stage of the process relate to Richard that previous concerns are resolved because of the correspondence between Richard and the General and the one issue remaining pertains to obedience?

- Can Richard remain outside the Oblate community life while exploring his options, being disposed to enter into community when an appointment can be arranged?

I did not hear again from the Oblates for another seven months. On December 2, 1985, I met with Fr. Harris a second time at the Provincial House. He shared with me a letter he had received four months earlier from Vicar General Francis George. The letter, dated August 8, 1985, was a reply on Fr. Jetté's behalf to Fr. Harris's letter of May 17. As the most significant thing about my second meeting with Fr. Harris was Fr. George's letter, I shall discuss its contents first and then describe the results of my brief exchange with Fr. Harris.

Fr. George informs Fr. Harris that most of his questions will have to be deferred pending further discussion in Rome. Though it seems vaguely implied that Fr. Jetté is satisfied with my answers to all of his questions except No. 3, concerning obedience, there is still a definite reluctance to say so. The only clear instruction to Fr. Harris is that he pursue two lines of inquiry with me.

The first line of inquiry concerns, of course, my disposition to obey, which, Fr. George echoes Fr. Jetté, has to be clarified "so that Richard's return to community will be on the same basis as that of any other Oblate." There is an obvious ambiguity at play in this line of questioning which shows why the process was not going anywhere, and I should like to pause a moment to explain it.

On the one hand, my *return* to community could not possibly be on the same basis as any other Oblate's because no other Oblate was in the position of having been uncanonically driven from community and of then having to negotiate what a return might entail. On the other hand, if we *achieved* the elusive goal of reintegration someday and I was truly *accepted* as a brother among brothers, then by definition my membership would be on the same terms as any other member's.

Now, in my view, it was simply perverse to keep raising a question about *that*, as if I was demanding some special status for myself within the Congregation. The issue before us had nothing to do with my disposition to obey the legitimate requests of my Superiors under *normal* conditions. It had to do, rather, with the *abnormal* conditions to which the leadership had consigned me and with what specifically they would have to do to correct those conditions. The leadership attempted to focus suspicion on my disposition to obey in order precisely to distract attention away from the four years of corporate malfeasance that created those conditions in the first place. This pattern of insinuation regarding obedience, combined with a fostering of collective amnesia, would be repeated time and again throughout the following decade. Indeed it provides the pretext for the present obedience.

The second line of inquiry recommended by Fr. Jetté was part of this leadership effort to shift attention away from themselves. "The second point," Fr. George continues,

> is perhaps more difficult, because it is more general. Fr. Wagner makes much of what he takes to be a "lack of confidence" in him on the part of his Superiors in the Congregation. This is a serious point, and it needs to be further pursued to see whether or not his reaction leaves room in the future for a healthy relationship between him and his future Superiors.

Fr. George then goes on to recommend that Fr. Harris "…pursue this point of 'lack of confidence' by trying to discover whether or not Richard thinks that there was any reason for his Superiors to lose confidence in him, mistaken though he might think those reasons to be."

All of this is an odd inversion of the actual sense of my remarks to Frs. Harris and Nourie in our first meeting. Nowhere in Fr. Harris's summary of that meeting does he quote me as using the phrase "lack of confidence," and certainly nowhere do I "make much" of my superiors' lack of confidence in me. The very word 'confidence' does not appear in the entire summary. Of the statements attributed to me that might be described as having something to do with confidence—those dealing with personal "validity" and "integrity"—all refer unmistakably to "unfinished business in the historical context which needs to be resolved," the need for "clarification of my status in the congregation," and the importance of having "my good name cleared." My confidence-related remarks, in other words, make nothing of my Superiors' "lack of confidence" in me and everything of my "lack of confidence" in them.

Yes, Fr. George does go on to observe that confidence works both ways: "In the same line [of questioning], I think I would try to discover if Richard realizes that he is asking for assurances that other Oblates don't demand and is himself manifesting a 'lack of confidence' in regard to his Superiors." But strikingly, Fr. George does *not* invite Fr. Harris to pursue further—or even, apparently, to be exposed to—the *reasons* I had for lacking confidence in the leadership, reasons such as I had elaborated in my letter to Fr. Jetté of June 11, 1984.

Again, Fr. Jetté's recommendation to focus attention on the leadership's lack of confidence in me was designed to deflect consideration of that detailed historical account and its recommendations. He wanted all and sundry to limit themselves to asking: What is wrong with *Fr. Wagner* that his superiors should lack confidence in him? And Fr. George's suggestion, working from the "opposite" direction, was to invite all and sundry also to start asking themselves: What is wrong with *Fr. Wagner* that he should lack confidence in his superiors?

So the question of confidence did cut both ways. It just happened to cut the same person.

The leadership used these lines of inquiry about confidence to help create the illusion that the suspicion I had of my Superiors was *my* problem and raised doubts about my ability to have healthy dealings with them in the future. For me to argue the unfairness and even illegality of the leadership's actions toward me—as I had done while exercising my canonical right to self-defense, a defense that the leadership itself had solicited—did not incline them to judge my case specifically on its merits but rather to judge me, for the very fact of defending myself, probably unfit to be in relationship with them.

There is another aspect of Fr. George's remarkable letter that I would like to discuss. In the same place where he recommends that Fr. Harris query me about whether I think there were reasons for my Superiors to lose confidence in me, he goes on to say,

> If there were reasons, and they seem to be objective, then even if they were mistaken it would seem that the actions taken with regard to Richard were not "personal." No one was out to get him personally. What was at stake was the meaning of our entire religious commitment and the effectiveness of our collective apostolate in front of the Church and the Christian

laity in the Church. This is a matter, which every Superior has to take with the utmost seriousness and if Richard cannot see that it will probably be hard for him to live in community under any Superior.

This *may* be the leadership's only attempt—and it would be a quite oblique one at that—to address any part of the body of my letter to Fr. Jetté. Fr. George mentions it at all, I think, only because it concerns him indirectly. The objective reasons he refers to are of course the scandal caused by my public self-identification as a gay priest and the implication this had for Fr. Jetté and his advisors that I had challenged the Oblates' "entire religious commitment" in plain sight of everyone. This, Fr. George is asserting, justifies the extreme measures that the general leadership adopted to quell the crisis, and if I cannot understand that, then my lack of empathy for the leadership's situation is still another reason why I am not suited for membership. (NOTE: This is classic Church sophistry. And one can easily see how this same thought pattern figures into covering up the worldwide clergy abuse scandal. Extreme means, even if they are illegal, are justified to quell a crisis.)

Of course, in my letter to Fr. Jetté I was not denying the leadership's right in 1981 to take appropriate steps to protect the collective apostolate from any dangers, as they perceived them. What I argued against was the nature of those perceptions and particularly the type of process that the leadership set in motion without ever pausing to consider their accuracy. The specific passage in my letter to Fr. Jetté to which Fr. George seems to be alluding concerns the document *Dismissal*, which Fr. George himself hand-delivered to Fr. Waldie. That document, you recall, invited Fr. Waldie to transpose Fr. Jetté's original assertions of my guilt of "living a false lifestyle" onto an obedience for the express purpose of procuring my dismissal. Here I quote from my June 11, 1984 letter to Fr. Jetté concerning that document:

I subsequently learned that the need to transpose all the preceding allegations onto the question of obedience was understood long before the meeting of June 7 [1981]. Two months earlier, on April 7, 1981, Fr. Francis George hand-delivered to Fr. Waldie a two-page document outlining the steps Fr. Waldie should take. I now believe that everything that followed April 7, including Fr. Waldie's letter of May 14, was an attempt to follow these guidelines. The document, entitled simply *Dismissal*, explains a great deal; and the meeting of June 7 was in quite large measure an attempt to fulfill its requirements.

Father, it may be irrelevant, and perhaps reflects an over-sensitivity on my part, but I must tell you of the sadness I felt when I first read this document. It lacks even the graciousness to refer to me by name, and is content to call me merely "R.W." This monogram seemed to me to indicate the extent to which the proceedings had become depersonalized and transformed into a purely abstract "situation." Furthermore, it seemed to me that the author could have cared less who "R.W." might be or how his present predicament had evolved or even what he might be accused of.

My position then—as now—was that the attempt to misappropriate my vow of obedience as the vehicle to attain my dismissal was—and is—wrong. And whatever may or may not have been the personal motives of those who did it, the consequences of that act "got" me in the most enduring, painful, and personal ways imaginable. Besides, if I were to be removed from the Congregation on a charge of technical disobedience, all other members of the Congregation, as well as everyone else watching from the sidelines, would interpret this as a confirmation of the original charges brought against me—that I was living a life incompatible with the teachings of the Church and with the vows I'd taken and I was encouraging others to do the same.

A significant factor in my growing sense of futility during this period was that more and more people were getting involved in my case, and they by no means agreed among themselves as to what the case was about or how to proceed with it. While being on the receiving end of all this "interest" necessarily made this problem more obvious to me than to them, it is to Fr. George's credit that he perceived the danger if not unfairness of so many people taking an active part. Though I could not share his optimism about issues already clarified, and though he left a number of people off his list, still the following remark by Fr. George represented to me potentially the most constructive part of his letter:

[Fr. Jetté] also mentioned that I might add any comments of my own. I hesitate to do so, for fear of complicating an already difficult situation. The dialogue originally was between Fr. Jetté and Fr. Waldie and Fr. Wagner. At one point Fr. Charles Breault had a very important conversation with Richard, and now you are taking Paul Waldie's place in the dialogue. Another voice only risks confusing the issues that have already been clarified.

Unfortunately, as we have seen, even Fr. George could not resist adding his voice to the din, and his insight passed by unobserved.

Now for a few words about the meeting with Fr. Harris at which he gave me a copy of Fr. George's letter. Fr. Harris's report to Fr. Jetté of January 3, 1986—which he did not mail to me until November 28—is not particularly useful, so I will rely on my own diary notes.

It was not a friendly meeting. My cursory reading of Fr. George's letter left me baffled. I could not understand what he was doing with the phrase "lack of confidence," though I could plainly see that he was continuing the leadership's studied disregard of my letter to Fr. Jetté —clearly another wasted effort on my part. That, combined with my awareness of the blocks of time that were allowed to fall away between letters and meetings, left me generally skeptical. For his part, Fr. Harris was ready to take up with gusto Fr. Jetté's two lines of inquiry. I demurred. The process thus far, fixated as it was on vague questions of disposition and confidence, was getting us nowhere. Meandering, formless, outside any canonical process of review or adjudication, it promised nothing but more of the same into the indefinite future. The longer I remained outside, the more blurred the process became, and the easy words of "solicitude" on everyone's lips did nothing to bring matters into clearer focus. I wanted definition, and that required specific procedures for coming to terms with the history of my situation and for determining my status. After again requesting an impartial hearing, I took my leave of Fr. Harris.

That was the last I would hear from him or any Oblate for another year. The fifth anniversary of the Oblates' break with me came and went almost unnoticed. My diary entry for August 1—the date that I had come to associate with Fr. Waldie's forwarding of the acts of dismissal to Rome in 1981—states merely: "Five years." Though I could scarcely attend Mass without experiencing profound sadness over my lost priesthood, I rarely thought of the Oblates, and almost never nostalgically.

In the first week of November I received a phone call from New York inviting me to participate on a talk show program (The Donahue Show) with Fr. John McNeill, SJ, the author of the classic work *The Church and the Homosexual*. I had great admiration for Fr. McNeill and considered our situations similar in many respects, so I did not hesitate to accept the honor of appearing with him.

The program aired nationally on November 12, 1986. In no time Fr. Harris was again present.

His first letter to me after his yearlong silence is noteworthy for what it reveals about the leadership's forgetful and fragmented grasp of events. Dated November 28, 1986, it included a copy of his report to Fr. Jetté on my meeting with Fr. Harris a year earlier. It upbraids me for my "independent behavior" in not obtaining my Provincial Superior's permission before doing such a program, and it proposed to take serious action accordingly. The most astonishing feature of his letter, however, is its attempt to characterize my TV appearance as a breach of promise. Fr. Harris reaches all the way back to my letters of February 26 and June 5, 1981—the very letters which Fr. Harris's predecessor had *not* accepted in order to push the dismissal process through. I quote Fr. Harris:

> [In 1981] without the approval of your superiors you addressed the issue of homosexuality in the media. When the administration called you to accountability you agreed to remain silent on this issue. In a letter dated June 5, 1981 to Father Paul Waldie, O.M.I. you state, "...I affirmed that I would never again pursue my ministry in the popular press or media, and I reaffirmed this in my letter of February 26."
>
> Participation in the show of November 12, 1986 is a breach of promise and contrary to the agreement entered into between you and the former provincial. This independent behavior without approval and contrary to the agreement, in my opinion, calls for action on my part.

These remarks were simply ignorant, and I called Fr. Harris at once to let him know my mind. Fr. Harris was peevish and condescending, and his statements on my case, as always, were rambling and vague. On December 5, I responded with a letter explaining the absurdity of his understanding of the situation, and I did not conceal my disgust with the "process" and his contributions to it:

> Your letter's tone of accusation and veiled threat, though in a way not surprising, is a little ridiculous in context. After five years of being made a pariah and of having to adapt my life in *every respect* to that of a layperson, and after a year of having heard no word from you, am I now being chastised

for acting as an independent agent? You talk as though, after all I have been through; I still have absolutely all of an Oblate's obligations but enjoy absolutely none of an Oblate's rights. In short, given my *de facto* status, any suggestion that I have acted irresponsibly seems strangely out of place. And to attach a letter that I expected to receive from you a year ago to one in which new actions are threatened against me suggests a peculiar sense of irony....

How many opportunities have been missed, Andrew, to write a different kind of letter than the one that I just received from you? How many opportunities have been squandered to reassure me that the community is resolved to bring this matter to a speedy and honorable conclusion? One appearance on TV and a year's indifference and lethargy become suddenly a stir. Yes, Andrew, I'm still alive. I did not disappear just because Fr. Waldie, Fr. Breault, Fr. George, and Fr. Jetté have all retired and left you holding the bag. And your what's-the-problem-now-Wagner tone changes nothing concerning your continuing responsibility in this.

Your suggestion that my appearance on the Donahue Show on November 12, 1986 somehow breaks a promise made to Fr. Waldie on February 26, 1981, wholly lacks plausibility because it neglects everything that happened after that date. Because the community failed to take up my pledge of February, 1981 as the basis for reconciliation—the very misstep that caused the convolutions of this case to begin with—all subsequent offers concerning media exposure and the like have to be viewed as part of ... on-going negotiations.

If we could clear up the matter of Fr. Jetté's original charges and *if* we could arrive at honorable terms of reconciliation, *then* I would agree to such and such conditions, including never again appearing on TV. These offers, too, were never taken up. All I received were more threats, more bullying, more demands, more aimless interviews, more delays, more long silences, and, finally, what amounted to a complete break. You seemed to just stop dealing with it. Perhaps you did so in the hope that it would go away, that you wouldn't have to hear about it anymore. Frankly I find it hard to understand how you can suggest that I have broken a promise or acted in bad faith without yourself blanching.

Another whole year of this business has been yawned away.   Only when I acted in accordance with my *de facto* independence and appeared on the Donahue Show, did you abruptly recall the outstanding business between us and begin to take action. And the question now, of course, is what action you propose to take. Had the community accepted my pledge of February 1981, or for that matter any of my subsequent offers, the Donahue Show would not have been done and you would not be reading this letter. Do you seriously propose to start the whole thing over *again*?

Evidently my point was well taken. Later I discovered that on November 6, 1986—six days before my TV appearance—Fr. Gilles Cazabon, the new Vicar General, had written to Fr. Harris to elicit "views" about "possible approaches" to my case. On January 19, 1987, Fr. Harris informed me that the Provincial Council, during its meeting in the first week of December—which was to have taken up the issue of my supposed "breach of promise"—decided instead "to forward a recommendation to the General Administration, requesting they set up an ad hoc committee to review the situation and make recommendations to the Provincial Council." "Hopefully," Fr. Harris concluded, "this procedure will enable us to continue the process in a pastoral way."

CHAPTER 4

1987 - 1989

Five months later, in early July 1987, I received an unexpected phone call from Fr. Ronald Carignan, OMI. (NOTE: He is the successor to Fr. Breault as Regional Councillor for the United States and predecessor of Fr. Waldie as provincial of the Western US Province—my province.) He invited me to meet with him at the Provincial House on July 14. With him would be Fr. Francis Morrissey, OMI, an Oblate canonist from St. Paul University, Ottawa, flown in to bring his expertise to bear on the "situation." Fr. Harris would also attend. This would be my first contact with the General Administration since Fr. Jetté's last letter to me in February 1985, and it would mark a turning point in my controversy with the Oblates. The purpose of the meeting—to quote Fr. Morrissey's official record—was "to clarify the canonical status of Rev. Richard Wagner, and to move towards a possible resolution of an unclear situation."

Just before the meeting begins, Fr. Morrissey takes me aside, introduces himself and tells me that he too is gay. With a wink, a nod and a pat on the back he lets me know that he is on my side and that we have a special bond in our gay priest identity. I'm astonished by the revelation, but I welcome his openness and his solidarity.

Fr. Carignan presided, but the meeting was entirely Fr. Morrissey's. I am sure Fr. Morrissey knew where he wanted the conversation to go and how to lead it there, which is why he was given the assignment. His official record is less a faithful account of our talk than the script he brought with him to direct it.

After the meeting was in progress, Fr. Carignan informed me that I would be assisted in obtaining any canonical counsel I might require. This was very odd. During our earlier telephone conversation, when he invited me to the meeting, I had specifically asked Fr. Carignan if I would need canonical representation, and he replied, "No, no, that would be a sign of bad faith."

Now Fr. Morrissey was about to confront me with a two-and-half-hour, highly nuanced, often confusing presentation designed to put before me all the canonical options and to nudge me toward the choice that the leadership had already decided upon before they arranged the meeting.

Fr. Morrissey began by listing ten "available options," which fell under four general headings: (a) Reintegration into the Congregation; (b) Absence; (c) Exclaustration; (d) Departure from the Congregation. He then listed the ten "available options," one option under the first heading, two under the second, three under the third, and four under the fourth:

1) Reintegration into the Congregation

2) Permission of absence for a ministry mandated by the Congregation

3) Absence for personal reasons

4) Voluntary exclaustration enabling Fr. Wagner to function as a priest.

5) Qualified exclaustration

6) Imposed exclaustration

7) Voluntary departure, but continuing in priesthood (secularization)

8) Voluntary departure with laicization

9) Dismissal from the Congregation

10) Dismissal from the Congregation and from the clerical state

After a cursory discussion, Fr. Morrissey eliminated three of the ten "available" options, and then classified the rest as "preferred options." Both categories of options were misnomers, which unnecessarily confused matters.

By far the majority of the "available options" were not options at all. Nos. 6, 9 and 10 in particular were, to speak bluntly, pure bluff. My six-year non-status in the Congregation was the leadership's own doing, not mine, as the fading away of the first dismissal process amply demonstrated. The leadership had arranged this meeting for the sole purpose of trying to maneuver out of the difficult situation they had gotten themselves into. Thus I knew that they had no basis whatsoever for the extreme canonical measures represented by Nos. 6, 9 and 10. But note how Fr. Morrissey characterized their elimination from the list. These options, his resume states, "would not be the preferred options, since they are not voluntary and could, in some instances, amount to a dishonorable discharge, thus jeopardizing possibilities of finding a bishop enabling Fr. Wagner to continue in priestly ministry."

Their appearance on the list, in other words, was for no other purpose than to give the impression that only leadership forbearance forbade their selection. (It is very important to observe that even in Fr. Morrissey's report, the option of finding a bishop was *assumed* even before we discussed and rejected reintegration—understood as a return to community—as a possible option.)

Nos. 2 and 3 dealt with the two forms of permitted absence from the Congregation—the first for a mandated ministry, the second for personal reasons. Both forms of absence presupposed normal standing in the Congregation, the very condition I had *not* enjoyed for six years. Since during all those years I had been protesting my uncanonical separation, for me at any point to request permission for a one-year absence for personal reasons would have been incoherent. As for absence for a mandated ministry—an option that would not emerge as viable until after my exoneration—the leadership blocked that by refusing to revoke the obedience of 1981.

So under the circumstances neither of these options was "available" either, although the second—after my exoneration—would become the best, indeed the only viable option from my point of view. The leadership, as events would make clear, never wanted it to emerge as a real option. Why, then, does it show up on Fr. Morrissey's list of "preferred options?" Its presence, along with absence for personal reasons, was, as I shall show later, very important in connection with an unspoken, secondary purpose which Fr. Morrissey brought with him to the meeting. That purpose was to quietly identify my status in the Congregation as "tolerated absence."

Following the Morrissey meeting, the leadership would habitually employ this term to characterize my standing as an Oblate, even though they would never define it. Why the term was introduced and regularly repeated, and above all what it meant in relation to the leadership's overall objective, are important subjects I shall return to in Chapter 4 of this narrative. Till then, I shall leave the term appropriately mysterious.

Options No. 7 and 8, two forms of voluntary departure, were very far from being preferred, and for the same familiar reason. I was not going to leave the Congregation voluntarily until I had my name cleared. No. 4, Voluntary Exclaustration, was not an immediate option because I had no bishop to sponsor me in a ministry. Thus everything presumably came down to a choice between the two remaining options: No. 1, Reintegration into the Congregation, and No. 4, Qualified Exclaustration, an indult to live outside the institute for up to three years but without the ability to function as a priest.

This was the option Fr. Morrissey had come all the way from Ottawa to get me to accept.

When it came time to discuss Reintegration, the result was predictable. At the very beginning of the meeting I had asked: "Why was I assured a number of years ago that I would be dismissed from the Congregation, and then nothing happened?" If the object of our meeting was to clarify my status, I reasoned, then we should begin by clarifying the events that made my status so unclear.

"In response to his (my) question," Fr. Morrissey's report reads, "it was noted that the Provincial Superior and Council had asked the General Administration to set up an ad hoc committee to review the dossier. Such a committee was established and reviewed the situation based on available documents. ...The present meeting is the result of this request." In other words, the history of my situation would *not* be a topic of conversation.

Nevertheless, when the topic of reintegration came up, I again insisted on the history. Reintegration, I stated, would depend on three things: an apology from the leadership for its wrongful treatment of me, acknowledgment of me as an Oblate in good standing, and permission to develop my ministerial connections outside the community as the most obvious way to prepare the groundwork for incardination. Fr. Harris's immediate retort was that reintegration would require that I reside in community, that I would not participate in unauthorized media presentations, that I would accept an obedience from him, and that my future ministry would have nothing to do with homosexuality.

Obviously Fr. Harris and I had entirely different notions of "reintegration." For him it meant simply reasserting authority over me and putting the history of my ordeal in a closet and forgetting it. But as I have observed, my departure from the Congregation by way of finding a bishop was already assumed even before we discussed reintegration. In view of that, and of the history of my six-year banishment, return to an Oblate community was out of the question. Consequently for me "reintegration" could only mean formal exoneration so that I would have a credible basis to seek a bishop and eventually leave the Congregation. In his report Fr. Morrissey described this possibility as "temporary reintegration" and declared it unacceptable to the General Administration because "this would in some way simply continue the status quo."

Fr. Morrissey was half wrong and half right in his assessment. He was half wrong because from my perspective achieving explicit exoneration after so long a banishment would hardly be the *status quo*. He was half right because if no steps were taken after exoneration to normalize my status in the form of an assignment, I would still be merely out in the cold with no real connection to the community.

The point, however—though it was conspicuously avoided at the time— was that exoneration would open up another, far more constructive possibility. It was highly artificial of Fr. Morrissey to limit the alternatives to either having a bishop immediately in hand or being consigned to priestly limbo while I went in search of one—much less forgetting the whole affair and moving into an Oblate house. I am thinking particularly of option No. 2, permission to be absent from the Institute to pursue a mandated ministry, a ministry that the leadership could easily have facilitated. But because the fundamental issues separating us were again slighted, such a creative alternative could not be entertained, and the meeting ended with Frs. Morrissey and Carignan emphatically urging me to accept Qualified Exclaustration as the *only* available option.

On July 20 Fr. Harris sent me a copy of Fr. Morrissey's report. After reflecting on it for almost a month, I wrote Fr. Carignan on August 17, 1987, to give him my decision. I am going to quote this letter in its entirety. It is important not only for its immediate purpose, but also for its summary of the whole pre-1988 era and for what it predicts, unwittingly, about the era soon to open up.

Dear Ron,

This letter is in response to our July 14, 1987 meeting at the Provincial House, during which you, Fr. Harris, and Fr. Morrissey urged me to accept Qualified Exclaustration as the only way to clarify my status and thus make a start on ending the incredibly protracted ordeal, which I have been made to suffer. This proposed option is, I regret to say, unacceptable, and I devote the rest of this letter to explaining why.

To begin with, it is important to set aside a condition which some would like to impose on our discussion but which

I find not only peculiar but also impossible. This condition stipulates that if we are to make progress toward remedying my predicament we must somehow suspend or bracket off or erase from our memories the very events that enable us to define it. In particular we are asked to forget the history of how the congregation, through a series of false and manufactured charges followed by years of indecision and neglect, created in its midst a *persona non grata* whom it then could neither induce to leave voluntarily (for he saw that as tantamount to admitting guilt) nor dismiss (for he was not guilty of any dismissible offense).

     In place of this history we are asked to substitute a convenient fiction, based on certain vague and legally immaterial "perceptions," that this case involves nothing more than a discredited but intractable member whom the congregation is bending over backwards to try to help. We are asked, in other words, to forget everything *except* the blank "perception" that I am unworthy to be an Oblate but that I remain deaf to the only "practical" alternatives available—all of which, it so happens, are punitive in nature.

     Obviously, the history of this trouble is the *only* thing that cries out for a solution. As you know, I have labored very long and very hard to keep that history in the foreground where it belongs, because as soon as it begins to slip away nothing about this unhappy business makes sense. Frankly I am amazed that there can still be misunderstanding as to my resolve on this point: The only question before us is the question of justice, and I am fully prepared to endure dismissal before I sacrifice my conscience and the principles involved.

     Given this context, what might we expect Qualified Exclaustration to accomplish? The main reason given for this option is that it will enable us to "to buy some time." But the formal relinquishment of my priesthood for what would almost certainly be a period of three years—is that not very costly time? And who, really, needs this time? Andrew made the surprising suggestion that it is *I* who need time, so as better to discern what I want to do. But I have spent every day of the last [six] years doing that; it has been for me a full-time occupation. Time and again, in the most unmistakable terms, without the least ambiguity, I have told the congregation where I stand. I require not another day, not another hour for discernment. So if I am not the one who needs time, perhaps the congregation needs it; but if the congregation needs it, why must I once again be the one to bear the cost?

Nothing more typifies the congregation's handling of this matter than its unconscionable squandering of time. Lately some have tried to interpret this stalling as actually something done for my benefit, as a kind of indulgence or favor, a sign of the congregation's long-suffering patience regarding me. But in truth it is just this kind of year in, year out temporizing that fosters the growth of those very "perceptions" which some would now have us believe are the substance of this case.

Its effect has been to obfuscate, not to clarify; to let memories grow dull, not to sharpen them. It is a well known fact that the longer an innocent person is made to linger under suspicion, the more an indifferent "perception" of guilt grows and solidifies around him. Conversely, the longer group responsibility for a bad situation is shirked, the more it becomes diffused and unassignable.

Clearly in my situation, where the original accusers have actually left the scene, responsibility is by now so thinly distributed that I fear my case has become little more than a fat dossier easily passed from hand to hand in a great circle, with no mechanism in place to bring a halt to its movement. And the more time we buy the worse it gets.

Of course, Ron, I know that it was your personal hope, as my friend, that the time gained by Qualified Exclaustration would provide a cooling off period—as though this case were not already in a state of deep freeze—during which we could approach various bishops to see if one might sponsor me in a ministry. But consider how implausible such a prospect is.

First of all, such a move would make my status more ambiguous, not less so. Not only would I continue to be *persona non grata*, with all the old unaddressed accusations still looming in the background, but I would be corralled into a temporary (though very long-term) situation which I neither need nor want and which the congregation—let's be frank about this—would be *hoping* might not elapse before my permanent exile could somehow or other be arranged.

So the quandary then would be: how, with my situation as weirdly ambiguous as this, could I possibly be presented to a bishop? What would one say to him? "Here is a discredited Oblate whose present status is Qualified Exclaustration but who we do not wish to return to us and whom we cannot persuade to leave—so would you be kind enough to take him off our hands?" I'm sorry to sound facetious, Ron, but the more thought I give to this proposed option the more I can't help seeing it in an ironic light.

Now once this bishop—who surely would have enough clerical prudence not to buy damaged goods—says NO, what happens then? Why, then everything reverts right back to where it is now: to the same *persona non grata* status, the same threatened sanctions, the same effort to force me out without having to face the history of why I am in this predicament in the first place. We will have come full circle and at the same time transformed seven years of neglect and forgetfulness into a round decade of the same.

Clearly this is the wrong way to go about it. It is putting the cart before the horse—an arrangement that, as Thoreau once quipped, is neither lovely nor useful. The only way this case can be justly settled is for the congregation to acknowledge those egregious actions and failures to act which destroyed my viability as an Oblate; to clear my name of all false, transposed, and manufactured charges; and to declare me an Oblate in good (if unusual) standing. In return I am more than willing, as I have been from the start, to tender the congregation such *reasonable* guarantees as it needs to protect its perceived interests.

Then, with an Oblate-endorsed explanation of this seven-year odyssey in hand, I could seek out a bishop, apply for exclaustration, and take up a worthwhile (if ever so quiet) ministry and so get on with my priestly life. If you consider this option to be no less implausible than the previous one, it at least has the virtue of putting the horse before the cart and of pulling in the right direction.

Ron, I trust you understand that in rejecting the option urged upon me I am not rejecting the process. I remain open, as ever, to a truly equitable solution.

———————

On August 27, I met again with Frs. Carignan and Harris at the Provincial House. Fr. Richard Haslam, OMI, the Provincial Secretary, was present as recorder. His sanitized report is typical of all the official accounts of my meetings with Oblate representatives. Frs. Carignan and Harris traded off posing questions, comments, and accusations, all the while protesting Oblate good will.

Fr. Carignan disliked my use of the term *persona non grata*, describing it as "toxic language", and pointedly instructed me "for your own good" to "keep a positive tone both verbally and in writing". Never mind that the term described my condition precisely, and that during my six years of banishment from community the leadership had given me absolutely nothing to be positive about. I was being told to pretend that my condition was not what it was, but simply a "misunderstanding" for which I bore all of the responsibility. Anything I might say that implied leadership wrongdoing was branded "negative" and a reflection of an attitude problem on my part.

(NOTE: I feel it is important to interject a bit of a confession here. People who were sexually abused as children, as I was by and Oblate priest superior when I was 14 years old, will always have trust issues later in life. This is particularly true with regards to authority figures in their lives, those who claim to be their advocates and allies and profess to have their best interest at heart. After all, it is precisely by means of manipulating and violating the child's trust that the sexual abuse can happen. I fully admit that I have these issues, even to this day.

So it should come as no surprise that I remained highly skeptical of the intentions of these Oblate superiors who insist they know what is best for me.)

Indeed the more I attempted to discuss the specifics of what clearing my name would entail as a prelude to seeking a bishop, the more Frs. Carignan and Harris worked to heap on me further insinuations of misconduct. In particular, during their numerous questions and comments, Frs. Carignan and Harris were consciously planting the phrase 'tolerated absence' into the record, and, as it turned out, that was far more important to their purpose than anything else that appeared to be going on.

But as in the Morrissey meeting, the general swirl of impressions prevented me from hearing anything significant in that innocuous-sounding label. I was trying to keep attention focused on the history of the controversy and on the need to restore my good standing as an Oblate. In view of that overriding interest, the label's recurrence in Fr. Carignan and Fr. Harris's remarks did not catch my ear in the way it perhaps should have. Again, I shall discuss the significance of this in considerable detail later.

Despite the down-in-the-ditch aspect of the meeting, it did prove decisive in a number of respects. The consensus reached at our previous meeting that I would leave the Congregation by way of finding a sponsoring bishop was reaffirmed. Moreover, while I pursued this option I would, in the words of Fr. Haslam's report, "remain an active member of the province." Even though I was in no sense an active member, I decided to give this phrase a diplomatic interpretation. Given our unusual situation, an obedience to move into Lenox Avenue (the provincial headquarters) or some other Oblate house would probably be more of a hindrance than a help in facilitating my departure.

In closing the meeting, Fr. Carignan suggested that we should do four things: "...develop a mutually acceptable chronology of events; move toward a statement of reconciliation; develop a statement on Father Wagner's views of the church's teachings on sexuality; [and] come to an agreement that Father Wagner not use the media at this time." In view of the glacial movements that had characterized the process up to then and the extreme reluctance to allow any hint of leadership malfeasance to be expressed in our meetings, I was not especially sanguine about Fr. Carignan's proposals. In fact, given their make-work quality and their obvious primary aim of bottling me up, I felt a distinct chill in the air.

Nevertheless I agreed to put together a draft chronology. With the emergence of a chance, however dim, to salvage my priesthood, I was willing to put my shoulder to the wheel one more time to see if I couldn't budge the leadership from its rut.

Over the next six weeks I re-read the dossier and composed my chronology, and I mailed it on October 9, 1987. I received no acknowledgment, however, until the following May 9, 1988, after placing several calls to Fr. Carignan and the Provincial House. Fr. Haslam, the Provincial Secretary, wrote to me on May 10, apologized for the oversight, and enclosed a copy of a draft chronology that he had prepared "some time ago at the request of the Provincial." (I should also like to note that after the August 27 meeting, Fr. Harris dropped out of the process altogether; except for this one reference to his assigning my case to Fr. Haslam, I would not hear from him again for another year.)

Fr. Haslam and I agreed to meet at St. Mary's parish in Oakland on May 19 to compare chronologies and work toward a mutually acceptable version. At the meeting we quickly became bogged down in differing "interpretations" and "perceptions." Typically Fr. Haslam would not admit even the possibility of wrongdoing by anyone in the Oblate leadership. Indeed he seemed to argue, in a way reminiscent of Fr. George, that the leadership's responsibilities to the community and to the Church are so overriding that it is entitled to act on its judgments even before determining whether those judgments might be rash or false. He did not seem to acknowledge any countervailing responsibilities to individual members, which must be weighed in the balance. Instead he recommended that I take a "positive view" of the General Administration's failure to follow through on my dismissal and to engage me in this six-year "dialogue."

As usual in such discussions, my removal from the Congregation throughout all those years was interpreted as an act of charity.

Fr. Haslam also denied that institutional homophobia was a strong factor behind the General Administration's rush to judgment in 1981, and that my suggestions of being persecuted for being gay were wholly unfounded. Fr. Haslam expressed the point this way in his minutes of our meeting: "I also asked Richard to take a close look, for his own sake, at some of his expressed feelings of being victimized. I felt there was no grounds for his feeling that the Oblates were trying to get rid of him merely because he was a gay person. He could take a more objective view."

For my part, I reiterated my wish for an apology from the General and Provincial administrations and a public affirmation of me as an Oblate in good standing. And at this point Fr. Haslam made a crucial suggestion, which I at once accepted. Fr. Haslam's minutes express our understanding as follows:

> We agreed that to move the situation forward to some point of further dialogue towards the goal of having him be able to find a Bishop, it might be helpful if he was willing to draw up *a minimal statement* of what he feels needs to be acknowledged by the Oblate Administration so that he could 'have his good name restored'. I did say that he should be realistic in this matter.

I immediately set to work on a draft statement and posted it to Fr. Carignan on May 21, 1988. I also sent a copy to Fr. Harris, receipt of which he promptly acknowledged on June 4.

In my cover letter to Fr. Carignan I explained that my draft statement asked for the minimum; that it was simple, straightforward, and correct in tone; and that it let the whole case rest at the point of natural resolution it had attained back on February 26, 1981. Here, then, is the complete text of my draft statement.

> We the undersigned take this opportunity to address a controversy of long-standing between the Congregation and one of its members. Our action here is not for the purpose of insinuating blame or bad faith on the part of anyone involved. Rather it is a determined effort to make peace where there has been unnecessary discord and to preserve the integrity of

the community by reaffirming the right to fair treatment of its members.

On February 8, 1981, the then Superior General of the Missionary Oblates of Mary Immaculate, wrote a letter to the then Provincial of the Western Province concerning Fr. Richard Wagner, OMI, a member of that province, and specifically concerning an article Fr. Wagner had published in the November 21, 1980 issue of the *National Catholic Reporter*. In his letter, the Superior General stated in part:

> *[Fr. Wagner's] declaration: "I, too, am a gay priest..."*
> *and the principles he expresses in that article are incompatible*
> *with the teachings of the Church and with the vows he has*
> *pronounced.*
>
> ...
>
> *If there isn't in him a sincere disposition to change his*
> *way of life and to fully accept the requisites of the commitments*
> *he has taken, the simplest solution would be that he personally*
> *ask to leave the priesthood and religious life. Otherwise—even*
> *though the solution would be a still more sorrowful one—he will*
> *be dismissed from the Congregation.*
>
> ...
>
> *By doing nothing we are not helping this confrere*
> *who has installed himself in a false life, nor are we helping the*
> *Religious Institute which looses all credibility.*

Of particular concern in these passages is the imputation of moral fault. This accusation seems to follow from the Superior General's judgment that Fr. Wagner's statement of his sexual orientation was one and the same as a statement of sexual activity on his part. Apparently unfamiliar with the distinction between sexual orientation and sexual behavior, the Superior General mistakenly concluded that Fr. Wagner had announced his adoption of "a false life" contrary to his professed life under vows.

The General's eagerness to protect the reputation and credibility of the Congregation, though laudable, had the unfortunate effect of compromising the reputation and credibility of Fr. Wagner. Times being what they were, an atmosphere of misinformation and apprehension pervaded the subject of homosexuality in religious life, and this no doubt compounded misunderstanding and led to needless polarization.

Without belaboring or discounting the sincere efforts at reconciliation, which were made during the intervening years, we now find it suitable to return to what we acknowledge and accept as Fr. Wagner's good faith response to the Superior General's charge. In his letter of February 26, 1981, Fr. Wagner stated in part:

I deny, unequivocally and in good conscience, what has been asserted against me. It has never been my practice to make public profession of my sins; that is a matter strictly between me and my confessor; and no one has the right to demand to know or presume to know that sacred confidentiality.

As for what I said in a public forum, my statements must be taken on their own merits and within their proper context. I have never in any public forum intentionally or knowingly affirmed or denied sexual activity on my part subsequent to my vows of celibacy and chastity. If in the judgment of my superiors I have made statements, which can be so construed, I am more than willing to deny that in my writing of these statements I intended that they should be so construed.

...

Father, from the beginning, as you well know, I have made no secret of my being gay. From the first I have tirelessly repeated the difference between being gay and being sexually active. And by no means is this distinction peculiar to me; psychologists and sexologists universally acknowledge the truth and usefulness of this distinction.

...

Let me say without further ado, however, that it was never my intention to advocate or defend sexual activity on the part of priests and religious, or in any way to challenge the teaching authority of the church in such matters.

...

If in the best judgment of my superiors they consider the article or any part of it to be advocating principles contrary to the teachings of the church, then I will freely renounce that article or any part of it, which has given offense.

...

Father, you know that I have never denied the teaching authority of the church. You also know that no teaching authority worthy of its name discourages or inhibits free inquiry. The questions and arguments with which I am routinely and inevitably confronted in my work—to which my piece in NCR witnesses—requires calm, deliberate, and reasoned answers. For they are not posed in a spirit of defiance; they are an invitation to open, honest, and direct dialogue. Our church is preeminently the church of reason; she never shirks dealing with the most complex issues in a dispassionate, detailed, and reasoned way.

We now declare this matter resolved. The Congregation is satisfied with Fr. Wagner's explanation of his offending remarks, his apology to whomever may have been offended by those remarks, and his re-affirmation of his commitment to religious life. We regret the hardships that Fr. Wagner has had to sustain in the course of this controversy and sincerely desire that his reputation and credibility as an Oblate and as a priest shall be restored, and we stand ready to assist him in discerning the future of his ministry.

This done, we now embrace Fr. Wagner without further reserve and restore to him all rights and privileges of membership in our Congregation.

[Signed]

Superior GeneralCounselors

I was determined that this should be the end of my ordeal. I wanted no more interrogations into my opinions and dispositions and no more haggling over relative perceptions concerning my case. I wanted immediate acknowledgment that my years of exile were unjustified, affirmation that I was an Oblate in good standing in the Congregation, and an explicit commitment by the leadership to assist me in finding a bishop so that I might eventually incardinate and save my priesthood. Consequently I put my intentions to Fr. Carignan in the bluntest terms:

> If the General Administration cannot bring itself to sign this document, or one of similar purpose, I will ask you to inform me in writing of the canonical recourse open to me. I must insist, in other words, that if this last effort at an in-house resolution fails we must broaden the forum to include experts and authorities from outside the Congregation.
>
> I anticipate your prompt reply.

In five weeks I received from Rome the following letter written by Fr. Marcello Zago, OMI, Superior General, dated June 17, 1988:

> Dear Father Wagner,
>
> In this first letter to you, I want to greet you most fraternally in the Lord. I regret the fact that we did not get to meet during my visit to California last November. Perhaps the future will provide an occasion for such a meeting.
>
> Early in my term of office as Superior General, your Provincial Superior, Father Andrew Harris asked me to review the difficult situation that has existed for some time now, between the Congregation and yourself. I did so along with Father Ronald Carignan, General Councillor for the United States. I read your statement on homosexuality in the November 21, 1980 issue of the National Catholic Reporter, the

subsequent exchange of letters and the reports of numerous and sincere attempts at reconciliation. Since then, Fr. Carignan has kept me informed of the more recent initiatives during the past year.

It appears to me that at the very beginning, the distinction between sexual orientation and sexual activity was not clearly made and your statement came to imply more than was intended. From this, there followed the perception that you had adopted a false life contrary to your professed religious commitment. In your letter of February 26, 1981 to Father Fernand Jetté [sic!], then Superior General of the Oblates, you unequivocally denied what had been implied. You stated that it was never your intention to advocate or defend sexual activity on the part of priests and religious or in any way challenge the teaching authority of the Church in such matters.

You also state in the same letter: "I have never in any public forum intentionally or knowingly affirmed or denied sexual activity on my part subsequent to my vows of celibacy and chastity. If in the judgment of my superiors I have made statements which can be so construed, I am more than willing to deny that in my writing of those statements, I intended that they should be so construed."

I want you to know, Richard, that I accept the good faith of your response in that letter. I accept the explanation of your remarks as well as your apology to whomever may have been offended by those remarks. Also know that I deeply regret the hardship you have had to sustain in the course of this controversy and I welcome the reaffirmation of your commitment to religious life. It is my sincere desire that your reputation and credibility be restored, both as an oblate and as a priest.

I urge you to be in close dialogue with your Provincial Superior, Father Andrew Harris. I am certain he stands ready to assist you in discerning your future.

You can well appreciate that I must ask you to refrain from any further public statements relating to homosexuality without the prior authorization of your major superior. I am requiring this because of my responsibility to protect the good name of the Congregation and uphold the integrity of the Church's teaching in this sensitive and difficult area.

> As Superior General, I embrace you as my brother
> Oblate and recognize that you have all the rights, responsibilities
> and privileges of membership in our Congregation.

———————

Fr. Zago's letter is disarming and can easily mislead the uninitiated. Its tone is friendly and gracious, it adopts the general approach to resolving the controversy and even some of the phrasing contained in my draft statement, and it eschews the insinuating rhetoric that characterized so much of the leadership's dealings with me. When I first read the letter, I had every hope that at last the way was open to recovering my priesthood. I received it as a "saving act," a pledge to make good on the corporate errors of the past, as well as an assurance of leadership help in facilitating my transition.

Nevertheless, there was much about Fr. Zago's letter that was disturbing, beginning with his unfamiliarity with the dossier as reflected in his belief that I had written my letter of February 26, 1981 to Fr. Jetté rather than to Fr. Waldie. That is why, even in the midst of expressing my effusive thanks in my reply of June 22, 1988, I paused to remark: "I still have many questions. The how's and why's whirl about my head. But it is not good to tempt the fates, and I must learn to accept this goodness without seeking to know its origin."

Naturally I immediately compared Fr. Zago's letter with my draft document and the silences and omissions that I saw in the former were even more unsettling. I can explain my uneasiness by showing how each document deals with the three general points that I felt any such statement had to address: (1) a public affirmation of me as Oblate in good standing through an acceptance of my explanation and apology to the Congregation of February 1981; (2) a minimal acknowledgment of the inappropriateness and injuriousness of my seven years of banishment; and (3) an assurance of General Administration support for my pursuit of an assignment that would lead to incardination.

Again, I was asking for a minimal statement, not for the leadership to cry "Uncle." But even the minimal expressions of my concerns were cut down in the final draft to the point where almost nothing was left—nothing save the astonishing fact of the Superior General accepting the explanation and apology that I had tendered to my Provincial Superior seven years earlier.

What many might consider to be one of the strongest aspects of Fr. Zago's letter was for me a disappointment. I am referring to the fact that it *was* a private letter with copies sent only to the three Oblate officials in the direct chain of command down to me: Vicar General Cazabon, Regional Councillor Carignan, and Provincial Harris. My draft statement had envisaged an official document signed not only by Fr. Zago but also by the members of his council, and it was crucial to me that it be generally shared with the membership.

The vast majority of Oblates knew nothing of developments in my case and most of them doubtless thought that the affair had long been settled with my departure. Many people interested in my case assumed that I had been dismissed back in 1981—some thought I had been excommunicated! And to this day, whenever I have occasion to disabuse someone of this notion, I am met with wide eyes and open mouths.

Fr. Zago's letter, from the time he sent it to me five years ago, has been a kind of leadership secret, with all inquiries concerning my case put off with remarks such as: "This difficult situation is being handled by the appropriate authorities in a way that protects the rights of all concerned."

So the public aspect of condition No. 1 was definitely not achieved. The remainder of that condition, however, appeared to be met. The General finally accepted the explanation and apology that I tendered to the Congregation in 1981 and he clearly affirmed my good standing in the community.

Fr. Zago's letter was even more troubling in its treatment of condition No. 2. Comparing my draft statement with Fr. Zago's version, I could plainly see that his letter was a studied attempt to delete anything that might appear to acknowledge leadership responsibility for my seven-year exile or indeed anything that might suggest something irregular in the leadership's treatment of me during those years. One can see this sidestepping of accountability in a few significant alterations. Thus the draft statement began:

> Our [the General Administration's] action here is not for the purpose of insinuating blame or bad faith on the part of anyone involved. Rather it is a determined effort to make peace where there has been *unnecessary discord* and to preserve the *integrity of the community* by reaffirming *the right to fair treatment* of its members. [Emphasis added.]

Fr. Zago simply dropped this statement from his version, as well as my draft statement's indulgent remark, "[Fr. Jetté's] eagerness to protect the reputation and credibility of the Congregation, though laudable, had the unfortunate effect of compromising the reputation and credibility of Fr. Wagner."

Now compare my last paragraph with Fr. Zago's next-to-last paragraph:

[Draft statement:] This done, we now embrace Fr. Wagner without further *reserve* and *restore* to him all rights and privileges of membership in our Congregation. [Emphasis added.]

[Fr. Zago's letter:] As Superior General, I embrace you as my brother Oblate and *recognize* that you have all the rights, responsibilities and privileges of membership in our Congregation. [Emphasis added.]

Note how my draft statement's tempered reference to the leadership's long-standing *reserve* about me and their consequent need to *restore* my rights and privileges was altered to a *recognition* of my rights and privileges. This almost invisible alteration had the effect of removing any suggestion that the leadership was responsible for having ever denied me my rights and privileges during this seven-year process. Not a single allusion to the unfairness and pointlessness of my ordeal or to what these implied for the rights of individual Oblates and the health of the community found its way into Fr. Zago's text.

My fretting such alterations may sound like quibbling since the very existence of Fr. Zago's letter would seem by itself to be a stunning concession. Accepting my defense of February 26, 1981 as "a good faith response" seven years after its original rejection by Fr. Waldie and four years after being slighted by Fr. Jetté would certainly seem to imply that the leadership was wrong to impose a coercive obedience in disregard of that defense, that they were wrong to proceed with the dismissal process knowing of that mistake, and that they were wrong to allow the process following that mistake to stagnate for seven years, thus consigning me to a limbo which effectively destroyed my membership in the Congregation.

Fr. Zago's letter would seem to imply, in other words, that the obedience of 1981 was, at long last, nullified. Nevertheless, an *explicit* acknowledgment of the *restoration* of my rights, however muted, was essential to what I was asking for. Without such an acknowledgment, my being embraced as a brother Oblate sounded more like a work of charity than an act of restitution, and it left the issue of the obedience of 1981 still lingering unaddressed in the dim past.

I might note here that while Fr. Zago was unwilling to use the word 'restore' in connection with my rights and privileges, he was willing to use it in connection with my reputation and credibility, as can be seen in the quotation below. These, he conceded, *were* lost, but not because of anything done by the leadership. I simply can't understand how I could have "lost" such things on my own. His scrupulous avoidance of the topic shows that he can't admit to even the possibility that the leadership's conduct between 1981 and 1988 had anything to do with these losses, and he wants his expressed desire for their restoration to be understood as a mark of his charity and good will, not his obligation.

He decidedly does not want anyone to interpret his deep "regret" for the hardships I endured as a regret for hardships *inflicted.*

Fr. Zago's 1988 letter fell far short on the all-important third condition as well, namely, a pledge to follow up his letter with good faith action in support of my transition to secular priesthood. Fr. Zago's letter was only a necessary condition for saving my priesthood, not the sufficient condition. If my transition was to have any chance of succeeding, the General would have to back up his gracious tone with no less gracious deeds.

Again, I was not making extraordinary demands; I was merely requesting that the General Administration indicate its willingness to exercise a positive influence during the difficult phase to come. Here is a pairing up of the relevant passages from my draft statement and Fr. Zago's letter:

> [Draft Statement:] We regret the hardships which Fr. Wagner has had to sustain in the course of this controversy and sincerely desire that his reputation and credibility as an Oblate and as a priest shall be restored, and *we stand ready to assist him* in discerning the future of his ministry. [Emphasis added].

> [Fr. Zago's Letter:]...I deeply regret the hardship you have had to sustain in the course of this controversy and I welcome the reaffirmation of your commitment to religious life. It is my sincere desire that your reputation and credibility be restored, both as an oblate and as a priest. I urge you to be in close dialogue with your Provincial Superior, Father Andrew Harris. *I am certain* he *stands ready to assist you* in discerning your future. [Emphasis added.]

This was a certainty I could not share. In fact, Fr. Zago's apparent intention to withdraw from the process made me quite apprehensive, especially in view of Fr. Harris's complete dependence on the General Leadership's guidance. I regret having to say so, but Fr. Harris was incapable of independent decision-making. His judgment was poor and often obscured by personal grudges and affectations of office. His long absences from the process and his sluggish responses to my letters and phone calls did nothing to facilitate understanding or trust between us. His musings on my case were rambling, jargon-laden, and often incoherent; yet his official involvement in my case had been continuous from the time of his membership on Fr. Waldie's provincial council when it voted to dismiss me back in 1981. Consequently my relationship to Fr. Harris had always been strained, as anyone familiar with the dossier at that juncture would have been clearly aware.

Why, then, with such serious reservations, did I nevertheless accept Fr. Zago's letter? Why did I not ask for clarifications and better assurances? The answers are fairly obvious. First, the full subtext of Fr. Zago's letter would not become visible to me until two years later (I shall discuss this in its appropriate place). Second, it was my first contact with Fr. Zago, and despite his changes to my draft statement, his tone *was* convincing. Third, Fr. Zago did accept the general terms of the solution that I had been proposing for years, and given the significance of this act in the overall historical context, perhaps his caution regarding more public and explicit statements of leadership accountability was understandable. Fourth, it seemed to me that the leadership had a clear interest, not to say duty, to foster the incardination process to a successful end. Fifth, if I was to elicit Fr. Zago's support despite his reluctance to commit himself in writing, a return gesture of acceptance and confidence seemed called for.

In short, I *wanted* to believe the best—so I placed my trust in Fr. Zago. Nevertheless, his wish to return my case exclusively into the hands of Fr. Harris was a very bad omen.

It was nearly three months after Fr. Zago's letter before I was able to make my first contact with Fr. Harris. I had tried numerous times to reach him by telephone but without success. On August 24, 1988, Fr. Carignan and I discussed over dinner the implications of Fr. Zago's letter and how the local leadership had received it. He assured me that Frs. Harris and Haslam were both pleased that there had finally been a breakthrough and he urged me to be in contact with them. Two days later I wrote Fr. Harris the following conciliatory letter.

Dear Andrew,

I thought I would contact you by letter, as I seem to be having some difficulty reaching you by phone. I realize you are busy and have been traveling a bit. At any rate, in the past written thoughts have served us best.

I had dinner with Ron Carignan on Wednesday evening. We spoke at length about the June 17, 1988 letter from Fr. Zago.

It was so good to hear that Fr. Zago's letter was well received by you and Dick Haslam. I was hoping for the best, of course, but since we have not really spoken I couldn't be sure of your reaction. I am greatly relieved.

Ron mentioned that we ought to sit down soon to discuss the particulars of our reconciliation. That could not happen soon enough for me. I am eager to get back to full-time ministry. As soon as there is a resumption of Oblate financial support, I will be able to diminish my load of house cleaning.

Another concern I have involves the use of a community car. I have been using the cars of friends these past years when I needed to travel outside of the city. Frankly, I believe that some of the joy with which these friends greeted the news from Rome was actually an expression of relief, no more would they be pestered for use of their car. I too am relieved. These people have been overly generous and it is high time that responsibility for such things return to me and my community.

I have many other concerns, such as how we can best get the word out concerning the happy resolution of this affair. Many people have been praying and supporting me, and I'm sure you will agree that we should share the good news. Surely the Province will want to know that this long ordeal is over. We persevered and our perseverance was rewarded.

Finally, I am sending along a bill from Pacific Presbyterian Medical Center, which arrived last week. I thought all the paper work for my physical in July—the first in 10 years—went directly to the insurance company. I guess I was mistaken. I have none of the directions for submitting such material, so I'll just include it here. I am sure that someone at the Provincial House will know what to do with it.

I will close now. It is so nice to be able to speak with the community again in amicable terms. I look forward to hearing from you soon.

––––––––––––

Fr. Harris wrote back on September 12. Except for his brief note of June 4, acknowledging receipt of his copy of my draft statement to Fr. Carignan, this was the first letter I received from him since the previous September, when he sent me the minutes of our August 27, 1987 meeting with Fr. Carignan. Here is the complete text of his reply:

Dear Richard:

Thank you for your letter of August 26, 1988, expressing enthusiasm relating to the correspondence of Father Zago, O.M.I. with you.

The General requests that we continue in dialogue so that you can be empowered to enter a ministry with the approval and faculties of a local Ordinary. Presently, you do not have diocesan faculties.

I informed you at a previous meeting [August 27, 1987] that the Council and myself decided we could no longer permit the present situation of "tolerated absence" to continue, as it is contrary to our Constitutions.

I request that you meet with Richard Haslam, O.M.I. and myself on Thursday morning, September 15, 10:30 a.m., at the Provincial House.

Kind personal regards.

I was taken aback by Fr. Harris's highhanded posture. To immediately follow up Fr. Zago's affirmation of me as an Oblate in good standing with rhetoric portraying me as an outlaw seemed inappropriate if not ludicrous. In less than three months I had gone from being an Oblate in good standing to being again on the outs, and nothing at all had happened in the interim.

Perhaps Fr. Harris merely misspoke. Perhaps he intended to say that now that the General had embraced me as an Oblate in good standing, we must work quickly to find an assignment that would at once normalize my status and facilitate the incardination process in accordance with our previous agreement and Fr. Zago's explicit instructions. As events would bear out, however, Fr. Harris meant exactly what he said. Despite Fr. Zago's letter, Fr. Harris regarded me as *absent*, living in *violation* of the Constitutions of the Institute, and he was going to see to it that I was brought into conformity.

Fr. Harris replicated the tone and substance of his letter in our meeting of September 15. His deportment was cold and insinuating. There was a spiteful, almost game-playing quality in his approach to the questions before us, a quality that even Fr. Haslam's highly partial minutes do not conceal. Under the circumstances, I saw no point in continuing the meeting and on departing I announced that I would write immediately to Fr. Carignan to inform him of the unfortunate turn of events. This I did on September 17.

———————

Dear Fr. Carignan,

    Following your and Fr. General's request at the end of June, I finally had an opportunity to meet with Fr. Harris on Thursday, September 15, 1988. You will recall that at our dinner meeting on August 24 I had asked you how the news of the reconciliation authored by Fr. General was received at the Provincial House. I was trying to anticipate Fr. Harris's mood before meeting with him. You said Frs. Harris and Haslam were happy with the news and looked forward to helping me during this time of transition. I gathered from your remarks that past ill feelings had been set aside and I prepared myself accordingly.

    I was completely caught off guard by the hostility I encountered.

    When Fr. Zago wrote to me in June and pronounced me an Oblate in good standing, I understood him to mean that our long-awaited reconciliation was finally at hand. All that remained was for Fr. Harris and I to sit down in a spirit of fraternal dialogue to formalize the unofficial ministry that I have had to pursue these past years in San Francisco. You will recall that prior to the Superior General's recent letter to me, you, Fr. Harris, and I arrived at an informal understanding about my future with the Oblates. I indicated that because of the unhappy history that had transpired between me and the local leadership, the best course of action for me to take would be to seek exclaustration leading to incardination in the San Francisco Archdiocese. Such a move, however, should presuppose an interim period during which I would have a formally defined ministry with tangible community support commensurate with my status as an Oblate in good standing. In view of my intention to seek exclaustration, would it not seem preferable, indeed logical, that the formal recognition of my ministry should incorporate the pastoral connections and work which I have labored so hard to cultivate here these past years?

Clearly, Frs. Harris and Haslam have a quite different understanding of the General's embrace of me as an Oblate in good standing and of what would constitute a practical ministry in this period of transition. Contrary to the Superior General's unqualified statement, Fr. Harris asserted that my status is "tolerated absence" and that therefore being an Oblate in good standing means nothing until and unless he and his council call me to a ministry. Furthermore, he spoke in such a manner as to imply that he and his council alone would decide upon the options available and make the ultimate choice.

I had first approached Fr. Harris with a suggestion that the community provide me with financial support and use of an Oblate car during my transition period. I would like, if possible, to get free of having to do house cleaning so that I might better focus on developing my ministry. I have accepted a position on the staff of a local parish and in time I will be able to develop a practice of pastoral counseling there. In any case, I cannot believe that making a living as a domestic is an appropriate use of a priestly vocation.

This proposal was brushed aside. When I stressed that such support was the reasonable expectation of any Oblate in good standing, I was accused of "quibbling." And when I observed, perhaps inappropriately, that my request for support was modest compared to the amount of income I had lost in past years, I was actually accused of "blackmailing" the community.

When I bracketed the question of income and asked that Fr. Harris make a speedy pastoral decision to recommend me for faculties in the San Francisco Archdiocese, he repeatedly said, "No, I won't do that." Is there some logic that I am missing in Fr. Harris's attitude? Is there an agenda agreed upon of which I have no knowledge?

Though I much regret it, I must confess that I raised my voice in anger and frustration. I am embarrassed and sorry for that. But I had come to the meeting thinking that we were within a few steps of reaching the end of this long journey, and suddenly old resentments and grudges were thrown onto the path to block the way. To minimize further aggravation, in the end I simply had no other choice but to excuse myself from the meeting.

I am writing, Ron, because I am fearful that the situation is regressing. In view of this, I would like to request that future negotiations be conducted by mail or in the presence of a mutually agreed upon mediator.

Thank you for your continuing interest. I trust that you will once again bring to these deliberations a healing influence.

Fr. Carignan never acknowledged this letter, and despite his frequent presence in the Bay Area (he has an office in Oakland), I would not hear from him again for two years.

Now I would like to convey to the reader my sense of where I stood at the time with the Provincial Administration and of the steps I would have to take if my transition was to have any hope of succeeding.

Despite being instructed to assist in this endeavor, Fr. Harris, in his first letter to me, picked up our relationship at exactly the low point where it had ended in July 1987. The letter had the same peremptory tone and accusatory rhetoric of the last stage of that unhappy pre-1988 era; and I had every reason to suspect, going into our September 15 meeting, that Fr. Zago's letter did nothing to affect the underlying Provincial attitude toward me. I had my worst fears confirmed during that unnerving encounter. Consequently at that meeting, and certainly following it, the overriding question for me was what kind of assistance if any I might expect from the Provincial Administration.

From the moment Fr. Zago's letter opened the way to my departure from the Oblates, I knew that I had a difficult task ahead of me and that success would depend on careful planning in close collaboration with the Province. On the other hand, aware that the General Administration had again absented itself from me and that I was going to have to deal exclusively with Fr. Harris, I did not intend to dawdle. Above all I did not want the sluggishness that typified Oblate treatment of me throughout the previous seven years to overcome this last opportunity to save my priesthood. (I should note again that already three months had elapsed between receipt of Fr. Zago's letter and Fr. Harris's first communication with me in mid-September, and even then it was I who had to initiate the contact.)

So in August I seized on what I saw as a godsend opportunity. I accepted, on the merits of Fr. Zago's letter, an invitation by Fr. Martin Greenlaw, Pastor of St. Robert's Church in San Bruno California (where I had been doing weekend supply work for some months previous) to become his part-time associate. I must stress here that no one in the Archdiocese—including Bishop McGrath who several times attended services I officiated—even hinted that there might be something irregular or suspect about my presence in the parish. Just the opposite. Fr. Greenlaw had full authority to grant me temporary faculties in his parish, and the staff and congregation of St. Robert's warmly accepted me and often commended me for my work.

When finally I did meet with Frs. Harris and Haslam in mid-September my overriding concern was to get my status in the Congregation fully normalized as quickly as possible. The worst thing that could happen was for my seven-year non-canonical condition to continue a significant time beyond the General's letter—and there we were three months beyond it already. Moreover, swift and full normalization was the minimal condition necessary for engaging Fr. Harris on the process to come. We were going to have to talk about the practical details of my ministerial transition and about how to coordinate our activities so that in due course we together could make a plausible approach to the Archdiocese. It was certain that unless we cleared away Fr. Harris's galling "tolerated absence" theme, built up a relationship of trust between us, and achieved clarity about what we were doing, there simply would be no incardination process.

Now the obvious way to normalize my status was a simple pastoral decision by Fr. Harris to request faculties for my part-time ministry at St. Robert's so that I could continue to develop the ministerial connections and possibilities that I had cultivated over the years in San Francisco. Besides satisfying Fr. Harris's demand that faculties be granted at the Archdiocesan level and that there be some sort of contractual arrangement, such a step would set an important precedent of Oblate support of my work in the Archdiocese, and would have a most reassuring affect on me personally.

I should have thought that anyone commissioned to assist in such a difficult endeavor would have been delighted to discover that the means to normalized my status and to begin the work of dialogue and discernment was immediately at hand. Not so Fr. Harris. At our September meeting he repeatedly refused to make the pastoral decision, insinuated that my position at St. Robert's was somehow illicit, and continued to harp on the theme of "tolerated absence." At the meeting's end he requested that I provide him with a description of my various ministerial activities and deferred any further decision until he could consult the Provincial Council scheduled to meet two months later. I objected to this delay, as it would put us five months beyond the General's letter. Instead of taking up my valid work at St. Robert's as the obvious first step to translating my recently confirmed *de jure* status into a *de facto* assignment and to reassuring me personally of his good will, Fr. Harris transformed it into a new point of disagreement between us, thus perpetuating the very "tolerated absence," which he habitually claimed was so noxious to him and the Oblate leadership.

In response to our meeting—and hearing no word from Fr. Carignan—I wrote to Fr. Harris on October 10, provided him with the requested information on my ministerial activities, asked a second time for financial support, and again urged him not to delay normalizing my status. I also requested that he excuse me from attending the Provincial Council meeting because I did not wish to engage in further acrimonious encounters with him. Nor did I wish to find myself again in the unequal position of facing a panel of inquisitive Oblates. Long experience had taught me that such group sessions were as short on results as they were long on confusion and pain. On the other hand, by not attending the meeting I certainly did not intend to forfeit my right to continuous consultation on decisions that were bound to have the profoundest influence on the shape of my future. In my closing remarks, I put the matter as delicately as I could:

> Finally, in light of what occurred at our September 15 meeting, I would like to request that I be excused from attending the upcoming Provincial Council session. Clearly we have personal difficulties communicating with one another face to face, and I think you will agree that we are ill-served by these unhappy encounters. I hope that the above description of my present ministerial activities, along with my explanation as to why I would like the local community to endorse them as my formal ministry, will be sufficient representation of me at the meeting. In any case, my written presence will allay any further possibility of misunderstanding and hurt feelings that seem to result when we are together. I would ask that you share this letter with the council members. Naturally I will provide you and the council with any additional information or clarification you may need.

It was just my right to on-going consultation that would be neglected in everything that followed.

Fr. Harris did not answer until November 19, when he provided me with a digest of the Provincial Council deliberations and informed me that the council had made two decisions about my fate:

The Provincial will initiate a dialogue with the pastor at St. Robert's, San Bruno, to explore the feasibility of assigning you to that parish.

The pastoral ministry you claim to have built up over the years in the city of San Francisco is to be terminated since there is no contract with the Archdiocese of San Francisco for that ministry. The subsidy you requested to continue this ministry will not be granted.

To summarize, this letter dismissed my request for immediate normalized standing based on my present ministry and in effect announced that Fr. Harris and his Council would alone and without consultation *with* me decide my future *for* me. In addition, they apparently expected me to terminate the very position, which Fr. Harris would then proceed to try to re-negotiate for me. The latter requirement seemed too peculiar to be true. Fr. Greenlaw, whose first communication from Fr. Harris was a copy of this letter, was also baffled by this requirement. He was also perplexed by the meaning of Fr. Harris's remark, "The tolerated absence which you are presently sustaining in San Francisco [must] be brought to a close."

Fr. Greenlaw sought clarification from me on both of these points: Was I an Oblate in good standing or not? And should he begin searching for a new part-time associate? I reassured him as best I could that however Fr. Harris might be using the term "tolerated absence,' Fr. Zago's letter must be considered to have priority, and I requested to remain on staff throughout whatever was coming. Interestingly, no further direct Provincial reference was made to the requirement to terminate at St. Robert's, and I would continue ministering there throughout the disastrous year and a half that ensued.

Another three months elapsed, leaving us eight months out from the General's letter with still no change in my *de facto* standing. Then on February 7, 1988, Fr. Harris wrote to inform me that Fr. Haslam had met with Fr. Greenlaw and arranged to have me appointed full-time parochial associate pastor at St. Robert's. Three years later, in an attempt to put a positive spin on Fr. Harris's conduct—see Fr. Nourie's letter to me of January 2, 1991—the leadership would argue that this arrangement was for two purposes: to build on my present ministerial activities and to satisfy Archdiocesan policy on candidates for incardination.

This argument's unstated conclusion would seem to be that my subsequent objections to this non-consultative arrangement were beside the point. Since Archdiocesan policy required five years of full-time parochial work, I had no substantial choice of assignments anyway, and besides I had already expressed a wish to remain at St. Robert's. There are a number of important issues collapsed into this formula that I would now like to separate out.

Fr. Harris's announcement to me reads in part, "Presently [Fr. Greenlaw] foresees he will need a full time associate pastor. He would like to invite you to accept." This is very misleading. In the first place, the supposed new position was never created. St. Robert's already had two full-time and two part-time associates, and whatever needs for a third full-time position Fr. Greenlaw may have "foreseen," the truth is that during the year and a half I continued on as part-time associate no new position was created and there was no further talk of doing so.

Fr. Greenlaw's "invitation" to me to accept this hypothetical position had a quite different cast in reality. Given Provincial insistence that my position at St. Robert's be a full-time parochial assignment and that it be contracted at the Archdiocesan level, Fr. Greenlaw expressed his willingness, if I wished to remain at St. Robert's, to do what he could to upgrade my part-time position to full-time to satisfy Oblate conditions for my continuing on there. Did I wish him to try? When I indicated that I would rather hold onto the bird I had in hand rather than chase one that *might* be in the bush that was the end of the "foreseen" full-time associate position.

Second, Fr. Harris was far beyond the stage of the transition process where we ought to have been then: he wanted to put on a roof before laying a foundation. The proposed contract negotiations with the Archdiocese concerning the yet non-existence full-time position were not assured of success under the most straightforward of circumstances, and in view of Fr. Harris's less than friendly attitude toward me I had no confidence at all in the kind of representations of me he was likely to make in such negotiations. Fr. Harris would fully confirm my apprehensions nine months later in his interview with Bishop McGrath, which I shall discuss in due course.

For now, I wish to ask the obvious question. What can explain Fr. Harris's determination not to have my status in the Congregation normalized except under conditions of a contracted full-time parochial assignment? Was it to facilitate the process? No! It was premature and non-consultative, and there were many types of assignments besides parish work that might have been explored. Was it to build on my ministry at St. Robert's? No! I was apparently required to terminate my ministry at St. Robert's pending a negotiated contract to minister there; and this, combined with the questions raised by the term 'tolerated absence,' had an unsettling affect on Fr. Greenlaw. Was it, then, to satisfy Archdiocesan policy on incardination? Very unlikely, as I shall discuss in a moment.

What, then, might explain it? There is one obvious answer. If the Oblates contracted with the Archdiocese to appoint me to a full-time parochial position, canon law would automatically oblige the Archdiocese to assume full financial responsibility for me, thus formally freeing the Oblates of all but token liability for my material upkeep. Had Fr. Harris succeeded in pushing through such a contract, he could have taken credit for killing three birds with one stone: he would have finally clarified my status in the Congregation *and* formally disposed of any practical obligation to me *and* put me on the straight road out.

Let me pause here for a few remarks on the important issue of Archdiocesan policy regarding candidates for incardination. First, at the time in question I myself knew nothing about this policy, since the outstanding issue then was solely Oblate policy toward me, not any Archdiocesan policies. Second, I doubt that Fr. Harris knew of Archdiocesan policy at that time either. None of his correspondence to me of that period alluded to such a policy, even though he insisted that my part-time ministry at St. Robert's was somehow irregular and that it be replaced with a full-time parochial assignment.

Fr. Harris's first mention of Archdiocesan policy did not occur until nearly a year later, when on January 2, 1990, he mailed me a memorandum of his meeting with Bishop McGrath the previous November. To judge from the memorandum, it would seem that Fr. Harris was first presented with the Archdiocesan policy during that meeting. Third, and most important, in my own, later discussions with Bishop McGrath he assured me that the policy was not inflexible and that it allowed exceptions both to the timeline and to the nature of the candidate's ministerial work before incardination.

A religious engaged in an approved and valued ministry within the Archdiocese, with the visible and full backing of his community, would stand a good chance of incardinating on that basis within a comparatively short time. And Bishop McGrath encouraged me to seek ministerial opportunities consistent with my education, aptitude, and gifts. An example that he suggested was work with AIDS patients, in which I had a particular concern, much experience, and unique qualifications; and the Oblates themselves had already shown interest in such work in San Francisco.

My point here is simply this: there *were* other options still to be explored, and plenty of them. The period for discernment and consultation had scarcely begun much less passed at the time Fr. Harris announced—not offered—that he had arranged to have me appointed full-time associate at St. Robert's. With patience, initiative, and a little constructive support by my community, a suitable and mutually acceptable ministry would have emerged in due season. Before any of this, however, had to come normalization of my status within the Congregation and confidence-building between me and the local leadership.

On February 24 I responded to Fr. Harris's announcement of a full-time parochial assignment. My letter was, I think, entirely to the point and correct in its appeal:

———————

Dear Andrew,

I received your letter of February 7, 1989, in which you announced that you are in the process of arranging a position for me as full time associate pastor at St. Robert's in San Bruno. As this is being done without consulting me, and as I do not wish the absence of any comment by me to be misconstrued as consent, I have decided to volunteer a response today. I do this in order to prevent any misunderstanding and especially to request that I be accorded the courtesy of a greater say in determining my future.

Of course I appreciate very much the contact which you have made with Fr. Greenlaw and your evident approval of my recent work at St. Robert's as reflected in your assumption that I should make it the sole focus of my ministry. However, I have never expressed to you or to Fr. Greenlaw an interest in parish work on a full-time basis. I am speaking here not only of preferences—which are of course important to any such decision—but also of aptitude, training, and gifts, which must surely feature prominently in any deliberation about a priest's assignment. When in your letter of September 21, 1988, you asked me to describe my present ministerial activities; it was not my impression that I was providing you with a list of possible options from which you would choose an assignment. I merely described what my ministerial activities had been. So far we have never discussed what I wish my ministry to be in the future, under normalized conditions. I fear that if we do not consult closely on this matter we may find ourselves at cross-purposes.

I am comfortable with my present status at St. Robert's. It provides for a great many of my needs during this time of transition. I am working in a recognized ministry in the Archdiocese, I am networking with the local clergy, and I am becoming aware of the varied ministerial opportunities available here. Among the many options that I would like to consider are:

chaplaincies, clinical/pastoral education programs, Catholic Social Services, retreat work, teaching, and so forth. I am also interested in continuing education programs, since I have been out of official ministry so many years.

I understand your wish to bring a quick closure to this matter. If the pressing issues before us are clarification of my status and obtaining faculties for me, my present position at St. Robert's should be sufficient to attain both of these ends. This will accord us the time for discernment and healing, which is of the utmost importance to all concerned.

I look forward to further dialogue.

———————

Fr. Harris reacted on April 10, 1989. His letter was cold, erratic, and threatening. He again swept aside my request that he seize on the opportunity immediately at hand:

> You assume that I approve the clerical ministry you are presently performing. The assumption is inaccurate. I consider the ministry irregular because it is not officially approved by the Provincial in Council nor is it officially approved by the local Ordinary. I will discuss the implications of this with the pastor of St. Robert's.

He followed this with a proposal to meet with Bishop McGrath to discuss alternative ministries. At this point Fr. Harris was evidently prepared to scuttle the St. Robert's option altogether—though he did not repeat his earlier demand that I terminate my current position there. There was no doubt that I was being coerced. Either I must accept the non-existent and doubtful position of third associate pastor at St. Robert's or else face a premature meeting with Bishop McGrath which could only result in the exposé of Fr. Harris's attitude toward me—the very thing I was hoping we might remedy before the start of formal, higher level contacts with the Archdiocese concerning incardination.

In my answer of April 21, I tried to show Fr. Harris the unreasonableness of his position and again urged him to engage me in a genuinely collaborative and constructive process.

———————

Dear Andrew,

Thank you for your letter of April 10, 1989. In reply I would like to dispel a misreading of my letter of February 24, 1989, and seek clarification on several aspects of your letter that puzzle me.

First, you state that in my last letter I indicated that I was not interested in an appointment as associate pastor at St. Robert's. This is not what I intended, and I would like now to correct any wrong impression I may have given. As you know I presently occupy part-time the very position to which you offered to appoint me full-time. I do so, I should add, very successfully and very happily. This is why I ended my letter by saying, "If the pressing issues before us are clarification of my status and obtaining faculties for me, my present position at St. Robert's should be sufficient to attain both of these ends. This will accord us the time for discernment and healing which is of the utmost importance to all concerned."

Second, you state that I was inaccurate to assume that you approve of my present ministry. I still fail to see how. This is the same ministry to which you in council expressed a willingness to assign me full-time. Consequently I can't help assuming that your objections, whatever they may be, have nothing to do with the *content* of that ministry. True, you have yet to approve of my ministry in the sense of formally assigning me to it; but that is a different sense of the word 'approve', and we should be careful not to mix the two senses. My question is simply this: If you tacitly approve of the content of my ministry in so far as you are willing to appoint me to it full-time, what germane objection can you have to appointing me to it part-time?

You say that you do not approve of my ministry because it is "irregular", and give two reasons why you consider it to be so. The first is that you have not formally approved of it in council. But as I have just observed, that is what we are waiting for: either that you formally approve the ministry or provide some explanation why it cannot be approved. As things stand, your first reason amounts to nothing more than the paradoxical assertion that you don't approve of my present ministry because you *haven't* approved of it—not because of any expressed defect in its content.

The second reason you consider my ministry to be "irregular" is that it has not been officially approved by the local Ordinary. But in all fairness, all that we need to obtain from the local Ordinary—at this time—is diocesan faculties, which will provide a more solid basis for my Oblate ministry at St. Robert's. How can the local Ordinary be expected to provide me with faculties if my local superior does not put me forward and request them? So this reason, too, has a hollow ring. Where, I ask again, is the obstruction?

I have maintained that the orderly way to pursue our common objective—and the only way that has any promise of success—is that you should put me forward for faculties on the basis of my present position at St. Robert's so that I can establish my credibility and reputation and have the grace period needed to explore and develop the possibilities of a full-scale secular assignment. Only then would I be in a position to request exclaustration and apply for incardination in the Archdiocese. We must not confuse my present ministry at St. Robert's, or my wish to attain faculties, with an augmented ministry to be developed sometime in the future. The list of possible ministries to which you refer in your letter was not intended as a list of options to replace my position at St. Robert's but as a list of further avenues to explore while I occupy that position. And by no means do I wish to exclude the possibility that this part-time position will be an essential part of my future ministry. In fact, I envision it that way.

Third, you state in your letter that you "will request an appointment with the Personnel Director in the Archdiocese to dialogue with him around possible ministry opportunities." Andrew, I view this offer in a very positive light, and I wish to thank you for the cooperative spirit it shows. However, given what I have discussed above, your seeking such an appointment for this purpose at this time strikes me as premature.

To achieve our objective we must be quite clear with one another about an orderly way to proceed so that when the time comes to approach the Archdiocese we are of one mind, acting in good faith, and with an honest will to succeed. We cannot go to the Personnel Director as to an employment office to check job listings on the bulletin board—not, that is, if we wish to save ourselves potential embarrassment. We both have too much self-respect to carry our hat in hand, shuffle our feet, and expect to be taken out of pity. I know you will agree that we must avoid being rash and disorderly in this, and must instead focus our energies in being cooperative, creative, and patient.

I spoke to Fr. Greenlaw this past Sunday and told him of your letter. He is eager to hear from you. I mentioned your desire to move this matter forward by approaching the Personal Director in the Archdiocese. He asked if you were referring to Bishop McGrath. Perhaps you can discuss this with him.

I consider this exchange of letters as the most efficient venue for dialogue at this time. As I said in my October 10, 1988 letter to you: "My written presence will allay any further possibility of misunderstanding and hurt feelings which seem to result when we are together."

Thank you again for your continuing efforts.

———————

Fr. Harris did not contact me again for five months, placing us a full year and three months beyond the General's letter with no resolution of my *de facto* status in sight. In his letter of September 21, 1989, Fr. Harris returned to the St. Robert's option. In all essentials, however, his new "offer" was the same ultimatum implied in his letter of April 10, only now he made it explicit and presented it as a compromise solution. Note that he posed the ultimatum to Fr. Greenlaw before he posed it to me. Again, there was no consultation going on at all. This is how his letter read in part:

In accordance with your wish [of April 21, 1989] and my desire I arranged an appointment with Father Greenlaw. I met with him last Monday, September 18 to discuss possible ministry options for you at St. Robert's. Because of the pastoral needs at St. Robert's [!] I proposed two options to the pastor for his consideration:

1. A full-time ministry at St. Robert's, with faculties from the local Ordinary.

> 2. A part-time ministry at St. Robert's, for a period
> of three months, with faculties from the local
> Ordinary. During the three months period you
> would be in dialogue with Bishop McGrath, clergy
> personnel director for the Archdiocese, to dialogue
> about the possibility of a full-time ministry for you
> in the Archdiocese.
>
> If at the end of three months a definite ministry cannot
> be arranged for you in the Archdiocese, I will request Father
> Greenlaw to terminate the part-time ministry at St. Robert's.

This was astounding. At last Fr. Harris was proposing to give me the coveted faculties for my part-time position at St. Robert's. However, he would do this not as the most efficient means to normalize my status and thus clear the way for *our* engaging in dialogue, but as a small limbo within my greater limbo in which he expected me—on my own, in three months time, with my Provincial publicly at odds with me and applying pressure on all concerned— to negotiate some alternative assignment with Bishop McGrath. Even more astounding, Fr. Harris's very first contact with Bishop McGrath was a copy of this ultimatum. As if the manifest coercive nature of this letter were not enough by itself to alert Bishop McGrath that all was not well between Fr. Wagner and his religious community, Fr. Harris again blurted out the by then obligatory and habitual phrase: "[N]either the General Administration nor the local Provincial Council can responsibly allow you to continue in a state of tolerated absence." *This* was Fr. Harris's formal introduction of me to the San Francisco Archdiocese.

Contrary to the Oblate leadership's official line—as reflected in the virtual cartoon of events to which Fr. Nourie signed his name on January 2, 1991—that it was I who failed to accept an assignment after Fr. Harris cleared the way for me, here is the precise point at which my efforts in San Francisco were brought to an end.

To be sure, the process would go on for another agonizing nine months, but there can be no doubt that at this time my once healthy ministry in San Francisco had become mortally infected. Any chance of ever attaining an assignment had disappeared. By dragging our disagreements into the open, Fr. Harris left me no choice but decisively to distance myself from him, and, equally important, to try to distance his actions from those of the Superior General of 15 months earlier. This I did in my letter of September 27, 1989. With copies sent to Fr. Greenlaw and Bishop McGrath in the Archdiocese and to Councillor General Carignan and Vicar General Cazabon in the Oblate General Administration, I provided a synopsis of my case from the very beginning, placing particular emphasis on Fr. Harris's negative attitudes and behaviors throughout. At the end of my letter I implored Fr. Harris to reconsider, but again to no avail. Following this letter, both Fr. Greenlaw and Bishop McGrath accorded me opportunities to further discuss with them my predicament. They were hospitable and sympathetic and encouraged me not to give up hope despite the bleak outlook. No one at all in the Oblate General Administration contacted me.

In a conversation with Bishop McGrath in mid-October, I asked if he would invite Fr. Harris to share perceptions of my situation. They met on November 22, 1989. Bishop McGrath shortly afterward gave me his sense of the meeting. It was not good. He told me frankly that Fr. Harris displayed a personal animus toward me; that he had difficulty drawing Fr. Harris out on the General's letter and on Fr. Harris's understanding of my status as an Oblate; that Fr. Harris was vague on whether he endorsed the incardination process; and that despite Fr. Harris's final grudging assent, he left the impression that he would not be sorry to see my priesthood destroyed.

Needless to say, Fr. Harris's memorandum of the meeting is in the starkest contrast to Bishop McGrath's account to me. At the meeting, Fr. Harris put before Bishop McGrath the same ultimatum he had laid down to me in his letter of September 21, 1989. I was to be given three months, with faculties, to cobble together a full-time ministry or be yanked from the Archdiocese. Fr. Harris's memorandum states that: "Bishop McGrath and the Provincial reached a consensus that a three (3) month time line is a reasonable period to pursue the search." Even in his cosmetic memorandum, however, Fr. Harris's cold, passive, unsympathetic demeanor is clearly in evidence. What could Bishop McGrath's response to Fr. Harris possibly have been under the circumstances? Let me suggest the words: "Well, if that's what you want—he's *your* man."

Looking back, it is not at all clear what if anything was decided at that meeting. Fr. Harris did not provide me with a copy of his memorandum until January 5, 1990, so it seems reasonable that my running the three-month gantlet— assuming I accepted the challenge—could only begin on or after that date. But in a singular omission, no date was ever set. At some point the provincial administration simply assumed that the "consensus" with Bishop McGrath was in effect. One can also see the uncertainty and confusion about the meeting's results by reading in tandem Fr. Harris's January 5 cover letter to his memorandum and an enclosed copy of his "follow-up letter" to Bishop McGrath, also dated January 5.

The cover letter to me begins: "On November 22, 1989, I met with the Clergy Personnel Director, Most Rev. Patrick McGrath ... to determine your status as priest/minister in the Archdiocese." But the letter to Bishop McGrath begins: "I am writing to clarify the ministry status of Father Richard Wagner, O.M.I. in the Archdiocese of San Francisco." It would appear that the November meeting resulted in insufficient clarity. After listing four points on which he needed clarification, Fr. Harris went on to say: "I would appreciate information on those issues prior to a Council meeting I have schedule for February 7, 1990."

Fr. Harris never informed me of the Bishop's reply, if any, to his follow-up queries; nor did he inform me of any Provincial Council deliberations or decisions until the following March 17, and only then after I had informed him that I was consulting a canonist and that the canonist had requested minutes of the February meeting.

Was the starting date of the three-month sprint supposed to have occurred after February 7? No. In his March 17 reply to my canonist's request, Fr. Harris wrote to me as follows: "At the February 7 council meeting we decided to place your situation on hold as we did not have clarity regarding your ministerial faculty status in the Archdiocese of San Francisco." Did Bishop McGrath not respond to Fr. Harris's January 5 follow-up letter? Clearly the "consensus" Fr. Harris supposedly reached with Bishop McGrath never took effect—not that it would have made any difference even if it had. My efforts in San Francisco, as I have observed, had for all practical purposes ended the previous September.

The "sincere efforts" on my behalf after September were in fact an embarrassing spectacle of Provincial muddle and disorder, with predictable results. A year and seven months after Fr. Zago's embrace of me as an Oblate in good standing, my last hope to save my priesthood was gone. I resigned my position as St. Robert's in June and my associate chaplaincy at St. Mary's Hospital—where I had also worked for over a year—in July. A postscript to all of this is a series of letters written by Bishop McGrath in response to parishioner queries about my sudden departure from St. Robert's. One such letter, written on July 9, 1990, reads as follows:

———————

Dear Mr. _____ :

I am most grateful for your letter and your kind words regarding Father Richard Wagner. I, too, believe that Father Wagner is a very fine priest and this Archdiocese is truly blessed by his presence.

Unfortunately, the events that have led to Father Wagner's departure from Saint Robert's Parish are between him and his order and do not come within the jurisdiction of this

Archdiocese. I pray that Father Wagner and his Order will be able to reach a satisfactory agreement within the near future.

Again, my sincere thanks for your interest in and support of Father Wagner.

Not wanting it to be said later that I left any stone unturned, I did submit three proposals for full-time ministry. With no community sponsorship at all, those last overturned stones revealed only dust. So when Fr. Harris wrote to me on June 24, 1990, to ask, "Now that I have returned [from a three-month trip to Europe] I wish to know if you have succeeded in finding a ministry, through the clergy personnel office, the Archdiocese would like you to undertake?"—I heard nothing but taunting from a man oblivious of his own actions. *When had my situation been taken off hold?* Anyway, nearly four months earlier, on March 2, I had already notified Fr. Harris that I had contacted a canon lawyer, and that action ought to have cued him that his cat-and-mouse game was up. Fr. Harris didn't deserve an answer.

On June 30, 1990, two years after the General's embrace of me and within months of Fr. Harris's retirement as Provincial, I wrote Fr. Harris a last letter. I summarized the history of his handling of my situation in the Congregation, requested that he excuse himself from any further involvement in my affairs, and announced my intention to appeal to Superior General Zago.

Moreover, I made it clear to him that I held the General Administration itself ultimately responsible for Fr. Harris's actions, as the Superior General had expressly commissioned him to assist me in the transition to my post-Oblate priesthood and Fr. Harris regularly deferred to Fr. Carignan for guidelines and instruction. Suddenly, after a silence of two years, Fr. Carignan wrote me on July 20, 1990.

His long silence is striking because since at least 1987, when the General Administration reentered the process after an absence of more than two years, he was the General Administration official most involved with my case and most responsible for Fr. Harris's handling of it. Not surprisingly, then, his letter of July 20 makes haste to defend Fr. Harris's record. On the same day, I received a letter signed by Fr. Harris, answering mine of June 30 by way of also defending his actions and informing me of my right of appeal. As these were obviously parts of a coordinated effort, I replied to both in a lengthy letter to Fr. Carignan on July 30, 1990. During a brief telephone conversation on August 12, Fr. Carignan informed me that if I wished to appeal to the Superior General I should do so by writing to Fr. Zago directly.

CHAPTER 5

1990 - 1993

On September 4, 1990, I mailed Fr. Zago a seven-page summary of Fr. Harris's conduct toward me since 1985. In introducing the summary, I made clear that I held the General Administration responsible for all that had happened to me:

> By invoking this option, I wish to give the General Administration the courtesy of one last opportunity to redeem in a just and thorough manner the treatment that has been meted out to me during this ten-year ordeal. Clearly, the ultimate responsibility for all that has happened lies with the General Administration, which—at the very least—has been negligent of my welfare and rights as an Oblate.

I stated that my appeal had two objectives: "a clear reiteration of my status to the local leadership such that they will unequivocally honor it in word and in deed" and "a full recompense of Oblate support accruing from June 1981."

I also requested specific information on what the appeal process entailed, as the Oblate *Constitutions and Rules* contained no information on the subject.

To seek reassurance on the impartiality of the process, I asked seven specific questions framed in terms of judicial due process as I understand it.

In conclusion, I announced that if the nature of the appeal process or its progress proved unsatisfactory after two months, I would appeal to The Sacred Congregation for Institutes of Consecrated Life. (Though there were plenty of reasons to do so, I never availed myself of the right to appeal outside the Congregation, for reasons I shall discuss in a moment.)

Fr. Zago's reply of October 3, 1990, was patronizing and dismissive. By addressed himself exclusively to "your grievance with your Provincial Superior", he simply ignored my explicit statements holding the General Administration accountable. He announced that my inquiry about the appeal process did not present "sufficient cause" for incorporating any of the guarantees of impartiality that I had enumerated to him. He reiterated my right to appeal to him as indicated in the *Constitutions and Rules* but offered no further information other than to quote Article 84 of that document: "An Oblate who feels an injustice has been done to him by a Superior may have recourse to higher authority." His response to my lengthy account of Fr. Harris's conduct relative to my ministry in San Francisco was a smattering of lines that are remarkable only for their evasive brevity:

> You did pursue the possibility of incardination in the Archdiocese of San Francisco. That option does not seem likely at this time. In the final analysis, incardination is a decision of the Bishop after considering the facts as he sees them....
>
> It seems to me that your interpretation of the motives, words and actions of your superiors have been most negative. I do encourage you to look within yourself to see if you have been doing all you can to help create an environment in which a workable resolution can be found to a situation that is of concern to all of us.

Like his predecessor and all Oblate officials with whom I have had to deal—and despite the one line in the *Constitutions and Rules* allowing for at least the possibility of leadership injustice—Fr. Zago assumes that leadership misconduct is impossible in principle, rendering it unnecessary to address the specifics of my case. His "judgment" concerning all that I had placed before him boiled down to something like this: Your case against the leadership does not have merit because if it did it would reflect negatively on the leadership.

Even to suggest such a thing indicates that you have a serious attitude problem. I recommend that you take a more cooperative approach and talk with your new Provincial Superior about other options.

This paraphrase is not the parody it might at first seem. Fr. Zago obviously had no intention of informing me of the appeal process or of weighing the merits of my case. His objective was simply to deflect my grievance and to lay the groundwork for a new dismissal process under the guise of indulging my pursuit of other options. This will take a bit of explaining; so let me now quote what I take to be the two most important passages in Fr. Zago's October 3 letter (they are separated by a paragraph in the text but definitely belong together):

> In has been over two years now since my June 17, 1988 letter to you. At the time I stated: "I embrace you as my brother Oblate and recognize that you have all the rights, responsibilities and privileges of membership in our Congregation." This statement still stands. ...I want to urge you once again to dialogue with Fr. Paul Nourie, OMI, your present Provincial superior concerning other options you might want to pursue in the future.

> Richard, I want to remind you that you have both rights and responsibilities within the Congregation. One of your responsibilities is to belong to and participate in the life and mission of a community. When I wrote to you in June of 1988, I did not sanction in any way, the continuation of your absence from community.

Since technically only a major superior can give an obedience, and since he can do this only under conditions of normal membership—the very conditions that were not restored despite Fr. Zago's supposed exoneration of me in 1988—it was imperative to quash the appeal, push everything back down to the provincial level, and get some semblance of normalcy going before a plausible obedience could be given. But the likelihood that I would resist coaxing in that direction made the general leadership's problem complicated.

The first complication, of course, was that the leadership had no explanation for my decade-old, non-canonical state, especially in view of my own numerous, connected, and documented accounts of that state's emergence and persistence. So at the same time that Fr. Zago was trying to persuade me to return to the province to explore other possibilities, he was also reverting to the old rhetorical attempt to shift the blame for my *de facto* dismissal. This he did simply by tapping back into to the innuendo of "absence" indulged in by Oblate officials since the summer of 1987.

Obviously, the leadership's rationale for this present obedience and hence for my dismissal revolves around the word 'absence.' At several points in the foregoing discussion I have deferred dealing with the emergence of this word and its application in my case till a later time. That time has now come.

I shall begin with the two quotations from Fr. Zago's letter of October 3, 1990. The key to these passages, and indeed to the entire letter, is the matter-of-fact appearance of the single word 'absence' and the assertion that the years of my *de facto* separation from the Institute were the result of an ongoing unsanctioned absence by me. Equally important is Fr. Zago's attempt to read back into his letter of June 1988 his present disapproval of this supposed culpable absence. In fact, neither the word 'absence' nor the sentiment of disapproval show up at all in that earlier missive, and I had come to think of that word as a verbal tic unique to Fr. Harris. (Recall my taking him to task for this in my letter of September 27, 1989.) In Fr. Zago's 1988 letter the only references to my non-canonical condition are the standard euphemisms "the difficult situation" and "the controversy." Fr. Zago injects disapproval into his 1988 exoneration of me simply by defining in 1990 one word that appears in the earlier letter.

Among the many ways Fr. Zago changed my original draft statement was to insert the word 'responsibilities' into a phrase where I saw no need for it, considering that my draft statement was seeking an acknowledgment, however muted, that my rights had been taken from me and needed to be restored. (A reassuring handshake and reaffirmation of my *de jure* status was not what I had in mind.) Where my draft statement had read, "We now embrace Fr. Wagner without further reserve and restore to him all rights and privileges of membership in our Congregation," Fr. Zago wrote, "I embrace you as my brother Oblate and recognize that you have all the rights, responsibilities and privileges of membership in our Congregation."

I have already discussed the unsettling effect that Fr. Zago's replacement of the word 'restore' with the word 'recognize' had on me. But the nestling of word 'responsibilities' between the words 'rights' and 'privileges' was not at all surprising coming from the supreme authority in the Congregation, and I made nothing of it.

I fully intended to fulfill my responsibilities in the context of the real history of my relationship with the Oblates, of the understandings I had arrived at with the General Administration on my mode of departure, and of the specific instructions that Fr. Zago gave me in his letter, namely: "to refrain from any further public statements relating to homosexuality without the prior authorization of your major superior" and "to be in close dialogue with your Provincial Superior … in discerning your future." It was Fr. Zago's 1990 definition of his 1988 use of the word 'responsibilities' to imply an additional instruction to "belong to and participate in the life and mission of a community" and the pairing of this retroactive instruction with his censuring use of the word 'absence' that had the effect of redefining the entire historical prelude to his letter.

In other words, Fr. Zago was attempting in 1990 to have his 1988 embrace of me viewed in complete abstraction from the events and understandings that led to its being written in the first place, that is, as a necessary precondition for my permanent departure from the Congregation, not for my return to an Oblate community.

In addition, Fr. Zago's 1990 suggestion that his 1988 embrace was tendered while he was in a disapproving state of mind transforms that embrace into something highly equivocal: it was grasping me as a brother Oblate with one hand while pointing an accusing finger at me with the other. This equivocation had the same effect on me as Fr. Harris's first communiqué after Fr. Zago's exoneration, when Fr. Harris stated to me, "[We can] no longer permit the present situation of 'tolerated absence' to continue, as it is contrary to our Constitutions."

If Fr. Zago actually did write his 1988 letter with this equivocation in mind—and it now seems that he did—then by accepting it as a pledge to make good on my seven-year banishment, I had misplaced my trust. Fr. Zago was merely placating me to forestall any appeal I might make outside the Congregation. At the same time he was invisibly espousing—or at least laying the groundwork for later claiming that he was—the now familiar corporate line: the uncanonical removal of me from the Congregation and the resultant stripping of my rights and privileges *never occurred* and that consequently my "absence" was my own doing, all those years merely "tolerated" by a solicitous leadership.

Needless to say, I *have* been "absent" from community, and the foregoing pages of this narrative have laid before you just how this situation occurred and who bears responsibility for it. It began with the leadership's uncanonical suspension of my membership during the seven years before 1988, and the leadership perpetuated it an additional five years after my exoneration because of their refusal to normalize my status as a first step toward dialogue about the specifics of my transition to secular priesthood. Where, then, did this label 'absence' come from and how did it come to connote an offense actively committed by me over a dozen years?

It first came up in my meeting with Frs. Carignan, Morrissey, and Harris on July 14, 1987. By that time I had been without canonical status for six years, amounting to dismissal in practice, and this placed the leadership in an awkward position to say the least. So the overriding objective of the meeting was, in the words of Fr. Morrissey's summary, "...to clarify the canonical status of Rev. Richard Wagner, and to move toward a possible resolution of an unclear situation."

How I came to lose canonical status in the first place was, as ever, not considered a pertinent topic of conversation. The "clarification" of my canonical status was supposed to have been Qualified Exclaustration, but along the way a backup category was surreptitiously introduced by way of defining the "unclear situation". This of course was the tag 'tolerated absence.'

Focused as I was on the question of status and on the process of elimination by which Fr. Morrissey was guiding me down the narrowing corridor of options toward the one door at the end, I took no particular notice of the harmless-sounding term. Even Fr. Morrissey's tidy summary of the meeting cannot conceal the confusing nature of the two-and-half-hour ordeal. Besides his numerous categories and sub-categories—most of which were ill-defined or not defined at all—I was simultaneously obliged to deal with the occasional interjections of two other people. I did not go back to reconstruct what had happened at that meeting until after I became aware of Fr. Harris's habitual finger-pointing use of the term, the cumulative effect of which was: Absent! Absent! Absent!

The leadership's sole means of establishing the appearance of my culpability has been the repetition of this label—applying pressure to make it stick, so to speak—combined with a studied avoidance of any reference to the actual history of the case. Now it is extremely interesting to see the specific way this innuendo got its start and developed over the years. Its ultimate origin, of course, extends all the way back to Fr. Jetté's "disposition to obey" theme, but as I have already dealt with that at length, I shall limit myself here to the specific word 'absence.'

Like any sleight-of-hand, the introduction of 'tolerated absence' depended essentially on distracting the viewer's attention. To repeat my earlier review, Qualified Exclaustration was arrived at by listing all the "available" options and then narrowing them down to "preferred" options. Fr. Morrissey listed ten "available" options, ranging from reintegration into the Congregation (i.e. return to community) to dismissal from the clerical state. Two of them were forms of canonical absence: permission for absence to fulfill a mandated ministry and permission for absence for personal reasons. He brought both forms of permitted absence together under one category, "Absence," and included them among the "Preferred" options. Here is how the section appears in Fr. Morrissey's summary:

2) Absence

Fr. Wagner's present condition could be considered to be a "tolerated absence." It is this state that both the Congregational authorities and Fr. Wagner do not wish to see continue.

Therefore, options 2 [permitted absence for a mandated ministry] and 3 [permitted absence for personal reasons] were not considered possible at this time.

What is going on here? Simply put, the section "Absence" provides the space for inserting the invidious label 'tolerated absence' into the process and for creating the illusion of my agreement to it as the fitting definition of my state during the preceding six years. It should have been enough for Fr. Morrissey simply to state (as he did in the case of "Departure," for example) that the two forms of permitted absence were not viable because both presupposed canonical standing in the Congregation, the very lack of which we were presumably meeting to correct. Instead Fr. Morrissey extracts a *third* category of absence from the hat into which he had originally placed only two, and he then briskly declares this third category to be Fr. Wagner's "present condition."

Though obvious once pointed out, only an attentive eye could have caught the move at the time. Observe the first sentence. Looking at it grammatically one can see that Fr. Morrissey phrases it in the passive voice, which should lead the alert reader to ask: *Who* is doing the considering here? Moreover, he poses the application of 'tolerated absence' to my state as only a possibility: it *could* be considered Fr. Wagner's present condition. The second sentence, however, transforms that possibility into an actuality simply by asserting that the Congregational authorities and Fr. Wagner *agree* that they do not wish that state *continue*.

Here, then, is the precise emergence of my "absence"—and never mind its "tolerant" nativity. Now in no sense did I agree to the definition of my state as 'tolerated absence.' Even in Fr. Morrissey's summary it appears as at best an aside, and since he did not number it among the ever-shrinking range of *options* being posed to me—which after all was the object toward which he was directing my attention—I did not notice it. What's more, no one ever attempt to define the term either during the meeting or at any time afterward. I could not help observing over time, however, that the leadership quietly employed the term as though it had some type of canonical reference.

Also, 'tolerated absence' seems to have had a vague time limit associated with it, because almost all future references to the term spoke of its continuation as unacceptable to the leadership. Clearly, despite its "tolerant" beginnings and after many repetitions, 'tolerated absence' came more and more to imply an unlawful absence by me indulged by the leadership—a condition that the leadership wished to end. The leadership's use of the term was an attempt to assign an offense to me through sheer innuendo and to conceal behind a mask of wearing benevolence its own uncanonical separation of me. Of course by 1990, when Fr. Zago himself adopted the rhetoric of absence, the misleading adjective 'tolerated' was finally jettisoned.

In its numerous uses in the official documentation 'tolerated absence' usually appeared in quotation marks, even though I can find no such term anywhere in the canons governing religious institutes.

Where, then, might it come from? I have been able to find one canon that seems to me the probable source. Canon 665 §2, which deals with unlawful absences, contains language that might explain the odd pairing of the words 'tolerated' and 'absence.' The canon reads: "Members unlawfully absent from the religious house with the intention of withdrawing from the power of their superiors are to be solicitously sought after by them and aided to return and persevere in their vocation." The quotation marks around "tolerated absence," in other words, do not indicate a quotation in the proper sense; they are scare quotes indicating a euphemistic reference to the state of affairs described in Canon 665 §2. While the absent member's superiors are solicitously pursuing him, they might be considered—according to Fr. Morrissey's apparent gloss—to be "tolerating" the member's unlawful absence. And the longer a community forbears taking legal action to separate the offending member, the more the community is presumably "tolerating" his misbehavior.

Now obviously in all their dealings with me—including the very meeting in which the tag 'tolerated absence' is first insinuated—Oblate officials are studiously employing (with some notable lapses) the language of solicitude. Unctuous reassurances of good will toward me and of resolute efforts on my behalf are a kind of ritual requirement that the leadership must perform if they are to have any chance of transforming their unlawful separation of me into an appearance of my unlawful withdrawal from their power. This explains the sense of the 'therefore' with which Fr. Morrissey begins the second sentence of the section "Absence": "Fr. Wagner has unlawfully absented himself from community for six years and during all that time the leadership has solicitously pursued him to return. Therefore the leadership cannot consider a mandated ministry, much less a one-year permitted absence for personal reasons, unless and until it can persuade Fr. Wagner to return to the fold."

Had Fr. Morrissey called 'tolerated absence' by its real name I would have immediately halted the session and demanded a hearing on the history of my case—the very thing Fr. Morrissey side-stepped at the beginning of our 1987 meeting and for which the leadership has shown the deepest aversion throughout this controversy.

I have noticed an interesting feature of Canon 665 §2 that may be pertinent. The canon does not directly state a time limit beyond which an unlawfully absent member *must* be dismissed. This would seem to imply that an unlawful absence *might* be "tolerated" for an indefinite period. To be sure, a sense for the probable intent of the law strongly suggests otherwise. Canon 665 §1 stipulates that permitted absences for reasons other than poor health, studies, or a mandated ministry can be granted for no more than one year, and even then only with the express consent of the granting superior's council. It would seem highly unlikely, therefore, that the Code intends to condone unlawful absences for periods greater than the upper limit placed on many lawful ones. In addition, Canon 696 §1 states that unlawful absences as mentioned in Canon 665 §2 *can* be cause for dismissal after six months.

The stipulation of a minimum time that must elapse before a dismissal process can begin might suggest an upper limit as well, but again it does not positively prescribe such. When we read the three relevant canons together, their sense would seem to be something like this. After a six-month unlawful absence, duly "tolerated," dismissal proceedings can be initiated. The absence might be further "tolerated" upwards to a year—the limit imposed on all permitted absences save those enumerated in Canon 665 §1—though probably not much more than that. On the other hand, the lack of a definite upper limit might permit a superior faced with a "unique" situation to extend indefinitely the period of solicitude prescribed in Canon 665 §2. Canon 665 §2, in other words, might provide the leadership with an explanation—should they someday be challenged to provide one—of their part in this extraordinarily protracted absence.

If they erred by exceeding an unstated canonical limit on how long an institute can tolerate an unlawful absence—they might argue—it was for nothing more vicious than long-suffering solicitude. Of course if this explanation is to work, the leadership must make the appearance of my culpable absence stick, which is to say that they must harken all the way back to the obedience of 1981. And there, again, is the annoying problem. As soon as the documentation of the past 12 years is laid out, the attempt to cover it up with the solicitude clause of Canon 665 §2—even on the most hyper-indulgent interpretation—is quite incredible.

The leadership is aware of this, which is why they have now resorted to this second contrived obedience. They are using this obedience to create a six-month cycle of absence in isolation from the long history of their uncanonical imposed absence. Evidently they assume that I have been sufficiently worn down not to undertake the arduous task of placing this obedience in context, thus allowing it to be reviewed by higher authorities on purely procedural grounds in complete abstraction from the history of the case.

This is the best I can do by way of identifying what lies behind the leadership's otherwise inscrutable insistence on the undefined term 'tolerated absence.'

Now let me briefly review the career of 'tolerated absence' after the Morrissey meeting. Its next appearance is in Fr. Haslam's summary of my follow-up meeting with Frs. Harris and Carignan in late August 1987; convened to discuss what options remained after I rejected Qualified Exclaustration. The very first item of business is to reassert my status as "tolerated absence," and again—reading Fr. Haslam's summary—an attempt seems to be afoot to elicit my agreement to this characterization:

> [Fr. Carignan] recalled that the meeting of July 14, 1987, had talked about Father Wagner's present situation as one of 'tolerated absence.'
>
> Father Harris shared his hope and that of the Provincial Council to bring satisfactory closure to the current status of Father Wagner: it was his understanding that Father Wagner also desired this. The Province administration cannot accept an on-going 'tolerated absence.'
>
> Father Wagner again expressed his desire to see a satisfactory conclusion to the situation.

Note again the almost invisible transition from "tolerated absence" having been merely *talked* about to its being an established status that the Provincial administration cannot accept. The term appears a third time toward the end of Fr. Haslam's summary, when the following remark is attributed to Fr. Harris: "It was important, however, to keep the focus of the present meeting on the question of tolerated absence and the value of ... seeking a Bishop."

The term next appears in Fr. Haslam's chronology of my case which he mailed to me the following October. His note for the meeting of July 14, 1987, takes a sentence directly from Fr. Morrissey's resume, but observe the change it undergoes: "Fr. Wagner's present condition *could* be considered to be a 'tolerated absence'" becomes "Fr. Wagner's condition *is* considered as one of 'tolerated absence'." [Emphasis added.]

I have already remarked how immediately after Fr. Zago's exoneration of me, Fr. Harris again confronted me with this label, suddenly declaring my state to be "contrary to our Constitutions." (I can find no reference to the term in the Oblate *Constitutions and Rules*.) In his letter of November 19, 1988, he attempts to further insinuate active culpability on my part: "The Council members reached a unanimous decision [that] the tolerated absence which *you* are presently *sustaining* in San Francisco be brought to a close." [Emphasis added.]

When the term appears in his letter of September 21, 1989, with copies sent to Bishop McGrath and Fr. Greenlaw, the time was long overdue for me to call him on it. In my reply of September 27, when I am distancing myself from him, I frame my discussion specifically in terms of what lay behind his accusatory use of the term 'tolerated absence':

> In the course of the last year or so you have become quite fond of the label "tolerated absence" and have never let pass an opportunity to point it at me like an accusing finger. I wish I could convey to you how much this label hurts me. It is demeaning because it imputes that I am a miscreant who has been allowed to get away with something far too long.

Afterward the term disappeared from Oblate communications, and no one used it again until a year later, when it showed up in Fr. Zago's letter of October 3, 1990—now, however, shorn of its lenient adjective: "When I wrote to you in June of 1988, I did not sanction in any way, the continuation of your absence from community." When I read this line, it was like the dropping of a veil. Since 1987, the leadership's repetition of the term 'tolerated absence' had been setting me up for just that moment. In my retort of November 5, 1990, I identified the rhetorical lineage of Fr. Zago's phrase "absence from community", and laid the orphaned 'absence' back on the doorstep from whence it originally came:

> Your remark [reaffirming] my Oblate status is highly equivocal and actually represents a step back from your letter of June 17, 1988. Indeed, it commits itself to the fraud— there really is no other word for it—that my "absence from community" is my fault and not the community's. ...You are poorly informed indeed if you honestly think that this case has

anything to do with some supposed refusal on my part to return to community or, for that matter, that the community itself is in the least bit interested in my return. Talk of reconciliation along those lines ended in 1985, when Fr. Jetté's initiative of two years earlier fell mysteriously silent in mid-dialogue.

The General Administration's false charges and contrived obedience of 1981 (read again the cynical instructions entitled *Dismissal* hand-delivered to Fr. Waldie at that time) resulted in my being *pushed out* and *kept out* of community life. By the time the General Administration resumed contact with me in 1987, I had already lived more than six years as *persona non grata*, without rights, material support, or Oblate fellowship of any kind. (I won't neglect to mention the Congregation's out-of-pocket payment for my emergency appendectomy in 1985 which forced the community to reenlist me on the insurance roles, from which my name had been dropped in 1981; this only confirms that the Oblates did and do have an ongoing obligation to me despite my *de facto* status as an outcast.)

The only "right" I had during this era was to be subjected from time to time to "hot light" interrogations.... Consequently, in my 1987 meeting with Frs. Carignan and Morrissey—when they informed me that the *only* option remaining to me was "qualified exclaustration"—I finally acceded to the clear and overwhelming desire of the Oblate leadership that I leave the Congregation. However, I agreed to take this route *only* through a normal process of exclaustration so that I might eventually incardinate in a diocese or seek my vocation in another religious institute. This meant that my name had to be cleared of all false charges, that the contrived obedience stemming from them had to be removed, and that I had to be declared an Oblate in good standing. Your letter of 1988 is in the direct line of the understanding I arrived at with Frs. Carignan and Morrissey about my route of departure. Indeed, ...the only use your letter could have had was as a passport out, so to speak, since it had no influence at all on my situation as an unwanted and excluded brother.

...Your latter-day adoption of Fr. Harris's bogus "continued absence" theme (spoken in a way to insinuate that I skipped out of community one day and ever after turned a deaf ear to calls for me to come home) might be seen as a transparent attempt to villainize the victim and force the case back to a simple issue of obedience and hence to a coerced "final solution."

Let me remind you that in 1981 the Provincial Council under Fr. Waldie's guidance and at the instigation of the General Administration voted unanimously for my dismissal. I have never been given a single word of explanation about what became of that dismissal process. For all I know it has merely been on hold all this time, pending some future, "cleaner" occasion to be started up again. I do know, however, that the Council's vote to dismiss me was never rescinded and that no one who was party to it, including of course Fr. Harris, has ever expressed the least qualm about it. That vote has always stood and still stands as the official expression of Provincial sentiment and intentions toward me. For this reason alone the implication that the community *wants* me to return is simply ludicrous.

But there is more. For ten years I have been denied even the simplest civilities, which any Oblate has the right to expect from his community. For example, I have never received a Provincial newsletter; I was not informed of the death of a brother Oblate or invited to attend his funeral; I have never been included in retreats or feast days; I have never been informed of the ordination and installation of new Oblates; I have never been invited to concelebrate Mass, etc.

Your letter of 1988 had no affect whatsoever on this systematic exclusion of me from anything and everything touching on community life. Still worse, for more than two years now your letter has been kept strictly under wraps, as confidential information not to be shared with the rank-and-file membership. No one in a non-leadership position has ever been informed officially of this supposed reconciliation. Now I ask you: What could explain this secrecy about your letter?

If the situation is as simple as the leadership tries to represent it, and I have been actively removing myself from my superiors' authority since some unspecified time before 1988; and if I have persisted in this absent state in all the years after 1988; and if, finally, the leadership denies any responsibility for my "absence" during all those years as well as any part in the destruction of my efforts in San Francisco—why did Fr. Zago not have me called me back to community at any time after he rebuffed my appeal in 1990? If the innuendo of absence had any basis in fact at all, what could possibly justify allowing that supposed absence to continue another three years?

There is only one answer. Fr. Zago and his advisors, following the general policy of their predecessors, have gotten themselves into a serious predicament; and like their predecessors they lack the courage to admit their mistakes and to seek a just and open solution.

Since the very beginning of this scandal the leadership has done little more than stall for time in the hope that eventually they might manipulate appearances to their advantage. In the beginning they were probably motivated by the concern that if they acknowledged their errors they would be undermining their authority. In time, however, their actions degenerated into a classic cover up. As so often happens in cases like this, the more they floundered to conceal the truth of their problem, the deeper into it they sank. Now the leadership is so hopelessly mired that they are prepared to resort to higher authority to pull them out. As long as they can conceal the shameful spectacle from the membership, the leaders are prepared to swallow their pride and let the Holy See clean up their mess for them.

Here by way of summary I shall outline the four elements of the leadership's strategy as it has emerged since Fr. Zago's letter of October 3, 1990. (1) To shift blame for the seven-year "absence" before 1988 onto me and to portray the leadership's role as one solely of long-suffering indulgence. (2) To portray the five-year "absence" after 1988 as a further period of indulgence and solicitude and to deny any responsibility for the sabotage of the incardination process. (3) To get me back into a normal-appearing relationship with the provincial administration so as to prepare the way for a plausible obedience. (4) To allow the predictable "absence" following such an obedience to last the canonically prescribed six months, thus creating an isolated cycle of absence that hopefully will eclipse the cumulative "absence" stretching back 12 years.

The leadership hopes that when the acts of dismissal based on the contrived six-month absence come up for canonical review, SCICL (The Sacred Congregation for Institutes of Consecrated Life) will consider the case on procedural grounds only, untainted by any reference to the larger history. Obviously the strategy has not work out as planned. As the documentation I have brought together here shows, elements (1) and (2) are without basis in fact and amount to nothing more than propaganda. Element (3) has not fallen into place either, as I have refused to allow the General Administration to be push my case back down the provincial level. Consequently, that leaves element (4), Fr. Zago's at last instructing Fr. Nourie to give me an obedience in the rather fantastic expectation that The Sacred Congregation for Institutes of Consecrated Life will be complicitous in helping Oblate officials save face before their own community.

The leadership's strategy was flawed for a more conspicuous reason: elements (1) and (2) are inconsistent with elements (3) and (4). Either I have been culpably absent for 12 years or I have not. If I have, then the grounds for my dismissal have existed all along, and the present obedience with its six-month timeline is superfluous and indeed a gratuitous abuse of the vow of obedience. If I have not, then the responsibility for my "absence" lies elsewhere, and the leadership must find another solution besides a dismissal process based on another trumped-up obedience.

The most striking thing about Fr. Zago's October 3, 1990 remark, "When I wrote to you in June of 1988, I did not sanction in any way the continuation of your absence from community" is that in fact he *did* "sanction" my "absence," indeed my *permanent* absence from community.

Fr. Zago provided that letter expressly to facilitate my departure from the Congregation, and no one familiar with my case could imagine that he did so to facilitate my rejoining an Oblate community. In other words, Fr. Zago did consent to my "absence"—if in no other way than by turning his back on the situation—during the entire two years I worked at St. Robert's and lobbied Fr. Harris to normalize my status. In his letter of October 3, 1990, replying to my intention to appeal, Fr. Zago contradicts himself on this point. At the same time that he declares my "absence from community" to be unacceptable, he reaffirms his embrace of me as an Oblate in good standing and goes on to say: "I want to urge you once again to dialogue with Fr. Paul Nourie, OMI, your present Provincial Superior concerning other options you might wish to pursue in the future."

And what options might those be? Two years later, on November 23, 1992, Fr. Nourie, in response to a query by me as to what practically speaking being an Oblate in good standing could possibly mean under such bizarre circumstances, replied: "For me it means that you can present yourself with [Fr. Zago's] letter, to any Bishop who will accept you into their diocese for ministry with the hope of incardination, and that we will support the effort in whatever way the Bishop is willing to work that out."

In other words, Fr. Zago was urging me not to return to community but to resume the *status quo* with yet a third provincial and thus, in principle at least, extend for an indefinite period the identical "absence" that he claimed to disapprove of. One might well ask, if Fr. Zago was so concerned about my unsanctioned "absence," why did he urge me to return to a condition defined precisely by that "absence"?

There were several benefits. Resuming the *status quo* at the provincial level would deflect my appeal and thus free the General Leadership from the uncomfortable duty of having to review and judge its own role in the egregious treatment of me. It would also dispose of the memory of that treatment under the guise of charitably according me a second chance to incardinate. Finally, return to the *status quo* at the provincial level—if more carefully managed than the botched return in 1988—would create an appearance of normalcy and thus open the way, after the inevitable second failure, to an eventual "normal" obedience. Such a scenario would have spared Fr. Zago the current messy alternative of having to instruct Fr. Nourie to place me under obedience.

Fr. Zago has been fond of saying that I have obligations as well as rights, the innuendo being that I do not live up to my obligations. In his last note to me, he said: "I cannot see how you can pretend to have a financial claim towards the Congregation from whom you received your formation without giving back the promised missionary commitment." My foregoing defense has demonstrated the hollowness of such a statement.

Nevertheless, I should like to close with some brief remarks on how well I have fulfilled my obligations. Despite the many efforts to shake me off during this ordeal, I have persevered with the Congregation. I have been constantly available to the leadership, I have been responsive to its every contact, and I have answered every question put to me. I have dialogued and argued and written at times to the point of exhaustion. I dare say that very few Oblates in the history of the organization have made themselves as *present* to their superiors as I have over the years. Almost any other man would have fled long ago to save his sanity.

Twice I refrained from appealing to authorities outside the Congregation for redress. The first time was in 1988, when instead of appealing to SCICL I accepted Fr. Zago's letter and set about preparing to leave voluntarily. The second time was in 1990. When I appealed to Fr. Zago, I announced again that I would appeal to SCICL within in a specified time if I did not get satisfaction. Again I eschewed that option and resolved to wait for the leadership to turn voluntarily toward a just settlement.

In his letter of 1988, Fr. Zago required that I be in close dialogue with Fr. Harris, which God knows I tried to do. He also required that I "refrain from any further public statements relating to homosexuality." I want it to go on record now that in the five years since Fr. Zago posed that requirement to me, I have honored it. I have refused to allow republication of my dissertation. I have not pursued academic opportunities offered me in the field. I have written no article on the subject. I have given no interviews to the press. I have made no television appearances. I have turned down speaking engagements. I have even declined to participate in informal symposia. In short, I have destroyed a career as spokesperson and social activist in a matter that is of the utmost personal and moral concern to me. And despite all that has happened, I am still respecting Fr. Zago's request.

But suppose I had no cause to worry about the *sub rosa* strategy I have just outlined, why would I not accept Fr. Zago's and Fr. Nourie's offer to engage again at the provincial level and seek another bishop? Here is my brief answer. If I discount that Fr. Nourie sat with Fr. Harris on the original Provincial Council which voted for my dismissal, and if I discount that he also sat on the Provincial Council during Fr. Harris's first term, and if I discount that on January 2, 1991, he lent his name to a document rationalizing Fr. Harris's conduct toward me—Fr. Nourie's proffered support was nothing more than an offer to sit back and wait. *You* go find a bishop, *you* talk him into accepting you, and whatever *he* agrees to work out with you, we'll support. That is the gist of what it means for me to be an Oblate in good standing. From the community nothing will be forthcoming: no creative thought, no initiative, no active presence, nothing that a bishop or anyone else would understand as convincing sponsorship—in short, failure guaranteed. I would have to do all the work, and what would that work be exactly? Mailing out resumes? Traveling the country to interview bishops? And who would pay my travel expenses, who would earn my salary while I was off conducting these clerical explorations? And what guarantee would I have that, even if I were able to accomplish this Herculean task; the current Provincial wouldn't sabotage the effort like Fr. Harris sabotaged my ministry in San Francisco? Then how much time would I be given before the drumbeat started up again: "Neither the General Administration nor the local Provincial Council can responsibly allow you to continue in a state of tolerated absence," etc., etc., etc.?

No! I have experienced enough heartache and disappointment for several lifetimes. My vocation as an Oblate was ruined long ago, and now I have resigned myself to the knowledge that my priesthood has been destroyed as well.

I have not, however, abandoned my quest for justice—for that is the last thing that I have to offer you as brothers. And believe me, if you allow the history of my degradation to be suppressed and forgotten, and if you allow that suppression and forgetfulness to stand as a precedent, then the gravest implications follow for every Oblate and indeed every religious as a bearer of rights.

I call upon the leadership at long last to bring themselves to accountability, and I maintain that the most minimal sense of equity toward a brother requires a voluntary and full restitution of all that has been denied me and taken from me. I maintain that anyone with a conscience (and a memory!)—undergoing what I have undergone, knowing what I know, losing what I have lost—would repudiate this obedience for what it so palpably is: a smokescreen to conceal 13 years of disregard for the rule of law.

CHAPTER 6

Afterward

No one on the provincial council who received a copy of the above document responded to me.

I received the two requisite canonical warnings from my provincial, each one stating unequivocally that, should I fail to do as I was told, I would suffer the consequences—dismissal from the congregation.

I didn't respond to the warnings. And once again, like in 1982, this new dismissal process was ratified by the standing provincial counsel and sent to the General house in Rome. This time, however, they were in dead earnest. The General Administration accepted the provincial recommendation that I be dismissed. They issued their decree of dismissal on May 13,1994.

The final document reads:

DECREE OF DISMISSAL

Whereas the Rev. Richard Joseph WAGNER, O.M.I., made first profession in the Congregation go the Missionary Oblates of Mary Immaculate on August 15, 1970;

Whereas in virtue of his profession, he is bound to obey lawful superiors in any matter pertaining directly or indirectly to the observance of the Constitutions and Rules of the Congregation (Const. Art. 27);

Whereas on July 28th, 1993, he received an order from Very Rev. Paul NOURIE, O.M.I., his Provincial Superior, assigning him in virtue of the vow of obedience to St. Benedict's Parish and Community in Seattle, Washington as of August 15, 1993;

Whereas Father Wagner did not report to his assigned place of residence;

Whereas after six months of illegitimate absence he received two canonical warnings from his Provincial Superior (dated February 20, 1994 and March 12, 1994), both of which indicated that he was illegitimately absent and that this constituted cause for dismissal; and these admonitions also indicated that he had the right of defense (Canon 696 §1);

Whereas Father Wagner presented a lengthy defense which did not address the issue of his formal disobedience; (NOTE: The General Administration dismisses everything you've just read with this clause. They suppress the history of the controversy and all of their misdeeds and no one is the wiser, not even the The Sacred Congregation for Institutes of Consecrated Life who will ratify this whitewashed version and acquiesce to the dismissal.)

Whereas, after the prescribed time had elapsed his Provincial Superior having gathered the pertinent acts, met April 28, 1994, with his Council to consider the dismissal of Father Wagner from the Congregation and that they were in favor of pursuing the dismissal;

Whereas the acts of the case were forwarded to the Very Rev. Marcello ZAGO, O.M.I., Superior General;

Whereas Father Zago met with the General Council of the Congregation in May 13, 1994, and collegially by secret ballot, they voted to dismiss Father Richard Joseph Wagner from the congregation.

It is hereby decreed as follows:

1.   Rev. Richard Joseph WAGNER, O.M.I., is dismissed from the Congregation of the Missionary Oblates of Mary Immaculate;

2.   This decree, in accordance with canon 700 is to be forwarded to the Holy See for confirmation;

3.   If this decree is confirmed, it is then to be communicated to Father Wagner, who, within ten days of receiving notification of the decree, may have recourse against it to the Congregation of Consecrated Life and Societies of Apostolic Life. If such recourse is had, the decree of dismissal is suspended pending the reply of the Holy See;

4.   In accordance with the prescriptions of Canon 702 §2, the Congregation of the Missionary Oblates of Mary Immaculate shall show equity and evangelical charity towards Father Wagner, so as to help him make a transition to his new situation.

Given at Rome, at the General House of the Missionary Oblates of May Immaculate, this thirteenth day of May, 1994.

Signed

Marcello ZAGO, O.M.I.
Superior General

And

Gilles COMEAU, O.M.I
General Secretary and Notary

And with this final document my once vibrant and holy vocation; my religious life, once so full of passion and promise, is aborted. In the end it is smothered and extinguished by a group of my brother priests anxious to preserve a fiction.

I keep asking myself, even all these years later, was this fratricide necessary; was it worth it? Was it worth subverting everything we Oblates held sacred? Was it worth flushing away all those years of my priestly formation and tens of thousands of dollars spent on my post-graduate education? Did I really pose that much of a threat?

Of course, this monstrous corporate malfeasance and canonical corruption prefigures the horrors of the international clergy abuse scandal that is still breaking today. And despite the hundreds of millions of dollars the Church will be made to pay out in restitution to survivors, the secrecy and sophistry continues unabated. It is this kind of profligate waste that is the real scandal of this murderous story. And no person of faith can remain unmoved.

GAY CATHOLIC PRIESTS:

A STUDY OF COGNITIVE AND AFFECTIVE DISSONANCE

by

RICHARD WAGNER, O.M.I., M.DIV.

Dissertation Committee

Wardell B. Pomeroy, Ph.D.

Erwin J. Haeberle, Ph.D.

Loretta Haroian, Ph.D.

Approved by the Dissertation Committee,

The Institute for Advanced Study of Human Sexuality San Francisco, California

Date: February 16, 1981

TABLE OF CONTENTS

LIST OF TABLES

CHAPTER 1

Review of Catholic Doctrine

On January 15, 1976 the Sacred Congregation for the Doctrine of Faith issued a document entitled: Declaration on Certain Questions Concerning. Sexual Ethics. This document, the most recent Vatican pronouncement concerning sexual morality, carried this paragraph as a preface to its discussion of homosexual behavior:

> At the present there are those who, basing themselves on observations in the psychological order, have begun to judge indulgently, and even excuse completely, homosexual relations between certain people. This they do in opposition to the constant teaching of the Magisterium and to the moral sense of the Christian people. (1)

More will be said about this document later. For now, however, this paragraph serves as an appropriate departure for this study of gay Roman Catholic priests. The entire presentation will attempt to isolate areas of conflict in both thought and feeling that surface in the lives of gay priests. This will be accomplished by focusing on the personal struggles of the individual priests who comprise this sample. There are two issues of equal importance to these priests. This study will highlight the conflicts these men may be experiencing, not only because they are gay, but also because they have made a public commitment to celibacy by virtue of their ordination.

To date nothing has been published concerning the sexual attitudes or behaviors of Catholic priests serving in public ministry. The veil of secrecy surrounding this vocation as well as the popular presumption that all priests are sexually abstinent has provided a camouflage for the sexually active priest. But as this study will illustrate, this situation is not without its negative consequences. The sexually active priest is faced with a paradox. The same circumstances that guarantee secrecy also perpetuate the need for secrecy.

By way of introduction, we begin with a brief historical survey of the development of thought within the Roman tradition concerning homosexuality and clerical celibacy. The purpose is to show the confusion surrounding theological speculation on these issues. This survey will begin with the Bible, move through the early Christian Fathers to Thomas Aquinas, and conclude with contemporary opinions.

First, the issue of homosexuality. Six passages in the Bible have traditionally been understood as dealing with homosexual activity. The following biblical quotations are taken from the New American Bible.

Perhaps the single most important passage is the Sodom and Gomorrah story in Genesis 19:4-11.

> Before they went to bed, all the townsmen of Sodom, both young and old - all the people to the last man - closed in on the house. They called to Lot and said to him, 'Where are the men who came to your house tonight? Bring them out to us that we might have intimacies with them.' Lot went out to meet them at the entrance. When he had shut the door behind him, he said, 'I beg you, my brothers, not to do this wicked thing. I have two daughters who have never had intercourse with men. Let me bring them out to you, and you may do with them as you please. But don't do anything to these men, for you know they have come under the shelter of my roof.' They replied, 'Stand back! This fellow,' they sneered, 'comes here as an immigrant, and now he dares to give orders! We'll treat you worse than them!'

With that, they pressed hard against Lot, moving in closer to
break down the door. But his guests put out their hands, pulled
Lot inside with them, and closed the door; at the same time they
struck the men at the entrance of the house, one and all, with
such a blinding light that they were utterly unable to reach the
doorway.

Another reference which is said to reflect a general condemnation of homosexual
behavior is found in the Old Testament Holiness Code, Leviticus 18:22; 20:13.

You shall not lie with a male as with a woman; such a thing is
an abomination.

If a man lies with a male as with a woman, both of them shall
be put to death for their abominable deed; they have forfeited
their lives.

In the New Testament, two Greek words - *malaikoi* and *arsenokoitai* — are
usually translated as direct references to homosexual activity. These terms appear
in 1 Corinthians 6:9 and 1 Timothy 1:10.

Can you not realize that the unholy will not fall heir to the
Kingdom of God? Do not deceive yourselves: no fornicators,
idolaters, or adulterers, no sodomites...

...fornicators, sexual perverts, kidnapers, liars, perjurers, and
those who in other ways flout the sound teaching... .

Finally, what appears to be the strongest condemnation of homosexual activity is
Romans 1:26-27.

God therefore delivered them up to disgraceful passions. Their
women exchanged natural intercourse for unnatural, and the
men gave up natural intercourse with women and burned with

lust for one another. Men did shameful things with men, and thus received in their own persons the penalty for their perversity.

In the Patristic Period there was unanimity on the sinfulness of homosexuality among the leading Church Fathers. Their attacks were based on the general supposition that homosexual acts are unnatural because they are non-procreative in nature. John Chrysostom is particularly emphatic in denouncing homosexual practices as unnatural.

> A certain new illicit love has entered our lives, an ugly and incurable disease has appeared, the most severe of all the plagues has been hurled down, a new and insufferable crime has been devised, not only are the laws established (by man) overthrown but even those of nature herself. (2)

Augustine contends that homosexual practices are transgressions of the command to love God and one's neighbor.

> ...those shameful acts against nature, such as were committed in Sodom, ought everywhere and always to be detested and punished. (3)

By the thirteenth century, social pressure against homosexuality through ecclesiastical decrees and national custom became codified in cannon law. Much of the credit for moving the Church in this direction belongs to Thomas Aquinas and his *Summa Theoloqica*. He states that homosexual acts are unnatural because they are against reason as well as the fact that such acts do not appear among animals.

> It must be noted that the nature of man may be spoken of either as that which is peculiar to man, and according to this all sins, insofar as they are against reason, are against nature (as is stated by Damascene); or as that which is common to man and other animals, according to which certain particular sins are said

to be against nature, as intercourse between males (which is specifically called the vice against nature) is contrary to the union of male and female which is natural to all animals. (4)

No serious challenge came from within the Church to this position until the latter part of this century. The publication of Fr. Charles Curran's *Catholic Moral Theology in Dialogue* in 1972 typified the contemporary movement for a cautious reassessment of moral theology regarding homosexuality.

> The homosexual is generally not responsible for his condition. …Therapy as an attempt to make the homosexual into a heterosexual, does not offer great promise for most homosexuals. Celibacy and sublimation are not always possible or even desirable for the homosexual. There are somewhat suitable homosexual unions, which afford their partners some human fulfillment and contentment. Obviously, such unions are better than homosexual promiscuity…the individual homosexual may morally come to the conclusion that a somewhat permanent homosexual union is the best, and sometimes the only, way for him to achieve some humanity. Homosexuality can never become an ideal. Attempts should be made to overcome this condition if possible; however, at times one may reluctantly accept homosexual unions as the only way in which some people can find a satisfying degree of humanity in their lives. (5)

In 1976 John McNeill S.J. published his work, *The Church and the Homosexual*, to date the first systematic attack on the scriptural and theological suppositions supporting the condemnation of homosexuality.

> It can, however, be argued 1) that what is referred to, especially in the New Testament, under the rubric of homosexuality is not the same reality at all or 2) that the biblical authors do not manifest the same understanding of that reality as we have today. Further it can be seriously questioned whether what is understood today as the true homosexual and his or her activity

is ever the object of explicit moral condemnation in Scripture. (6)

Throughout the Old Testament Sodom is referred to as a symbol of utter destruction occasioned by sins of such magnitude as to merit exemplary punishment. However, nowhere in the Old Testament is that sin identified explicitly with homosexual behavior. (7)

There is no reason to assume that Aquinas had any more awareness than the Church Fathers of the homosexual condition. Rather, it is almost certain that in his references to homosexual practices he is assuming that these are merely sexual indulgences undertaken from a motive of lust by otherwise heterosexual persons. (8)

The greater part of both moral and psychological thinking concerning homosexuality tends to be prejudiced at its source, because it begins with a questionable presupposition. That presupposition, frequently explicit, maintains that the heterosexual condition is somehow the very essence of the human and at the very center of the mature human personality. (9)

If the findings of this study are correct, then the Church's attitude toward homosexuals is another example of structured social injustice, equally based in questionable interpretation of Scripture, prejudice, and blind adherence to merely human traditions, which have been falsely interpreted as the law of nature and of God. In fact, as we have seen, it is the same age-old tradition of male control, domination and oppression of women, which underlies the oppression of the homosexual. (10)

Despite the attempt at opening a dialogue, the last official word remains the Vatican's *Declaration on Certain Questions Concerning Sexual Ethics*. What is noteworthy is that this is the first official statement on homosexuality, which admits the possibility of a homosexual orientation, even though it continues to view homosexuality as pathological in nature.

A distinction is drawn, and it seems with some reason, between homosexuals whose tendency comes from a false education, from a lack of normal sexual development, from habit, from bad example, or from other similar causes, and is transitory or at least not incurable; and homosexuals who are definitely such because of some kind of innate instinct or a pathological constitution judged to be incurable.

In regard to this second category of subjects, some people conclude that their tendency is so natural that it justifies in their case homosexual relations within a sincere communion of life and love analogous to marriage, insofar as such homosexuals feel incapable of enduring a solitary life.

In the pastoral field, these homosexuals must certainly be treated with understanding and sustained in hope of overcoming their personal difficulties and their inability to fit into society. Their culpability will be judged with prudence. But no pastoral method can be employed which would give moral justification to these acts on the grounds that they would be consonant with the condition of such people. For according to the objective moral order, homosexual relations are acts, which lack an essential and indispensable finality. In Sacred Scripture they are condemned as a serious depravity and even presented as the sad consequence of rejecting God. This judgment of Scripture does not of course permit us to conclude that all those who suffer from this anomaly are personally responsible for it, but it does attest to the fact that homosexual acts are intrinsically disordered and can in no case be approved of. (11)

The history of theological speculation and Church reform regarding clerical celibacy is an equally complex issue. Authors are often indiscriminate in their use of spiritual and ascetical notions such as chastity, virginity, and sexual abstinence when defining celibacy, even though the word itself simply denotes a renunciation of marriage. Because of this it is often impossible to determine the precise ecclesiastical expectations for the clerical celibate. Is one to assume that a public commitment to celibacy entails more than commitment to remain single? While this question remains unanswered the popular interpretation holds sway: celibacy means sexual abstinence.

There is a remarkable difference between the Old and New Testaments with regard to the celibate lifestyle. The Old Testament stresses the virtue of premarital virginity while it promotes the values of married life. Marriage is considered honorable and compulsory for all, and to be unmarried and childless is deemed shameful. The New Testament, on the other hand, emphasizes the value of permanent virginity as a means of worshiping God. This is apparent in the example and teaching of Jesus.

> Some men are incapable of sexual activity from birth; some have been deliberately made so; and some there are who have freely renounced sex for the sake of God's reign. Let him accept this teaching who can. (12)

St. Paul praised celibacy and virginity as a more perfect state, since it is the condition for a more fervent consecration to God.

> Are you bound to a wife? Then do not seek your freedom. Are you free of a wife? If so do not go in search of one. Should you marry, however, you will not be committing a sin. Neither does a virgin commit sin if she marries. But such people will have trials in this life, and these I should like to spare you. (13)

The Patristic Period, the first three or four Christian centuries, saw no laws promulgated against clerical marriage.

> Clement of Alexandria commenting on the Pauline texts stated that marriage, if used properly, is a way of salvation for all: priests, deacons, and laymen. (14)

The earliest legislation comes from the fourth century. The Spanish Council of Elvira in 305 decreed that all clergy were to abstain from their wives. The decree did not forbid marriage; it simply required abstinence.

> We decree that all bishops, priests, and deacons, and all clerics engaged in the ministry are forbidden entirely to live with their wives and to beget children: Whoever shall do so will be deposed from the clerical dignity. (15)

Emphasis on celibacy accompanied the rise of monasticism, which replaced martyrdom as the supreme form of witness to Jesus. The first ecumenical and universal council to require celibacy was the First Lateran Council in 1123. It forbade marriage for the clergy and required that marriages already contracted should be broken. The final formulation of the mandate for clerical celibacy came as a result of the Reformation at the Council of Trent in 1563.

While the celibacy controversy continues to be an issue in the Church, very little contemporary thought has been brought to the discussion. One exception is Donald Goergen's O.P. work *The Sexual Celibate*. The author combines a mixture of contemporary psychology and traditional theology in his discussion of the celibate lifestyle. Goergen maintains that although the clerical celibate forswears his right to marry he is free to develop affectional friendships. Goergen does not suggest that genital sexuality is proper to the celibate, but he does maintain that celibacy does not mean being asexual.

> The sexual life of a celibate person is going to manifest itself primarily in the affective bonds of permanent and steadfast human friendships, which are exemplifications of God's way of loving. (16)

The primary concern of this section has been the history of clerical celibacy. But one must not overlook the church's demand for sexual abstinence for all its members not validly married. Of particular concern here is the implication for the homosexual. In 1973 the committee on pastoral research and practice of the National Conference of Catholic Bishops approved for distribution and published a paper entitled: *Principles To Guide Confessors in Questions of Homosexuality*. It serves as an accurate indication of official Catholic teaching and pastoral practice regarding homosexuality today.

Since all homosexual acts are assumed to be intrinsically evil by nature apart from any other consideration, confessors are advised to help homosexuals to work out an 'ascetical plan of life.' Each homosexual has the obligation to control his tendency by every means within his power, particularly by psychological and spiritual counsel. It is difficult for the homosexual to remain chaste in his environment, and he may slip into sin for a variety of reasons, including loneliness and compulsive tendencies and the pull of homosexual companions. But generally, he is responsible for his actions. (17)

The dilemma of the gay priest, the cognitive and affective dissonance present in his life, is due in great measure to the confusion surrounding the issues of homosexuality and celibacy and their moral and theological implications. Dubious interpretations of Scripture, ambiguous terminology, and diffuse prejudices and fears have all contributed to the confusion. Identifying the difficulties gay priests encounter in personally assessing the impact of theological speculation and pastoral directives in regard to homosexuality and celibacy is one of the intents of the study that follows.

CHAPTER 2

Methodology

Purpose of the Study

The present investigation was undertaken with several purposes in mind. First, there was an effort to identify the various sexual dimensions present in the histories of a sample of fifty Roman Catholic priests who self-identify as gay. This encompassed more than a survey of the nature and frequency of each subject's sexual behavior. It was also an attempt to capture a feeling for each respondent's growth in his appreciation of himself as a sexual being. Second, there was an effort to examine areas of ambivalence or conflict in thought and feeling regarding the gay priest's "double" social and cultural identity. Third, all of this was undertaken as a step toward an appreciation of the unique position of the gay priest.

It must be pointed out from the beginning that any conclusion about the number of gay men in the Roman Catholic priesthood or the degree, if any, they are exhibiting a particular behavior or characteristic, is not the aim of this study. On the contrary, the fortuitous nature of this sample precludes such generalizations. Also something should be said about the use of the term "gay." The choice of this term over the more pervasively used "homosexual" or "homophile" is more than a personal preference. It is used to indicate a higher degree of homoerotic self-awareness. Though an individual might experience homoerotic feelings, and even give them physical expression, the term "gay" would not be used to describe him unless his homoeroticism was part of his self-identification. In other words, the term "gay" is used to denote a person's conscious effort to integrate his homosexual orientation with the rest of his personality. This conscious effort presupposes a conceptual framework in terms of which the person tries to understand himself and interact with others. It is important to point out that this definition does not necessarily denote a sexually active lifestyle. It is possible for an individual to self-identify as gay without having had a single overt same-sex experience.

Procedure

This study is divided into two large sections corresponding to the two instruments used to facilitate the inquiry. The first section deals with the respondents' sex histories, while the second is concerned with the respondents' attitudes with respect to their double identity as gay priests.

The sex history selected was an adaptation of the one developed by Kinsey. Its design enabled an in-depth assessment of each subject's current behaviors as well as the biographical context out of which he is now acting. The sex history was administered in a face-to-face interview, which generally took about 90 minutes. The attitude inventory comprised thirty-four questions. These were divided among four areas of concern: **a) conflicts of conviction; b) conflicts in lifestyle; c) conflicts of identity**; and **d) conflicts in sexual behavior**, as well as introductory and summary sections. The respondent was given the questionnaire at the end of the sex history interview with the instruction to return it to the interviewer by mail when completed. Both the sex history and the attitude inventory bore identical code numbers to insure proper coordination of the data.

I was aware that the design and length of the attitude inventory would present problems in the analysis of the data gathered. However, the written responses to the questions would be potentially more enlightening to the unique sphere of this study. It would allow for a greater breadth of expression for the respondent than the statistically advantageous multiple-choice questionnaire.

Statistics

The gathering of the sample of fifty gay Catholic priests was the most difficult part of the process. The circumstances which militate against the participation of gay lay people in studies of their sexual attitudes and behaviors were considerably compounded in this study of gay priests. The fear of disclosure, possible reprisals, ambivalent attitudes, and feelings of guilt were some of the concerns that stood in the way. In fact, only one thing made the process possible. The gay priest, like any marginal personality, needs a support system. There is an informal network of gay priests operative in just about every section of the country. It was this network that was utilized in the recruitment of respondents. A considerable amount of energy and time was exerted in having the sample of fifty represent the broadest geographical distribution possible. This began by contacting key priests in different parts of the country. These individuals acted as liaisons with priests in their vicinity. The liaisons were given copies of a brief description of the proposed study and were asked to distribute them to the contacts they had. If anyone showed an interest in participating in the study his name, address, and telephone number were forwarded to the interviewer. A personal contact was then made for the purpose of setting an interview date. In some cases travel plans dictated the amount of time available in a particular locale

The final sample of fifty gay priests reflects 68% of the seventy-three total contacts made. The remaining twenty-three individuals were not able to participate for a number of reasons. Five were not included because of scheduling difficulties. Twelve were not included because they reconsidered the risk involved and decided against granting the initial interview. Four possible subjects, while undergoing the sex history interview, excluded themselves from the study by not returning the attitude inventory questionnaire. And finally, the interviewer had to disqualify two other respondents: one because he had resigned the active ministry, the other because he was a priest imposter.

Definitions

In an effort to aid the reader in understanding some distinctive terminology used throughout this presentation a brief list of terms are here defined. These definitions reflect the use intended by the author within the context of this particular study.

Catholic priest. A man properly ordained as a public minister in the Roman Catholic tradition, serving in the active ministry. The Catholic priesthood can be divided into two major groups: secular priests, and religious priests.
Secular priest. A priest ordained to serve in a particular diocese or archdiocese. His immediate superior being the local bishop, archbishop, or cardinal.

Religious priest. A priest ordained as a member of an established community or congregation such as the Jesuits or Franciscans. His immediate superior being a provincial or abbot. He is also distinctive in as much as he professes public vows of poverty, chastity and obedience and lives in accordance with specific rules of life as outlined by his community or congregation. The term "religious" may also refer to any individual associated by vow with a particular community or congregation but who is not an ordained priest - such as a lay brother, sister, nun, or monk.

Living in community. The living situation of both secular and religious priests who are living with other priests or religious in an established community house or rectory.

Celibacy. The public profession to remain unmarried made by every Catholic priest at the time of his ordination.

Chastity. One of the three vows professed by a religious man or woman upon being accepted into a community or congregation. It reflects a commitment to the virtue of purity.

BDSM. The mutual exchange of power within the context of a sexual situation. This may include forms of bondage, discipline, and/or humiliation.

Fist fucking. The insertion of a hand or fist into the rectum of a partner.

Analinctus. Anal-oral contact, "rimming."

CHAPTER 3

The Sample

This chapter is designed to provide an overview of basic demographic characteristics, aspects of sexual development, and current sexual behavior of the respondents in this study. For the sake of convenience, complete results of this part of the study are gathered in the tables, which appear at the end of this chapter (pages 31 - 40). When relevant the reader is referred to these tables. Frequent use is made, both in the text and in the tables, of Gebhard and Johnson's *The Kinsey Data: Marginal Tabulations of the 1938 - 1963 Interviews Conducted the Institute for Sex Research* (Philadelphia: W.B. Saunders, 1979). Use of the statistics contained in that volume permit ready comparison with the present sample of Roman Catholic priests.

Demographics

Though the sample of respondents in this study was of necessity a fortuitous one, a major effort was made to recruit respondents from all over the United States. The majority, twenty-one (42%), reside in California, while seventeen (34%) live in the Northeast - seven in Massachusetts, five in Pennsylvania, three in New York, and two in New Jersey. An additional seven respondents (14%) live in the Midwest - one in Minnesota, one in Michigan, four in Illinois, and one in Iowa.

The remaining five respondents (10%) reside in the Northwest - three in Idaho and two in Washington.

All but two of the respondents were Caucasian; one was black and one identified himself as brown.

The respondents ranged in age from 27 to 58 years. The mean age was 36.4 years, the median was 35 years, and the mode was 32 years. Since all of the respondents are by profession Roman Catholic priests all have achieved a high level of education. Thirty-one (62%) surpassed the theological Master's degree mandatory for ordination into the priesthood. Eighteen (36%) had two Master's degrees, while five (10%) had three Master's degrees. Eight respondents (16%) had attained doctoral degrees.

Sexual Development

The sex history interview began with an evaluation of the personal recreational habits of the respondents. A list of eleven activities was presented to the subject. He was then asked to give the frequency with which he engaged in each activity. (See Table 1, pg. 163)

Four of the respondents (8%) reported that they were recovering alcoholics. It was impossible to determine the percentage of others who might currently be experiencing problems with alcohol. The sample as a whole, however, displayed a high level of awareness about the dangers of alcohol addiction both within the gay community and among their vocational peers. An even greater awareness was expressed about the dangers of using other drugs, although the use of marijuana was considered the least dangerous. It is interesting to note that the respondents in California reported a greater familiarity with and personal use of all the drugs listed. Of recreational activities, the most popular outlet reported was reading. This was followed by cooking, even among respondents who have little opportunity to cook.

The next part of the sex history concerned family background. The results of these questions appear in Tables 2-4 (pg. 163-164). Only seven of the respondents (14%) reported having lived on an operating farm for longer than one year. The balance of the respondents were urban, suburban, or small town dwellers all their lives. Thirty respondents (60%) reported that their fathers were still living. Thirty-eight (76%) reported that their mothers were still living. Two respondents reported that their mothers had died prior to the respondents' adolescence; one other reported that his father deserted his family prior to the respondent reaching adolescence. The remaining forty-seven respondents were able to answer questions about the quality of their relationships with their parents, as well as the quality of the relationship their parents shared. Tables 2-4 reflect answers given to these questions concerning relationships, both intra-parental and between the respondents and each of his parents. The rating is based on each respondent's recollection from adolescence.

Generally the respondents recalled that the quality of their parents' relationship during the period of the respondent's adolescence to be average or above average. As for the relationship between parent and son, the affectional ties were reported to be healthier and stronger between mother and son than between father and son. Of the forty-seven respondents able to make the comparison, 51.1% rated the maternal relationship higher, while only 4.2% rated the paternal relationship higher. 44.7% gave an equal rating for both parents.

Five respondents (10%) were an only child. The forty-five respondents who indicated having siblings reported a range of between 1 and 13 other children in their families. The mean number of siblings was 2.9. Eight respondents (16%) were aware that they were not the only gay sibling in their immediate family. Five had a gay brother, three had a lesbian sister.

After ascertaining aspects of family background, questions were asked about the nature of each of the respondent's early sex education. The procedure was to record the age at which each respondent had his first fairly accurate notion of suggested sexual topics. Following this the respondent was asked what the source of information was for each of the topics. (See Table 5 pg. 164).

Predominantly, same-sex peer groups were responsible for the greatest amount of early sex information for this sample. The only significant exception was the source of information about menstruation, which was more often the home. When the respondents were asked the extent of more formal sex education in school, only sixteen (32%) remembered receiving formal education of any kind. Of these, the types of education most often mentioned were "family life" courses in high school or "morality" courses in graduate level college. Only seventeen of the respondents (34%) considered one or both of his parents to be influential in their sex education. Mothers were slightly favored over fathers.

Next the respondents were asked to estimate their approximate age at the onset of a number of variables signaling the advent of puberty. Each was asked to recall his age when pubic hair began to grow, when his voice began to change, when his first ejaculation occurred, and when his rapid growth spurt ended. Using this information, a further calculation was made to establish the approximate onset of puberty for each respondent. The mean age of the onset of puberty for this sample was 13.9 years; the median age was 13 years. These figures compare with the mean age of 13.7 years established by Kinsey). In addition to these questions, each respondent was asked to recall his feelings about going through all the pubertal changes. The majority, thirty (60%) recalled negative feelings. These feelings ranged from a general discomfort on the part of some to a real dread and fear on the part of others. The positive feelings reported by the remaining twenty respondents (40%) were also on a continuum. There were those who recalled feeling "okay," and those who were overjoyed at the prospect of imminent manhood.

Inquiry into the extent of each respondent's preadolescent sex play was also made. Twenty respondents (40%) reported engaging in heterosexual sex play before reaching puberty. The mean age at the onset of this activity was 6.9 years. All of the reported partners of the respondents were the same age to within one year. The techniques employed were limited to showing genitalia or a combination of showing and touching. The frequency ranged from 1 to 15 occurrences, although the majority reported no more than one or two occurrences total. There was a slightly higher occurrence of preadolescent homosexual sex play by this sample. Twenty-seven respondents (54%) reported such behavior. The mean age at onset was 7.8 years, and once again all the reported partners were within one year of age of the respondent; and the techniques employed generally included no more than showing and touching of each other's genitalia. However, four respondents reported mouth-to-genital contact and/or anal intercourse. The frequency ranged from one occurrence total to one occurrence a week for three years. Most respondents, however, reported less than five occurrences total. These figures compare with 54.4% found in the Kinsey sample. (2) This population reflected a 9.21 years mean age at onset. (3)

In addition to preadolescent sex play, respondents were asked about preadolescent sexual contact with adults. Five respondents (10%) reported having had such contact, and all were same-sex in nature. Three of these respondents reported one occurrence each. These consisted of a stranger approaching them in a public place, such as a movie theater or a park. There was mutual touching and showing of genitalia involved and masturbation on the part of the adult. These encounters provoked similar reactions in all three respondents. There was a mixture of fear and excitement.

The other two respondents reporting preadolescent sexual contact with an adult had their contact with an older brother. The frequency of contact for both of these was at least twice a month for over a year. One of the two reported being coerced into the activity and finding it dissatisfying. The other respondent, however, reported very positive feelings because the sexual interest expressed was mutual.

Sexual Behavior

The respondents were asked about the age of onset and current frequency of masturbation. Table 6 (pg. 165) charts the onset of masturbation. The mean age of first masturbation for this sample was 13.1 years. The first incident of masturbation occurred through self-discovery on the part of thirty-three (66%) of the respondents. Seventeen (34%) learned of masturbation through the instruction of another. Only seven respondents recalled fearing physical harm as a result of masturbation, and all seven resolved their fears within two years of onset. When questioned about guilt associated with masturbation, only seven recalled being free of guilt from the beginning. Of the forty-three others who initially experienced guilt over masturbation all but six have currently resolved their guilt. It is interesting to note that the thirty-seven who initially experienced guilt and then resolved it were unable to do so until the average age of 23.7 years.

Current frequency of masturbation varies greatly among this sample. One respondent reported his current rate at three times a day, while two others reported their rate at no more than once a month. Only one respondent reported that he was currently abstaining. Of the respondents currently engaging in masturbation, the mean frequency is 3.45 times a week, the median frequency is three times a week, and the mode once a week. By way of comparison, Kinsey found a mean frequency of 1.42 times a week, and a median frequency of .73 times a week for college educated males between the ages of 26 and 30. (4)

A minority of the total sample, fourteen (28%), had engaged in heterosexual intercourse. Of these, none has had heterosexual intercourse within the past year. The mean age of first coitus for this group was 26.7 years. Six of these respondents reported having just one other-sex partner, while the most other-sex partners reported was four. When these fourteen respondents were questioned about their attitudes concerning coitus, all but one expressed neutral to negative attitudes. The one respondent who expressed a positive attitude believed that he might initiate further heterosexual contacts in the future. Most of those who expressed neutral to negative attitudes saw their coital experiences as motivated by a desire to prove their masculinity or to overcome fears about being gay. Others reported that the reason for their not continuing to seek heterosexual partners was that such outlet was less satisfying than their same-sex outlets.

During the interview attention also was given to determining the source and extent of sexual arousability for each respondent. Table 7 (pg. 166) represents the responses made by this sample to a selection of erotic stimuli. Not surprisingly, this sample's psychosexual response was predominantly homoerotic. And it is interesting to note that even when a given stimulus involved no distinction between other or same-sex, the respondents made clear their preference. That is, the vast majority of respondents who reported being aroused by sexually explicit photos and movies, live sex shows and reading love stories, volunteered that such stimuli were arousing only if they were homoerotic in nature.

The interviewer also inquired about the presence and extent of the respondent's participation in more exotic sexual outlets, such as sex accompanied by physical force, exhibitionism, voyeurism, bestiality, and fetishes. The only areas that received positive responses beyond curiosity were sex with animals and fetishes. Eleven respondents (22%) reported having had at least one post-pubertal sexual contact with an animal. None, however, reported more than three such contacts. Kinsey found that 22.4% of his sample had had sexual contact with animals. (5) The source of contact for this sample was exclusively domestic animals, primarily dogs. And the type of contact most often reported was allowing the animal to lick the respondent's genitalia.

Twelve of the respondents (24%) reported having a fetish. Of these, seven had clothing fetishes. Items most often mentioned were jockstraps, swimwear, and leather articles. Four others reported fetishes for parts of the body, specifically hands and feet. Finally one reported a fetish for bondage and discipline.

The next phase of the interview dealt directly with the respondents' homosexual activity from first post-pubertal same-sex contact to current same-sex behavior. Questioning began by focusing on the onset, nature, and frequency of the respondents' same-sex contacts. Table 8 (pg. 167) gives the ages at which the respondents had their first post-pubertal experience. The mean age of first contact for this group was 19.9 years, the median age 16 years, and the mode 12 years. Eight respondents (16%) reported that their first same-sex contact was with a stranger: a bar pickup, hustler, or the like. This compares with 12% in the Kinsey sample. (6) The remaining forty-two (84%) reported that their first same-sex contact occurred with a friend.

Concerning sexual techniques involved in this first experience, thirty-three (66%) reported that it involved mutual masturbation, ten (20%) reported oral-genital contact, and six (12%) frictation. This compares with 59.7% mutual masturbation, 6.2% oral-genital, and 5.8% frictation in the Kinsey sample. (7) Only one person in this group reported that his first same-sex contact occurred within a sadomasochistic scenario.

Forty-eight of the respondents (96%) recalled enjoying their first same- sex experience. The two who did not indicated as the reason the unsatisfactory nature of their partners. Nevertheless, despite the overwhelming majority reporting enjoyment, this first encounter was also a source of much guilt. Only eleven (22%) indicated experiencing no guilt over their first same-sex experience.

Next the interviewer asked each respondent to recall his age the first time he engaged in a selection of suggested sexual techniques. (See Table 9, pg. 167) It is noteworthy that when the technique suggested requires more of a physical involvement, there is a progressive increase in the median age and a gradual decrease in the number of respondents who have engaged in it. Thus, while nearly all the respondents, forty-nine, have been active in the masturbation of a partner, only thirty-five have been passive in anal intercourse, and at a considerably older age. Interestingly enough, when those who had not participated in given techniques were asked why, the majority suggested that some of the techniques (particularly anal intercourse) demanded more of a personal commitment. As one respondent put it: *"It is like coming-out. The more you become comfortable with your sexuality the more you are willing to explore new avenues of expression."*

After determining the age at which each respondent had his first same-sex contact involving selected techniques, he was asked the frequency with which he engages in those techniques. The results of this question are reflected in Table 10 (pg. 168). Kissing was the activity most often engaged in by the respondents. Active oral-genital contact on the part of the respondent was the next most frequent. Sadomasochistic techniques of bondage and discipline were the least frequently used.

This line of questioning continued by asking the respondent about his current favorite technique, the one he would most like to use in every sexual encounter. The results were: oral-genital twenty-four (48%), masturbation five (10%), anal intercourse nine (18%), kissing three (6%), frictation six (12%), bondage one (2%), analinctus one (2%), and "fist fucking" one (2%).

The interview continued with an investigation of the frequency of same-sex contact in high school, in college, and currently. The results are reflected in Table 11 (pg. 169). At present, the mean frequency of same-sex contact is two times per week. Only two respondents indicated that they are currently abstaining. After determining the frequency of same-sex contacts, the respondents were asked to give the total number of same-sex contacts made in the course of their lives. In many cases the number had to be approximated, especially when the total number exceeded 100 partners. The fifty respondents averaged 226.8 partners. Of some note is the fact that nine respondents (18%) in this sample had no more than ten partners total, while eleven (22%) reported 500 or more. Kinsey found that 39.2% of his sample had no more than ten partners, while 8.4% reported having had more than 500. (8)

Thirty respondents (60%) reported that .the majority of their partners were approximately the same age as themselves. Only three respondents (6%) reported that the majority of their partners were distinctly older than themselves, but seventeen (34%) said that the majority of their partners were distinctly younger than themselves. Following this, the respondents were asked the extent of their partnering with men living with heterosexual spouses. Twenty-five respondents (50%) were aware of having had such partners. These respondents averaged 6.4 such partners. Each respondent was asked the extent of his sexual partnering with homosexual "virgins," that is, with individuals for whom that contact would have been their first same-sex experience. Twenty-two respondents (44%) recalled such contact. These respondents averaged 4.6 such partners. It is important to note that the majority of the respondents who express their sexuality in more anonymous situations, such as bathhouses or cruising areas, found it difficult to respond accurately to these questions.

Each respondent was questioned about the duration of his longest continuous sexual relationship (affair). Forty respondents (80%) reported having had at least one relationship lasting longer than one month. The mean duration of the reported relationships was just over two years, 24.3 months. (See Table 12, pg. 170). For comparison, Table 13 (pg. 170) represents the percentage of total partners with whom the respondent had but one contact. When asked about the number of partners the respondents could recall being in love with, forty-three respondents reported being in love with an average of 5.2 partners. Seven respondents indicated that they had never been in love with any of their partners. Thirty-one respondents (62%) reported a familiarity with group sex. Of these, seventeen currently engaged in such activity on a regular basis. When inquiry was made into the nature of the group sex contact, most of the respondents indicated that their experiences had been in bathhouses and/or with two other friends. As to the level of enjoyment of group sex experiences, twenty-three (72.2%) reported that they enjoyed their encounters and circumstances. most probably would repeat such behavior under the right The remaining eight (34.6%) found their experiences with group sex dissatisfactory and indicated that they would most probably not pursue such contact in the future.

Each respondent was asked about his contact with male prostitutes. Twelve respondents (24%) indicated having used the services of a hustler. Five of these reported that their total number of contacts did not exceed two or three, while four others reported that this type of outlet comprised the bulk of their same-sex contacts. The most contacts with male prostitutes reported by an individual were twice a month for two years. Respondents were also asked if they engaged in sex in particularly vulnerable places such as bookstores public toilets, parks, and the like. Twenty-three (46%) reported doing so, though only seven of these indicated that they enjoyed this type of outlet and were currently engaging in it. The respondents were asked if they had ever encountered any difficulty or harassment from the police for being gay. Six (12%) said that they had. All reported that harassments were associated with cruising in public places. Two individuals reported having been arrested in a sex-related situation. However, no charges were brought to bear and both were released.

Investigation was made as to the percentage of the respondents' friends who are gay. The mean percentage reported was 53.8%. (See Table 14, pg. 171) Each respondent was also asked the percentage of his non-gay friends who knew that he was gay. The mean percentage reported was 36.6%. (See Table 15, pg. 171)

The interviewer then familiarized the respondent with the seven-point (0-6) heterosexual-homosexual rating scale developed by Kinsey. Each respondent was then asked to rate himself on that scale, taking into account his behaviors as well as his fantasies. At the same time, the interviewer rated the individual on the basis of information gained through the interview. It is significant that the interviewer disagreed with 40% of the respondents' self-evaluations, and in each case believed that the respondent should have rated himself closer to the homosexual end of the continuum. For example, the individual who exhibits little or no heterosexual contact and who is exclusively homoerotic in his fantasies could not be a Kinsey "4", even though he might consider himself as such. The interviewer would more likely rate this individual as a Kinsey "5" or "6". (See Table 16, pg. 172)

The sex history concluded with a few general questions regarding the respondents' attitudes about being gay. Each respondent was asked if he had ever regretted being gay. Sixteen (32%) reported never experiencing any regrets. Nineteen (38%) reported that they had regretted being gay in the past, but no longer do so. The remaining fifteen (30%) are currently experiencing such regret. The reasons given were loneliness and society's disapproval, but the most frequent reason was that their gay lifestyle was in conflict with generally held religious beliefs.

Concerning the respondents' gay identity, a series of questions were asked. Each respondent was first asked if he thought he would continue in a gay lifestyle in the future. Forty-nine respondents (98%) said that they intended to do so. Each respondent was then asked if he would want to change his gay orientation if he were able. Once again forty-nine (98%) showed no desire to change even if they were able. Finally the question was raised as to the ability of the respondent to change his gay orientation if he wanted to. A somewhat smaller majority, forty-five (90%), believed they could not change even if they wanted to. It is interesting to note that Kinsey found a much smaller percentage, 58.2% of his sample, had no desire to change their orientation; 53.3% of his sample believed they could not change even if they wanted to. (9)

Finally, each respondent was asked what he believed accounted for his being gay. Twenty (40%) had no opinion on the origin of their gayness. Ten (20%) thought that their being gay was biologically caused, that is, that they were born homosexual or that it "just came naturally." Fifteen other respondents (30%) believed that their being gay was psychologically caused, that is, the result of a distant father, or a dominant mother, or an arrested psychosexual development. Seven respondents (14%) felt that the fact most contributive to their being gay was living in an all-male environment. Finally, four others (8%) believed that they had learned their sexual orientation, as well as its expression, as if by chance.

Table 1
Personal Recreational Habits [Footnote 10]

Activity	Often		Periodic		Seldom		Never	
	Present Sample	Kinsey Margnls	Present Sample	Kinsey Margnls	Present Sample	Kinsey Margnls	Present Sample	Kinsey Margnls
Movies	36	47.6 (N+3814)	50*	20.0	14*	28.5	--	3.3
Dancing	24	40.6 (N+3817)	42*	14.4	28	23.8	6*	20.1
Reading	58		28		14		--	
Cooking	64		8		14		14	
Television	10		28		60		2	
Gambing	2	4.7 (N=3800)	8	5.9	34	34.7	56	58.3
Smoking	26*	39.1 (N=3809)	2	11.0	4	12.9	68*	33.2
Drinking	36*	9.6 (N=3870)	32*	20.1	24*	49.6	8	20.0
Marijuana	8		30		38		24	
Cocaine, MDA, LSD**	2		4		18		76	
Poppers*	12		26		24		38	

* Indicates statistically significant difference at the .05 level.
** Methylenedioxyamphetamine
*** Amyl Nitrite

Table 2
Interparental Relationship
At The Respondent's Ages 14-17 [Footnote 11]
(N=47)

Rating	Percentage	
	Present Sample	**Kinsey Margnls.**
Very Good	40.4*	57.6 (N=3693)
Good	27.6	26.5
Fair	15.0	9.0
Poor	17.0	6.9

*Indicates statistically significant difference at the .05 level

Table 3
Relationship With Father
At Ages 14-17 [Footnote 12]
(N=49)

Rating	Percentage	
	Present Sample	**Kinsey Margnls.**
Very Good	24.5*	52.6 (N=4266)
Good	32.6	28.4
Fair	28.6*	11.1
Poor	14.3	7.9

*Indicates statistically significant difference at the .05 level

Table 4
Relationship With Mother
At Ages 14-17 [Footnote 13]
(N=48)

Rating	Percentage	
	Present Sample	**Kinsey Margnls.**
Very Good	43.7*	70.6 (N=4552)
Good	47.9*	18.8
Fair	6.2	6.7
Poor	2.1	4.0

*Indicates statistically significant difference at the .05 level

Table 5
Age And Source Of Early Sex Information [Footnote 14]
(N=50)

Sexual Topic	Mean Age	Home		School		Peers		Reading	
		Present Sample	Kinsey Margnls	Present Sample	Kinsey Margnls	Present Sample	Kinsey Margnls	Present Sample	Kinsey Margnls
Intercourse	11.4	10	9.3 (N=4551)	12*	0.6	68	73.9	10	3.9
Pregnancy	11.4	18	22.5 (N=4394)	18*	1.0	56	53.0	8	8.1
Menstruation	13.2	34	16.8 (N=4067)	26*	5.9	26	53.4	14	13.8
Prostitution	13.7	14	4.6 (N=3615)	10	1.1	56	80.7	20	8.5
Homosexuality	14.4	14		4		58		24	

*Indicates statistically significant difference at the .05 level

Age	Percentage	
Table 6 **Age At First Masturbation** **Resulting In Ejaculation** [Footnote 15]		
	Present Sample	**Kinsey Margnls.**
8	4	0.1 (N=4443)
9	--	0.3
10	10	2.4
11	16	7.3
12	16	20.6
13	24	26.7
14	12	20.4
15	2	7.4
16	4	4.7
17	4	2.5
18	2	1.9
19	2	1.1
20	--	1.0
21	--	0.8
22	--	0.3
23	2	0.4
24	--	0.2
25	--	0.2
33	2	--
No significant difference is indicated at the .05 level		

Table 7 Sexual Arousability [Footnote 16]				
Item	**Found It Arousing**		**Didn't Find It Arousing**	
	Present Sample	Kinsey Margnls.	Present Sample	Kinsey Margnls.
The sight or thought of the other sex	20 (N=50)		80	
The sight or thought of the same sex	84 (N=50)		16	
Viewing sexually explicit photographs	72 (N=50)	64.6 (N=4305)	28	21.6
Viewing live sex shows	73.3* (N=50)	52.2 (N=3961)	26.7	35.9
Viewing sexually explicit movies	81.3 (N=50)		18.7	31.9
Reading love stories	81.3* (N=50)	61.8 (N=4524)	18.7*	78.9
Seeing yourself nude	66* (N=50)	16.8 (N=4655)	34	
Watching yourself masturbate	66 (N=50)		34	
Biting during sex	44 (N=50)		56	
Being bitten during sex play	36 (N=50)		64	
See animals have sex	12 (N=50)	21.4 (N=4641)	88*	67.6

*Indicates statistically significant difference at the .05 level

Age	Percentage	
	Present Sample	**Kinsey Margnls.**
11	4	6.9 (N=945)
12	24	19.6
13	8*	20.5
14	8*	21.5
15	2	7.9
16	4	5.2
17	6	3.3
18	2	3.4
19	4	1.9
20	--	1.8
21	2	0.8
22	4	0.6
23	4	0.8
24	4	0.6
25	4	0.6
25-30	4	0.9
31-35	10*	0.1
36-40	4	0.1
41+	4	0.1

**Table 8
Age At First Postpubertal
Same-Sex Contact [Footnote 17]
(N=50)**

*Indicates statistically significant difference at the .05 level

**Table 9
Sexual Techniques
Age At Which First Attempted**

Technique	Mean	Median	Age Range
Masturbation (Active) N=49	21.6	19	11-47
Masturbation (Passive) N=49	21.9	19	11-48
Oral-genital (Active) N=48	24.6	24	13-49
Oral-genital (Passive) N=45	26.3	27	13-48
Anal Intercourse (Active) N=38	29.0	28	14-52
Anal Intercourse (Passive) N=35	29.0	28	13-53

<table>
<thead>
<tr>
<th colspan="2" rowspan="2">Activity</th>
<th colspan="2">Often</th>
<th colspan="2">Periodic</th>
<th colspan="2">Seldom</th>
<th colspan="2">Never</th>
</tr>
</thead>
<tbody>
<tr>
<td colspan="2"></td>
<td>Present Sample</td>
<td>Kinsey Margnls.</td>
<td>Present Sample</td>
<td>Kinsey Margnls.</td>
<td>Present Sample</td>
<td>Kinsey Margnls.</td>
<td>Present Sample</td>
<td>Kinsey Margnls.</td>
</tr>
</tbody>
</table>

Table 10
Sexual Techniques - Frequency Of Occurence [Footnote 18]
(N=50)

Activity	Often Present Sample	Often Kinsey Margnls.	Periodic Present Sample	Periodic Kinsey Margnls.	Seldom Present Sample	Seldom Kinsey Margnls.	Never Present Sample	Never Kinsey Margnls.
Respondent kissing partner	80	77.2 (N=592)	18*	4.7	2	7.3	--	8.4
Partner kissing respondent	82		18		--		--	20.1
Respondent's mouth on partner's breast and nipples	32	39.3 (N=488)	46*	6.8	20	16.4	2*	31.8
Partner's mouth on respondent's breast and nipples	34*	46.3 (N=598)	40*	6.9	24	16.1	2*	25.4
Respondent's mouth on partner's penis	58		36		6		--	
Partner's mouth on respondent's penis	62		34		4		--	
Analinctus by respondent on partner	2*	16.2 (N=531)	6	4.1	42*	12.2	50*	56.3
Analinctus by partner on respondent	4*	19.7 (N=578)	10	6.4	56*	25.3	30*	32.7
Respondent tying-up or spanking partner	2	2.4 (N=497)	6	0.4	14	3.8	78	78.9
Partner tying-up or spanking respondent	2	2.5 (N=660)	6	0.3	10	3.2	82	86.5

*Indicates statistically significant difference at the .05 level

# of contacts per month	High School	College	Currently
Table 11 **Frequency Of Same-Sex Contact**			
.04 or less	4	4	4
.06	-	2	-
.08	-	-	2
.58	-	-	2
.41	2	-	-
.33	-	2	-
.25	-	2	2
.16	4	4	2
.12	-	2	-
.5	2	2	12
1.0	6	4	6
2.0	4	2	16
8.0	6	2	18
12.0	2	2	16
24.0	-	-	4
30.0	-	-	2
32.0	-	-	2
	N=17 mean freq. 3.2	N=18 mean freq. 2.3 per month	N=48 mean freq. 2 per month

Table 12
Duration Of Longest Continuous Same-Sex Relationship [Footnote 19]

Duration	Percentage	
	Present Sample	Kinsey Margnls.
1 month	2	3.7 (N=587)
2-3 months	8	8.2
4-5 months	4	4.9
6-7 months	8	6.5
8-9 months	6	2.4
10-11 months	2	0.5
1 year	6	9.5
13-18 months	14	4.8
19-23 months	--	0.5
2 years	4	14.5
3 years	8	9.9
4 years	10	8.2
5 years	4	6.3
7 years	2	2.9
12 year	2	--

No significant difference is indicated at the .05 level

Table 13
Partners With Which The Respondent Had Only One Contact [Footnote 20]
(N=50)

Percent of Partners	Percentage	
	Present Sample	Kinsey Margnls.
0	20*	6.7 (N=586)
1-10	6	4.9
11-20	4	8.0
21-30	2	8.5
31-40	2	5.1
41-50	12	13.8
51-60	4	3.4
61-70	--	6.8
71-80	18	16.5
81-90	18	9.6
91-100	14	5.5

*Indicates statistically significant difference at the .05 level

Table 14
Percent of Friends Who Are Gay [Footnote 21]
(N=50)

Percent of Friends	Percentage	
	Present Sample	Kinsey Margnls.
0	--	9.0 (N=469)
1-5	2	1.3
6-10	2	2.3
11-20	8	1.5
21-30	8	5.3
31-40	6	3.8
41-50	22	11.9
51-60	14	2.8
61-70	2	3.2
71-80	20	15.8
81-90	10	14.5
91-100	2	10.4

No significant difference is indicated at the .05 level

Table 15
Percent Of Heterosexual Friends Who
Know Respondent Is Gay
(N=50)

Percent of Friends	Percentage
0	12
1-5	20
6-10	15
11-20	8
21-30	6
31-40	--
41-50	14
51-60	--
61-70	2
71-80	8
81-90	10
91-100	8

Table 16 **Heterosexual - Homosexual Rating Scale** [Footnote 22] **(N=50)**			
Categories	**Respondent's** **Self-evaluation**		**Interviewer's Evaluation**
	Present Sample	**Kinsey** **Margnls.**	**Present Sample**
"4" mainly homosexual but with substantial heterosexual	6*	32.1 (N=246)	2
"5" mainly homosexual but with little heterosexual	44*	12.2	8
"6" entirely homosexual	50*	26.8	90

CHAPTER 4

Results

The Attitude Inventory

Once the sex history interview was completed, the interviewer presented each respondent with a copy of the attitude inventory questionnaire. He was given instructions for its completion and was asked to return it to the interviewer by mail. Both the sex history and the attitude inventory questionnaire bore identical code numbers to insure proper coordination of the data as it was received. When all the questionnaires were gathered each was read for the purpose of statistically analyzing the replies. Later each was read again in order to gather from the whole group some sample responses to be included in this presentation.

It is important to point out at the beginning that since the attitude inventory questionnaire was designed to elicit the respondents' thoughts and feelings on certain issues, and since the format used was highly subjective, the analysis of the replies was made more difficult. Determination of the number of possible categories into which the responses to each question fell was, at times, arbitrary. However, the main consideration in such calculations was to insure a faithful representation of the respondents' attitudes.

The attitude inventory comprised thirty-four questions. Twelve of the questions were divided between introductory and summary sections. The remaining twenty-two questions were divided among the four areas of possible dissonance to be studied. These areas are defined as follows:

a) Conflicts Of Conviction. An investigation of the potential areas of dissonance involved for the respondent as he evaluates his own thoughts and feelings in light of traditional church teachings. The respondents were asked to categorize their thoughts and feelings concerning the church's official positions regarding homosexuality and mandatory celibacy for priests. Each was asked to evaluate his own commitment to celibacy, that is, what he envisioned the celibate lifestyle to mean in his own life. Further questioning focused upon the possible guilt involved for the respondent should his personal views on these topics conflict with traditional church teachings.

b) Conflicts In Lifestyle. An inquiry into the possible dissonance present for the respondent when faced with traditional expectations of the priestly life. The respondents were asked if they are living within the confines of established communities or rectories, and if they have a preference for living alone. Each was questioned regarding the extent his priestly life has fulfilled his needs for intimacy. Further questioning focused upon the freedom afforded the respondent by virtue of his priestly life as it compares to the freedom enjoyed by his gay lay peers.

c) Conflicts Of Identity. An examination of the conceivable dissonance the respondent may experience as he considers his dual identity as a priest and as a gay man. The respondents were asked if they would be concerned if their fellow priests might come to know that they are gay; or if their gay peers might come to know that they are priests. Each was asked to categorize the type of involvement he has with the gay community,' and if he feared blackmail or any other kind of retaliation in light of this involvement.

d) <u>Conflicts In Sexual Behavior</u>. An investigation of the potential dissonance present for the respondent as he ponders his sexual needs and expectations in light of his realized outlets. The respondents were asked if being a priest enhanced or detracted from their sexuality. Inquiry was made into the number of respondents who have lovers, and to what extent those without sought to develop such a relationship. Particular attention was paid to the viability of monogamy in these relationships.

For the sake of convenience, a complete statistical breakdown of the replies to all the questions follows at the end of this chapter.

The attitude inventory questionnaire began with a series of eight preliminary questions designed to gather information about the respondents' backgrounds, both religious and sexual. The first six such questions were demographic in character, deserving only brief attention at this time. The statistical breakdown at the end of the chapter will provide an analysis of the responses to each of these questions.

The fifty respondents reside in four broad geographical areas: the Northeast, Midwest, Northwest, and West. Sixteen respondents (32%) entered seminary during their high school years; twenty-four (48%) during college; and ten (20%) as graduate students. The median age of the respondents at the time of their ordination was 26 years. The ages ranged from 24 to 42 years. The median age at which the respondents began to self-identify as gay was 23.1 years. The ages ranged from 11 to 45 years. The median age, at which the respondents started to "come out," that is, identify themselves as gay to others, was 27.3 years. For most, coming out was a slow and cautious process. Only six (12%) reported that their coming out was simultaneous with self-identification. The longest reported interval between an individual's self-identification and his coming out to others was 26 years. This respondent's gay identity remained a secret from age 13 to age 39. The majority of the respondents had not discussed their gay identity with either their parents or their ecclesiastical superiors. Only fourteen (28%) had come out to their parents. (Four respondents' parents had died before they could share this information). And only eighteen (36%) had come out to their bishops or provincials.

Beginning with question 7 a format of presenting the questions along with analysis and selected replies will be followed.

Question 7:

IF YOU WERE AWARE OF YOUR GAY ORIENTATION IN SEMINARY, DID YOU EVER LEAVE OR CONSIDER LEAVING BECAUSE OF THAT?

Thirty-one respondents (62%) reported being aware of their gay orientation in seminary. The remaining nineteen (38%) had not clearly identified themselves at that time.

Of the respondents who were aware of their gay orientation during seminary, twenty-four seriously considered leaving, or actually did leave for a period, because of their gayness. Some who considered leaving or who did leave for a time believed they were unfit to continue.

> I considered leaving out of a sense of 'responsibility' to the church, and fidelity to existing morality. A noble sacrifice.

> I often considered leaving because I was gay. I never did because no one I told could believe it, they thought I would outgrow it.

> I not only considered leaving, but in fact did leave after three years in seminary. After I worked a few things out I was able to return and feel good about my decision to continue.

Others considered leaving seminary or did leave because they fell in love or were sexually active at the time.

> I became infatuated with a seminarian one class above me. I left for two years.

> I did not leave the seminary, but did leave the active ministry for two years because of sexual activity.

I chose to leave the active ministry for a while because I fell in love with another priest.

Of the respondents who were aware of their gay orientation during seminary, only seven never considered leaving.

I was aware of tendencies but dismissed them to environment and the system and stayed.

I never seriously considered leaving because it seemed that celibacy was the only way open to a gay person, whether in the seminary or out.

On the contrary, I felt more honest in my decision-making regarding priesthood.

There were too many like me there to feel I had to leave, so I didn't.

A few of the nineteen respondents who were not aware of their gay orientation during seminary offered that they would have left had they known of their gayness.

They told us that if you were gay it was a sign from God that you should quit. I honestly would have quit if I believed I was gay at the time. This attitude in the seminary was responsible for the incredible repression operative in my life until recently.

Question 8:

DID YOU EVER HAVE ANY SAME-SEX EXPERIENCES IN SEMINARY? HOW DID YOU FEEL ABOUT THEM THEN? NOW?

Twenty-eight respondents (56%) reported having had at least one same-sex contact while in seminary. The remaining twenty-two (44%) reported no same-sex contact.

The majority of the respondents who reported same-sex contact in seminary recalled negative feelings surrounding the events when they occurred, but now view them as growth or learning experiences.

> I was guilty at first. Now I see it was an expression of genuine affection. It was a growing experience that I needed.

> At first I felt very bad about them. Gradually, I grew to accept these experiences. Now I see them as the experiences through which I learned how to entrust myself to others in love relationships.

> I was frightened that it would be found out. I thought it meant I didn't have a vocation. Now I just laugh.

Other respondents recalled experiencing ambivalent feelings as a result of their same-sex experiences in seminary, but now consider those experiences in a positive light.

> I had sex a couple of times. Then I felt guilt, but joyous as well that someone could love me that much. Now I feel grateful for them. They put me in touch with my ability to be gentle and affectionate.

> I had sex with two classmates. I felt some growing freedom and a great deal of confusion back then. Now I look back on them as 'graced' events. I feel good about them now.

Two respondents recalled negative feelings surrounding their seminary same-sex contacts and continue to see those experiences negatively.

> I was afraid that I was going to be dismissed because we were caught in the act. As I look back now I wish it could have been more fulfilling.

> There was some embracing in the dark, allowing myself to be kissed and asking a friend to let me get into bed with him. The latter wrecked our friendship. I still have pain thinking about this.

Some of the respondents who reported no same-sex contacts while in seminary offered comments on the subject.

> I had no sex while in seminary. I am glad I didn't have to deal with my sexuality until after ordination.

> I didn't have sex in seminary -- only during vacation with non-seminarians. When I later learned how much was going on in the seminary, I was somewhat chagrined.

Section 1
CONFLICTS OF CONVICITON

Question 9:

WHAT IS YOUR ATTITUDE TOWARD THE CHURCH'S OFFICIAL POSITION REGARDING HOMOSEXUALITY?

The responses to this question indicate an almost unanimous disapproval of the church's official position on homosexuality. Forty-six respondents (92%) strongly disagreed with the current position of the church. The remaining four (8%) voiced mixed reactions.

The majority of the respondents rejected the church's position on homosexuality because of its narrowness, especially in the context of its rigid attitude toward sexuality in general.

I find it very narrow and rigid, a view not unlike the church's fixation with respect to all of sexuality. It is, in fact, the church's evident unwillingness to take a fresh look at sexuality that makes me feel more free to do so myself.

We are, in effect, being held hostage for the sake of the church's primary concern for marital (heterosexual) sexuality. Any 'give' in regard to us would crack the criterion for marriage, so…

For the church to accept homosexuality as a given condition of someone's life means a rethinking and revision of attitudes toward all of sexuality.

I believe the church's position must broaden to include the legitimacy and holiness of non-procreative sexuality.

Other respondents based their rejection of the church's position either on the church's lack of compassion or on its lack of knowledge about the subject, while some offered that the church's position is politically and economically rather than morally motivated.

> It is sad and a scandal that the church's love and compassion is so rarely extended to sexual minorities in a public manner.

> I remember how I rationalized and taught the official position to parishioners and penitents before I came to accept my own sexuality. In the vacuum of no experience, the arguments made sense. Now I see the official teachings to be thoroughly misdirected.

> It is completely out of line with the information that we now have through the natural sciences as well as scriptural exegesis. It continues to be extremely oppressive in light of all this.

> I think of the church's present attitude toward homosexuality as a political/economic issue rather than a moral one.

Four respondents offered mixed reactions.

> It is the beginning in a direction of compassion, but far from hitting the mark in accepting people for who they are.

> My attitude is ambiguous. It is unrealistic for the church to accept homosexuals for persons and condemn the emotional and psychological and physical expression of that condition. I also feel that there are positive Christian values about life and sexuality that the church could proclaim to the gay community that is at best neurotic. Unfortunately, the church has no credibility when it speaks about sexuality.

Question 10:

WHAT IS YOUR ATTITUDE TOWARD THE CHURCH'S OFFICIAL POSITION REGARDING MANDATORY CELIBACY FOR PRIESTS?

Forty-five respondents (90%) strongly rejected the church's requirement of mandatory celibacy for priests, while four (8%) disagreed with the requirement in a qualified way. Only one respondent whole-heartedly supported mandatory celibacy.

Those rejecting the requirement of mandatory celibacy for priests did so for a number of reasons, the most common being that a virtue cannot or ought not be mandated.

> I believe rather strongly that celibacy is a valid and much needed witness in our culture. It should not, however, be mandatory. Optional may have value; mandatory has none.

> Mandatory celibacy is a contradiction in terms. How can a gift or charism be mandated?

> This is part of the idiocy that abounds in the church. I see no scriptural or sound theological basis for the practice. I think there should be an option.

Others disagreed with the tradition of celibacy because of its current application to all priests. These respondents believed that celibacy should be required of religious priests by virtue of their special commitment to the church but that secular priests should be allowed an option.

> I believe that celibacy is a gift from God and can be embraced freely within religious life. It should not, however, be mandatory for diocesan clergy.

> I think that a mandate for celibacy on the part of either heterosexual or homosexual persons in the context of a religious

order or congregation is legitimate. Diocesan priesthood should have optional 'celibacy.'

Some respondents indicated that the requirement of celibacy was futile because it was not adhered to.

> I think the rule should be changed as soon as possible. We don't follow the rule anyway. I bumped into an auxiliary bishop at a gay hotel and saw the ordinary of a diocese at a gay bar across country.

One respondent felt that the celibate lifestyle is in total accord with priestly ministry.

> I support mandatory celibacy for the priesthood, more so now that ministry is finally being seen as not merely confined to priesthood. I find no objection to reserving the sacrificial and sacramental aspects of ministry to a clergy totally dedicated by lifestyle to Christ and the church.

Question 11:

HOW DO YOU UNDERSTAND YOUR COMMITMENT TO CELIBACY?

Responses to this question fall into five fairly distinct categories. It is important to note that some respondents equate "celibacy" and "chastity" while others do not.

Eleven respondents (22%) equate celibacy with total sexual abstinence. Some of these indicated that, though this was their understanding of celibacy, they either do not conform to it or oppose it as a binding rule.

Celibacy means no genital contact with anyone of any kind. This is my requirement. Hopefully, it will lead me to become more gentle and loving.

As it is generally understood; in the physical sense. That is, absence of genital activity with others and oneself.

In the traditional sense, meaning no sexual activity. I am beginning to question this understanding. If warm loving sexual relationships help a priest to be a better minister to his community, then why not enter into them, for his own sake as well.

The way that all the laity does -- priests don't screw. This presents an immediate conflict in my life because my lifestyle does not reflect that. However, I would rather live in conflict than play theological 'mind-fuck' games with myself and others.

Eleven other respondents (22%) understood celibacy as a commitment to forego traditional heterosexual marriage or the homosexual equivalent, that is, a permanent exclusive relationship.

I took the promise of celibacy, which means, as the church understands it, not to marry. So I'm keeping that promise. Celibacy for me means no heterosexual marriage -that's all I ever envisioned it to be.

To me, my promise of celibacy means that I have promised my bishop that I will not get married.

It means that I will not get married to a woman. A ridiculous rule imposed on me, a gay man.

It means the lack of a physical-psychological commitment to another person.

I understand celibacy to mean 'un-marriable' (in the gay context - no covenant with a life-long lover).

I understand celibacy to be for priests a commitment to remain unmarried which for me as a gay man means not to have a lover in the genital, sexual sense.

Thirteen respondents (26%) understood celibacy as a commitment to regulate their sexuality in terms of general Christian moral values, without believing that this precludes sexual expression.

I understand my clerical promise to celibacy as a commitment to put my sexuality in line with the person-oriented and love-oriented directives of the gospel.

Both celibacy and chastity in my understanding have little or nothing to do with my genitals. To see it as a genital issue is to blur the value of these virtues. It is like trying to define a pacifist as one who doesn't carry a gun. Obviously it is more than that. Pacifism, like celibacy and chastity, is a total demeanor, a way one looks at the world.

Chastity means learning how to love people properly. To my mind there are numerous occasions when the proper way to love an individual is non-genital; my mother for example. At the same time there are clearly numerous occasions when genital expression would be proper and appropriate.

I understand my promise to be celibate to be primarily that I am free emotionally and psychologically to be a witness and a minister of God's love in the world. My understanding of these virtues does not preclude genital sex.

Eight respondents (16%) understood celibacy in terms of a commitment to God, gospel values, or a more than usual openness to the needs of others, without explicitly indicating the role, if any, sexuality might have in such a commitment.

I understand it most clearly in terms of availability to many people. I see it also as a mystery of faith: it is a contradiction of so much that is human.

I see it as a sign of the breadth of God's love. Just as I see marriage as a sign of the depth of his love. When I am most genuinely celibate I should then be most open and available to the needs of all with whom I come in contact.

The call to enter life deeply, calling me to participation, involvement and vulnerability.

Saying to the Lord, 'Be my all my everything.'

Finally, seven respondents (14%) expressed confusion on the subject of celibacy, or expressed a feeling of being torn between conflicting interpretations of its meaning. Some offered no definite opinion on the subject.

I have never come to understand it. All I know is that I have been ordained to serve the Lord's people.

With a great deal of confusion! The ideal might be good or was good at a point in history but now it has tremendous political and manipulative overtones. I understand it in the best way I know how — as a process in which I am 'becoming' but in no way means 'fixed'.

In all honesty I am not able to answer right now. I see chastity as an ideal; and I am working toward that. I am sexually active now and I see this as an essential phase in my growth and development. I know with moral certainty that I am so much better off now spiritually and humanly than when I was repressing and suppressing all sexual desire and fantasy.

This one area is causing me personal anguish now. I know that traditionally chastity, as a public profession, has been equated with celibacy. I know in fact that chastity and celibacy are not the same. I guess I just don't have the guts at present to make the distinction.

Question 12:

ARE YOU EXPERIENCING ANY GUILT IN RECONCILING THE CHURCH'S POSITION ON HOMOSEXUALITY AND CELIBACY AND YOUR OWN LIFESTYLE? IF NOT, HOW ARE YOU PUTTING THESE THINGS TOGETHER?

The majority of the respondents, thirty (60%), remarked that they are currently experiencing no guilt in reconciling the church's positions on homosexuality and celibacy and their own lifestyles.

> There is no guilt. The church is wrong. The God I believe in is a God who speaks of love, acceptance and especially relationships. The two times I became seriously suicidal over being gay were sinful, the love relationships that I try to develop with others is not sinful. I now leave a relationship feeling more human, more alive, more spiritual.

> Now I am not experiencing any guilt. I have put a lot of work into knowing and accepting myself. I take responsibility for my life and I follow my conscience, having given due consideration to the church's teachings.

> With the help of two years of therapy and much personal reflection, I am no longer experiencing guilt.

> I am not; but I'm also not trying to reconcile the irreconcilable. I try to keep my professional and personal life separate but in tandem.

Only two specified that they are experiencing no guilt, since they are currently sexually abstemious.

At present I am a homosexual in orientation only, not in lifestyle. As long as I remain celibate, there is no guilt, regardless of my opinions on the official church teaching.

A number of individuals reported experiencing no guilt but went on to specify a variety of other qualms and concerns.

Guilt, no! Regret that I cannot be more open and honest, yes. I sincerely regret the necessary dishonesty that makes me appear publicly to be committed to a celibate lifestyle, whereas I am not. But few gays in our society have the luxury of complete honesty. 'Dissent in and for the church' is not simply a matter of theological speculation; it has always been a matter of praxis as well. Like all human beings I need affirmation and support, but approval is not so urgent a need.

No guilt. However, fear of discovery in regards to my sexual activity. Putting it together — I'd say the church has her view and I mine. I consider my view to be healthy and in line with the more intelligent view of scripture and psychology.

I don't feel guilty, but I feel selfish and outside the mainstream. The tension will have to resolve itself soon.

I think that the church is wrong on homosexuality so I don't feel guilty in that regard. I would be more apt to feel it with regard to my choice of celibacy. I feel dissatisfaction, resentment, anger, confusion and fear.

Seven respondents (14%) indicated that they are experiencing a little guilt.

There is little to no guilt since I am more or less celibate in the traditional understanding of the term.

Very little. I am relatively celibate at present. I have done three and a half years of therapy, and have read widely on the issue.

Very little guilt. I see the traditional 'wisdom' as not relating at all to my experience of life and of God. Yet after dealing with some of the unsatisfactory aspects of gay life I feel tempted to return to traditional celibacy. I am also uncomfortable about having a deep commitment to another person as endangering my commitment to God and the church. Yet since my gay lifestyle has helped me very much to be a loving person it has also enriched my priesthood and I have to weigh that factor.

Thirteen respondents (26%) indicated that they are experiencing a good deal of guilt as they try to reconcile the church's position on celibacy and/or homosexuality and their own lifestyles.

The only time that I feel guilty is when I compare my lifestyle with what a 'typical' Catholic would expect a priest to be. I feel no guilt when I compare myself and my lifestyle to my own expectations or those of the gospel.

There is some guilt, yes. Yet I feel psychologically compelled to do what I am doing. I wish I could reconcile it with my public commitment and witness to chastity and celibacy.

Initially there was a lot of guilt, but as I live my life I'm getting tired of feeling guilty. I realize that guilt is my way of holding back and not exploring my sexuality.

I have no guilt in reconciling the church's position and my orientation. I do have guilt in reconciling the church's position and my activity; especially as regards possible scandal.

My only guilt is that my celibacy may be a cop-out.

Question 13:

HOW WOULD YOU CHARACTERIZE THE DIFFERENCE BETWEEN THE CHURCH'S ATTITUDE TOWARD SEXUALITY AND THAT OF THE GAY COMMUNITY?

All but four of the respondents made value judgments in their characterizations of the church's and gay community's attitudes toward sexuality. The four who made no value judgments stated what they perceived to be the difference in attitudes but offered no opinion on their relative merits.

The forty-six responses reflecting value judgments fall into four categories of general emphasis. The first category is characterized by a negative appraisal of the church's attitude and a positive appraisal of the gay community's. Eighteen respondents (36%) characterized the difference in this way.

> Church leaders stress that the only way sexuality can be valuable and responsible is if it is open to procreation. The gay community sees sexuality in broader terms; that is, the value of sexuality is in the loving.

> I see the gay community accepting itself as persons whom God loves and made and who are trying to integrate their sexuality within their whale life. Sexuality is a big plus for gays; for the church it is a minus, limited and negative.

> The church still sees sexuality as the source of so much evil; the gay community, despite its many weaknesses, sees sexuality as a liberating force.

> The church is not altogether happy about sex. In fact we seem to have more hang-ups about sex than we do about war and racism. In this regard the gay community presents a challenge to the church and society.

> The church is 'sure' without being responsibly informed. The gay community is an emerging liberated minority, with all the eventually un-fortunate excesses, events and feelings that characterize an enthusiastic, newly liberated group.

The second category indicated a positive appraisal of the church's attitudes and a negative appraisal of the gay community's attitudes. Only one respondent stated the difference this way.

> The church seems rightly to emphasize that love and sexuality is much more than genitality. The gay community seems very sophomoric in this regard.

The third category indicated an emphasis on the negative aspects of both the church's and gay community's attitudes toward sexuality. Twenty-six of the respondents (52%) offered such characterizations.

> The gay community as I have experienced it admits that it screws around more than the church is willing to admit that her members do. Other than that I am surprised how much alike the two are. There is an amazing amount of guilt, sexual negativity, and 'hang-ups' between the two.

> The church deals with ideals to the exclusion of the real; the gay community is the opposite.

> The attitudes of both the church and the gay community are very unrealistic. The church's attitude is that it idealizes sex as the highest expression of mutual love between a man and a woman in marriage while ignoring the other emotional and psychological expressions of sexuality that are legitimately human. On the other hand, it seems the gay community tolerates and defends all forms of sexuality; even when they are neurotic, inhuman and even psychotic.

> I do not think there is much difference. Both seem to view sexuality in terms of isolated acts of genital expression.

> While the church may be overly concerned to draw lines, the gay community seems unwilling to draw any.

> The gay community has a wide range of experience though little reflection upon that experience is being done. The church, on the other hand, has lots of reflection on precious little experience.

The fourth category indicates an emphasis on the positive aspects of both the church's and gay community's attitudes. Only one respondent offered such a characterization.

> The church's attitude toward sexuality is understood in a biological/natural law context. The gay community understands sexuality in a personalistic context. Both are valid to my way of thinking.

The four respondents (8%) who refrained from making a value judgment outlined the particular attitudes, as they understood them.

> The official church's teaching certainly proscribes any genital sex outside the context of marriage. The gay community generally would allow any sort of sexual activity, with some stressing faithfulness and others being tolerant or even encouraging sexual activity with someone regardless of any possible primary commitment.

Question 14:

IF YOU HAVE READ ANY OF THE FOLLOWING BOOKS, PLEASE RATE THEM ACCORDING TO THEIR HELPFULNESS TO YOU.

1) **VERY HELPFUL,**
2) **HELPFUL**
3) **NOT VERY HELPFUL,**
4) **NOT AT ALL HELPFUL**

1) *The Church and the Homosexual*; John McNeill, SJ. Sheed Andrews & McMeel, Kansas City, 1976
2) *Another Kind of Love*; Richard Woods, OP. The Thomas. Moore Press, Chicago, 1977

3) *Jonathan Loved David, Homosexuality in Biblical Times*; Tom Horner, The Westminister Press, Philadelphia, 1978

4) *Is the Homosexual My Neighbor, Another Christian View*; Famey-Mollenkott, Scanzoni; Harper & Roe, New York, 1978

5) *The Sexual Celibate*; Donald Goergen, OP. Seabury Press, New York, 1974

During the past decade a number of books have been published which have dealt with the subject of homosexuality and Christianity. However, like the ones mentioned above, these books call into question the "traditional wisdom." From all reports they have enjoyed a large readership. Question 14 was formulated to establish the connection, if any this suggested list of books might have had on the attitude development of the respondents.

The respondents reported a remarkable familiarity with the suggested publications, and for the most part found them helpful in supporting and solidifying their attitudes. A majority reported reading three of the five titles. The most widely read was McNeill's *The Church and the Homosexual*. Forty-four respondents (88%) read the book, and 95.5% of them reported it to be helpful or very helpful. *The Sexual Celibate* and *Another Kind of Love* were the next most widely read, forty (80%) and thirty (60%) respondents reporting respectively. Once again the majority of these readers found the books helpful. The least read title was also the least helpful, proportionately, to its readers. *Jonathan Loved David* had but ten readers (20%), four of them reporting it to be not very helpful or not helpful at all. (The reader is reminded that a complete statistical breakdown of the responses to this and all the questions can be found at the end of this chapter).

Section 2
CONFLICTS IN LIFESTYLE

Question 15:

DO YOU LIVE IN COMMUNITY? IF YOU DO, ARE ANY OTHER MEMBERS OF YOUR COMMUNITY GAY?

At present, thirty-one respondents (62%) are living in formally established community houses or rectories. The remaining nineteen (38%) have other living arrangements, such as student housing or private apartments.

Just over half of the respondents (sixteen) who are living in community report that there are other gay priests or religious living with them. The remaining fifteen respondents were not aware of living with other gays.

Question 16:

WOULD YOU PREFER TO LIVE ALONE? WHAT WOULD BE THE ADVANTAGES AND DISADVANTAGES?

Both those living alone and those not currently living alone identified similar advantages and disadvantages. The most commonly cited advantage was privacy and freedom of movement, and the most commonly cited disadvantage was loneliness.

Twenty-five respondents (50%) reported a preference for living alone.

> I prefer to live alone for the freedom of personal lifestyle. Yet I realize the cost; support of others.

I have lived alone for two of the past ten years. I prefer this arrangement. Advantages - solitude, this helps me with my work and prayer and reflection. Disadvantages - I like to have people to live with, with whom I can share.

Five respondents (10%) indicated a preference for living alone but qualified their preference by stipulating a desire to live with a lover or close companion.

I would prefer to live alone with a lover. Living alone would give me the advantage of coming and going more freely. I would also feel less restricted about who comes to see me.

I would truly relish living alone but would prefer to live with a friend and companion for the joy of being close to someone I deeply loved.

Twenty respondents (40%) rejected the idea of living alone.

I would not prefer to live alone. The only advantage would be privacy. Disadvantages - possible loneliness, more intense than occurs now at times in community, and non-support on levels of communal prayer.

I would not prefer to live alone. For me the disadvantage of an empty house, not even someone to bitch about, is stronger than the advantage of the freedom (license) involved.

Living alone would only intensify my loneliness.

Question 17:

ARE THERE ANY INTIMACY NEEDS THAT YOU EXPERIENCE THAT ARE NOT BEING MET BY YOUR PRIESTLY OR RELIGIOUS LIFESTYLE?

Forty-four respondents (88%) reported being unfulfilled in terms of intimacy by their priestly or religious lifestyle. The remaining six respondents (12%) reported being generally content.

The frustration apparent in the responses of those who reported being unfulfilled was deafening. The areas most frequently identified as the cause of frustration were:

a) The inadequacy of the respondents' living condition.

> I really don't have a home. I live in a rectory. I am unable to bring friends to my house for entertainment or just to be with them. I can't even be myself at home.

b) The desire for a lover.

> I don't know how my need for intimacy and personal fulfillment, a sense of loving deeply and being loved, could be met in the traditional (celibate) lifestyle. The traditional expectations allow for me only the sterile, rational, efficient, feelingless lifestyle that I now see as inhuman.

> I feel a need and desire for a very close and affectionate relationship with a man. I'm not sure that I would need this permanently, but I do need to experience it right now at the stage I'm presently in.

> I feel a need to be wanted. I want to mean something special to someone. This need is not met by my priestly lifestyle. If anything, my priestly experience has told me that I'm expendable.

c) The need for an intimate, non-sexual relationship.

> I need to be held and touched. I need overt affection both from men and women. This would not necessarily include genital activity.

d) The need for the company of women and children.

> I have the need to be with women and children.

e) The need to be self-directed.

> The basic intimacy need that I have that is not being met in religious life is the need to be taken seriously. Superiors and peers fail to understand that I might have a say in what is best for me.

General comments of dissatisfaction were also voiced.

> All my intimacy needs are met by others, outside religious life. If I would have waited for those in community to minister to my needs I would have died waiting.

> Religious life does not meet any of my needs for intimacy.

The remaining six respondents (12%) reported being generally satisfied in their priestly and religious lifestyles.

> Presently there is a growing attempt with moderate success to integrate the ideals of community and religious intimacy with my own emotional needs, desires and demands.

Question 18:

DO YOU ENVY THE FREEDOM OF GAY LAYMEN? HOW WOULD YOU DESCRIBE THIS FREEDOM — POLITICAL, PSYCHOLOGICAL, SEXUAL, ETC.?

Replies to this question fall into three major categories. The first category includes respondents who reported being envious of at least some of the freedoms of their gay lay peers; the second category comprises those who reported not being envious of any freedoms; and the third category consists of those who expressed mixed feelings.

Eighteen respondents (36%) indicated being envious of at least some of the freedoms of their gay lay peers. Many of these emphasized sexual freedom.

> Gays have a greater sexual freedom (to find a lover).

> I feel a layperson has the space to grow in sexual maturity, while I have to struggle for this same space. I sometimes envy the sexual freedom of lay gay persons. It would involve for me the freedom from other people's expectations and freedom from being such a public figure.

> I believe gay laymen have greater sexual freedom. Political and spiritual and psychological freedom depends on the individual. I believe I have each of these.

Others in this group cited political freedom as enviable, either the freedom to openly associate with gays and act politically on their behalf or the freedom from the political limitations of life in the Church.

> If I were not a priest in my current position, I would like to get politically involved with gay issues.

Gay laymen are freer to be associated with gay groups that are public. In this diocese I would be suspended if I were seen in public doing anything pro-gay.

I envy them to the extent that they don't have to experience the oppressive structures of the church on a personal and professional level. In this diocese we are told where to live and paid a very inadequate salary. There is little if any real concern for the individual priest.

Twenty-two respondents (44%) reported not being envious of any of the supposed freedoms of their gay lay peers.

I used to envy gay laymen until I took a leave of absence. I found that I had much the same freedom or lack of it.

I have all the freedoms they do.

I envy nothing of the freedom that a gay layperson might have because I have fought for the same freedoms for myself.

The only freedom that gay laymen have that I see is an inner freedom, which I feel already. My limitations are self-imposed, and freely chosen.

What freedom? To be gay in our society is to be enslaved.

The remaining ten respondents (20%) reported mixed reactions. Often these replies express envy but are qualified by statements indicating that the envy is unfounded.

I envy freedom of lay gay men but often believe I am making a judgment about their freedom, which is too simplistic.

I often envy younger gay men because I wish that I had dealt with the gay issue when I was their age. I also see an illusion in this because I tend to romanticize the life of young gays today. They have their crises too.

I feel envy only when my gayness gets the best of me, like when I'm drunk, horny, or going into the Village.

Question 19:

DO YOU CONSIDER YOUR CELIBATE LIFESTYLE TO BE A FREEING EXPERIENCE — POLITICALLY, PSYCHOLOGICALLY, SEXUALLY, SPIRITUALLY, ETC.?

Replies to this question also fall into three general groups. The first consists of respondents who indicated that their celibate lifestyle is a freeing experience in one sense or another; the second comprises those who did not see celibacy as at all freeing; and the third includes those who gave mixed or qualified answers.

Twenty respondents (40%) reported their celibate lifestyle to be a freeing experience in one way or another. The most frequent characterization of this freedom was exemption from traditional heterosexual marriage.

I feel celibacy is a freeing experience in that I never felt I had to marry a woman to avoid society's suspicion. I feel free being with other men in public as it is expected that a priest's companions will be other males.

I would be imprisoned if I were married.

Roughly corresponding to these responses were those stressing freedom from complex relationships.

I have experienced the limitations of being in relationships. Prophecy must come from the totally free person; and relationships do limit that freedom.

> I feel free now. At age thirty-three I feel especially relieved in
> terms of not having to deal with complex relationships.

Other respondents indicated more generally that celibacy allowed a greater availability to ministry.

> Yes, I find it to be freeing. It allows me to be more available to
> be of service.

> I experience celibacy as freeing, to be available to minister to
> others. It also frees me to decide how to use my time, energy
> and resources for a greater good.

Eighteen respondents (36%) did not consider their celibate lifestyle to be a freeing experience. In responding to this question the majority simply answered "no." Most of those who elaborated focused on the sexual and/or political restrictions of celibacy.

> I feel I am restricted both sexually and politically.

> I don't feel free politically, in the sense of being able to engage
> actively in the gay liberation movement.

> I don't consider such a lifestyle freeing in any way.

Twelve respondents (24%) indicated that celibacy was in some respect freeing but qualified their answer in a specific way.

> I am freer as a celibate to focus, in my prayer life, on the Lord
> as my lover. My attention is not divided. That is not to say that
> if I had a lover my prayer life would suffer. On the contrary, a
> lover could well enhance it.

> Celibacy is the freedom from not having to marry. Yet as a
> lifestyle I would want a partner to live and share my life with.

Section 3
CONFLICTS OF IDENTITY

Question 20:

DOES IT CONCERN YOU THAT YOUR FELLOW PRIESTS OR RELIGIOUS MIGHT COME TO KNOW THAT YOU ARE GAY?

All respondents reported being concerned to some degree about having their gay identity become known to fellow priests and religious. Twenty-six respondents (52%) expressed unequivocal concern ranging from fear of possible reprisals to worry about being stereotyped and/or discredited.

> I feel called to ministry in a high school. If I was known to be gay I am sure that I no longer would be welcome in that ministry.

> I am sure I would lose my current position if they knew.

> They might become suspicious about the men who visit me in the rectory.

> I do not want most of my fellow priests to know that I am gay. I feel they will look down on me, discredit my work and read into the positions I take on many issues. I simply do not trust most priests.

> I fear being categorized and labeled by all the gay myths. I would not want to be seen only as 'gay', as if that is all there is to me.

The remaining twenty-four respondents (48%) offered mixed responses.

These respondents tend to be more open about their sexual orientation, but they too express concern about having their sexual identity known. These concerns range from eliciting hostility and mistrust from their religious peers to being subjected to unusual demands or expectations from them.

> I am as 'out' as can be. Yet I continue to pay a dear price for this posture. Many of my fellow priests are uncomfortable with me, others are outright hostile. The ones who associate with me do so at their own expense; guilt by association.

> I am rather open about being gay and am generally not concerned, although there are a sizeable number of my fellow priests that I wouldn't trust with anything, let alone this information.

> I don't so much mind other priests knowing I am gay. I do mind being propositioned by closeted priests who have found this out. It is most uncomfortable because some are real powerful people and when I don't return the interest I jeopardize my position in the diocese.

My being as open as I am has brought me many other priests who struggle with their own gayness. One problem is that they tend to live vicariously through me rather than living for themselves.

Question 21:

HAVE YOU EVER EXPERIENCED ANY HOSTILITY OR OPPRESSION FROM YOUR RELIGIOUS PEERS OR SUPERIORS WHO HAVE COME TO KNOW THAT YOU ARE GAY?

Thirty respondents (60%) reported never experiencing hostility or oppression from religious superiors or peers because of their gay identity. It should be noted that the majority of those who elaborated on their answers offered that the absence of hostility or oppression was the result of keeping their sexual identity hidden or of being discriminating about those they disclosed their identity to.

I have never experienced open hostility or oppression. Most, of course, don't know about me.

I haven't experienced any hostility; but I have been very discriminating in revealing my gayness.

I make sure that the people I share this information with can handle it. If I have the least bit of information that they won't be able to, I choose not to disclose myself. This really cuts down on the possibility of any hostility or oppression.

Fifteen respondents (30%) indicated experiencing some measure of hostility or oppression. Some were quite specific.

I am very open about my orientation. I have experienced a lot of hostility from both superiors and peers. It is worth it all to be out there for those more timid than myself who need to see that putting all this together is possible.

After one of my community members alerted our superior that I had gone to a gay bar with some other community members, I have been put under obedience to stay away from such places. Since then I have experienced coldness from some of the men I live with.

I don't have a position in a diocese at the present time because I am gay and hold the convictions I do.

I have experienced hostility from only one peer who is himself gay but closeted.

The remaining five respondents (10%) gave ambiguous replies.

I have experienced some hostility but generally I have found people accepting. Being black in the church short circuits any other marginality.

Question 22:

DOES IT CONCERN YOU THAT A GAY LAY PERSON MIGHT COME TO KNOW THAT YOU ARE A PRIEST?

A large majority of the respondents reported being concerned to some degree about having their identity, as a priest, become known to gay lay peers. Twenty-eight respondents (56%) expressed an unequivocal concern. These concerns ranged from uneasiness about possible scandal to lay persons to difficulties forming relationships.

> I feel uneasy when a gay layman finds out I'm a priest when I am out in a cruising situation. I don't want to make the church or my religion appear bad to others who do no understand the complex situation I'm trying to negotiate.

> In some respects it has been more difficult for me to 'come out' as a priest in the gay community than it was to come out as gay. I still have some concern about this with sexual partners on first meeting, but primarily in terms of whether or not they will be able to deal with it.

> I found that most gay laypersons tend to maintain a certain distance as regards a gay relationship with a priest.

Twenty respondents (40%) indicated more openness about their priestly identity but nonetheless specified caution depending on a certain degree of supportiveness and confidentiality.

> I am slow to reveal that I am a priest to a layperson until a certain level of trust develops. In several cases so far the reaction of the gay person has been, 'So what if you are a priest, you are also a man and a sexual man.' I have felt very affirmed by this acceptance as a person and not simply as a cleric.

> I have had some good experiences as well as bad. The risk is always there. However, the need for companionship outweighs the risk most of the time.

I don't mind; if they keep their mouth shut.

Only two respondents (4%) gave answers suggesting either no problem in revealing their priestly identity or a substantial degree of comfort doing so.

I have no concern in revealing myself as a priest in social settings. In professional settings I prefer to keep my personal life to myself.

I am becoming more and more comfortable with gay lay people knowing I am a priest.

Question 23:

HAVE YOU EVER EXPERIENCED HOSTILITY OR OPPRESSION FROM YOUR GAY LAY PEERS WHO HAVE COME TO KNOW THAT YOU ARE A PRIEST?

Thirty respondents (60%) reported never experiencing hostility or oppression from gay lay peers because of their priestly identity. As with question 21, many were quick to add that the absence of negativity was the result of keeping their vocational identity hidden or exercising caution about those to whom they disclose their identity.

I have never experienced any hostility, but then again I'm 'out' as a priest to very few.

Just three others know about my priesthood. All have been supportive. The risk has to be minimal before I even consider disclosure.

Seventeen respondents (34%) indicated some measure of hostility or oppression from gay lay peers. The most frequently cited reasons for this negativity were the gay laypersons' own sexual ambivalence or their adoption of a double standard in relation to the respondents.

Yes I have. I can safely say, however, that the majority of those who would want to control my sexuality are those who are afraid of their own.

The hostility that I have experienced from gay peers has generally to do with their lack of appreciation of the gift of sexuality. If they saw their sexuality as a healthy and wholesome thing they surely wouldn't be alarmed to learn that their priests and ministers celebrate their gift with them.

When it comes to sexuality, I have experienced a double standard; one for them and one for me.

Some, whether out of fear or occasionally envy, want Father to be 'good' for them, and not 'bad' like them.

Finally, three respondents (6%) gave ambiguous or tangential replies.

I have experienced no more than the stereotypical expectations laid on any cleric.

Question 24:

DO YOU FEAR OPEN ASSOCIATION WITH THE GAY COMMUNITY?

Thirty-two respondents (64%) indicated having no fear of open association with the gay community. Some of these suggested that the gay community was the only real community they have.

I know that I would just wither and die if I didn't have the 'free-flow' association I have with the gay community. The fellowship I feel through my sexuality is much stronger than the fellowship I feel through my religious ties.

I don't fear association with the gay community because that is
the only real community I have. The church is the oppressor; the
gay community is often my only support.

Eighteen respondents (36%) reported some degree of fear or caution.
Confidentiality was a frequently cited reason.

If I could be sure the gay people I associate with could respect
the confidentiality I need, the fear I have would be diminished.

I just don't trust the gay community.

I am cautious but I do not hide.

Others in this same group indicated a variety of reasons, such as fear of
disappointing straight friends or fear of the sexual temptation present in the gay
community.

I am certainly not ashamed of my involvement with the gay
community as a minister. I do not see any danger in this type of
involvement. However, I fear the temptation that I experience
when I am around attractive gay men. I fear being unfaithful to
my vows.

I don't want to hurt my straight friends, particularly the women
who fantasize about me.

Question 25:

DO YOU FEAR BLACKMAIL?

Forty-three respondents (86%) reported no fear of blackmail. The remaining
seven (14%) felt that there was reason for fear. Although most respondents replied
to this question with a simple "yes" or "no", a few elaborated.

My family has a great deal of money and I would use every cent of it to sue to the hilt anyone who tried to blackmail me. This is America not Medieval Europe or Nazi Germany. As a citizen I have rights and should never have to live fear.

I used to fear blackmail but no longer. Yet I do not know how I would react if the occasion ever arose.

Question 26:

ARE YOU ACTIVE IN THE GAY COMMUNITY POLITICALLY? MINISTERIALLY? SOCIALLY?

All respondents reported being active in one or more of the suggested areas of possible activity. The majority of the respondents indicated being active in all three areas. Thirty-one respondents (62%) reported being active politically, forty (80%) ministerially, and thirty-nine (78%) socially. Few elaborated on their simple "yes" or "no" responses to the three suggested areas, but those who did focused on personal and communal needs for such activity.

I always vote for gay causes. Likewise, I would always be willing to counsel a gay priest or layperson to help him adjust as a human and as a Christian.

I am active in Dignity — as a member, minister and counselor. I socialize with individuals beyond Dignity events. I am beginning to become active politically. There is a tremendous need being fulfilled here.

It pains me greatly that I cannot be more active politically even though I see a great need for such activity. I would risk confrontation with my bishop who has absolutely forbidden such activism.

One respondent indicated only marginal social activity.

I do my socializing with other gays in cities other than the one that I work in.

Section 4
CONFLICTS IN SEXUAL BEHAVIOR

Question 27:

DOES YOUR BEING A PRIEST ENHANCE OR DETRACT FROM YOUR SEXUALITY?

Eighteen respondents (36%) felt that their priesthood enhanced their sexuality, fifteen (30%) felt that it detracted from their sexuality, and seventeen (34%) felt that it enhanced in some ways and detracted in others. It should be borne in mind that sexuality, in many of these responses, does not necessarily refer to overt genitality though in many cases it clearly does.

The eighteen who felt that priesthood enhanced their sexuality gave similar reasons. In most cases the emphasis is on the ways in which priesthood and sexuality complement and enrich one another in the whole personality.

> My sexuality is me. My priesthood is me. They need not be separated. I used to think of my gay sexuality as if it were a stereo component that could be plugged in or taken out; but I have learned to integrate my priesthood and my sexuality into my personhood.

> Being a priest does not restrict my sexuality. My priesthood enriches my life and my whole self. That is what I share with another. It is a gift.

> Being a priest has enabled me to discover and use my personal gifts and talents that have enriched me as a person, and thereby enhanced my sexuality.

I think it enhances it by making it possible for me to integrate sexuality and spirituality.

My sexuality is enhanced because I am more ready to put sexuality into the context of prayer and worship for myself and for those who see me as a teacher and leader.

One respondent in this group offered that his priesthood was enhanced because it enabled him to escape the stereotypes of heterosexual masculinity.

It enhances my sexuality by separating my masculinity from the heterosexual stereotypes of genital sexuality.

The fifteen respondents who indicated that their priesthood detracted from their sexuality gave as the most common reason the unrealistic expectations surrounding the profession.

Priesthood detracts from my sexuality. It involves a lot of baggage guilt, repression, suppression, fear, social pressure, and just unreal expectations.

In my experience thus far, it is only rarely that someone can relate to me just as another person without having the fact of my priesthood overshadow the relationship. As a result, I resent the expectations that have been attached to priesthood; I feel like a marked man and I wish I could be freed.

Other respondents in this group indicated that their priesthood in various ways diminished their ability to accept or enjoy their sexuality.

I have allowed my priesthood to be a denial of my sexuality.

It doesn't enhance it in any way that I can see. It detracts from acting sexually in a relaxed way, the way I would like to.

> Priestly celibacy in general seems to detract from my sexuality
> because of the loneliness that comes from having so little outlet
> for my sexual energies.

The seventeen respondents who indicated that priesthood both enhanced and detracted from their sexuality often paired the ability to care and love which their vocation engenders with the lack of opportunity to explore sexual expression.

> Being a priest forces me to look for the meaning of sexuality
> beyond pure genital expression. On the other hand, I have little
> opportunity for sexual expression.

> My priesthood enhances my sexuality in terms of the depth of
> caring; detracts in terms of freedom to act.

Some among this group assessed the situation in a more practical way.

> My being a priest is a definite 'turn-on' for some, for others it
> is a sure 'turn-off'.

Question 28:

DO YOU EVER PRETEND TO BE STRAIGHT? WHEN? WHY? HOW DO YOU FEEL ABOUT IT?

Twenty-nine respondents (58%) reported that they do not pretend to be straight. However, a significant proportion of those who elaborated on their answers specified that when it is presumed they are straight they do nothing that would alter the presumption.

> I have never been asked whether I am gay or straight. The
> presumption is that I am straight. I have never found it necessary
> to make my sexual orientation public. I simply am, or try to be
> myself.

I sometimes do not deny the presumption that I am straight, but I do not pretend to be.

I am conscious of no pretense at all, as the subject of my sexual orientation has never come up.

Since I am able to 'pass' without difficulty, I have not recently felt the need to pretend. Obviously I do not yet feel able to share fully the truth of my situation. This I do regret.

Twelve respondents (24%) indicated that they pretend to be straight in most situations or in all professional situations.

At times I pretend to be straight. I pretend whenever my position would appear to be in jeopardy, or when I feel that people would reject me.

I pretend when I am acting in my professional capacity. I usually feel exhausted afterwards because it takes so much energy.

I pretend when I am with parishioners, but I don't feel that I have to imitate a rough, crude 'macho-man'.

So much of the gay life, the tackiness and bitchiness, is negative and destructive that I prefer to act 'straight' even in the gay scene.

Seven (14%) remarked that they pretend to be straight sometimes or in relation to specific people.

I pretend mostly with women. They interpret my interest and comments as heterosexual.

I always pretend when I am with straight people. I feel phony about it.

I pretend with my married friends. I feel somewhat dishonest.

Two respondents (4%) did not fall into any of the previous categories because of their ambiguous replies.

I do not pretend to be straight, but often I pretend to be naive about sexual experiences in professional settings. I believe it is necessary to play this game at times.

In general I am thought to be straight by my peers. However, in a few instances I have even flaunted my relationship with women so that my straight image would be secure. I am less inclined to act this way now. I am no longer afraid to be seen in the company of gays. This seems to be in direct proportion to my comfortableness with myself as a gay person.

Question 29:

DO YOU HAVE A LOVER?

DO YOU EXPECT THIS RELATIONSHIP TO BE MONOGAMOUS?

Thirteen respondents (26%) reported currently having a lover. Of these, six specified that they expected the relationship to be monogamous.

I am working on one, but I think he feels guilty. I try to understand, but all he does is lay trips on me. Who needs another trip? We have been monogamous; at least I know I have been.

The remaining seven respondents specified a preference for an "open" relationship.

Yes, I have a lover. We met in a local gay bar over three and a half years ago. We have lived together for two and a half. Both my lover and I have agreed to an open relationship, with an expectation of honest communication between us.

I have a lover of two years. Our arrangement works out beautifully for both of us. The monogamy that we experience is of the heart and mind not of the genitals.

Yes, we met in June. Our understanding of the relationship is such that we are free to determine how sexual expression fits into other friendships in our lives. If either of us chooses to sexualize a friendship outside our primary relationship with each other, I don't think that it would unbalance our relationship.

Question 30:

IF YOU DON'T HAVE A LOVER, WOULD YOU WANT ONE? WHY? WOULD YOU EXPECT THIS RELATIONSHP TO BE MONOGAMOUS?

Thirty-seven respondents (74%) reported currently not having a lover. Twenty-five of these remarked that they would like to have a lover. Twelve indicated no interest in pursuing such a relationship.

Of the twenty-five respondents who would like to have a lover, thirteen indicated that they would expect the relationship to be monogamous.

Right now, more than anything else, I would like to have a lover. I feel a deep need for this. I am very much alone and unfulfilled without one. I would expect, even demand, the relationship to be monogamous.

The support and closeness and on-going presence appear very attractive. I would hope the relationship would be sexually exclusive while it lasted.

I think that my own capability to love and be loved would be best realized in a loving relationship with another man. I would want to live in this relationship monogamously.

Yes, it is a bit awkward for me to admit, I would like to have a lover. I have paid money for anonymous sex and I have close friends who exclude sex from the relationship. The one thing that I have a strong need for is a close friend who includes sex as an expression of the relationship. I am sure that I would want it to be monogamous.

Twelve respondents who remarked that they would like a lover indicated that monogamy would not be imperative.

Yes, I am actively looking for a lover. I need a significant other in my life. This is a deep psychological need for me. I would never expect a lover to be monogamous.

There is something very enlivening in having a person I can share my life with. There is a deep desire in me for such a person. I would not expect our relationship to be automatically monogamous.

I think I would like a friend where there is a certain sexual aura (perhaps even genital expression). Monogamy for me, but not necessarily for my partner.

The twelve respondents who indicated no interest in having a lover gave as reasons: traditional celibacy, commitment to ministry, or fear of the consequences of such a relationship.

I no longer seek a lover because it is incompatible with my understanding of celibacy.

Since my work comes first and that alone consumes all of my time, I don't see how I could have a lover at this time and do justice to the relationship.

I don't know about a lover. I would fear what it might do to both of us; my priesthood and his relationship to God.

As a summary, the Attitude Inventory concluded with a series of four questions. These were designed to complete the picture of attitudes established by the previous thirty questions.

Question 31:

DO YOU THINK IT IS EASY BEING GAY TODAY?

The majority of the respondents, forty (80%), felt that being gay today was not easy. The reasons given were nearly as diverse as the replies themselves.

> It is harder now than ever. Because the achievements made by the gay community have lulled most of us into a sense of complacency. We can't stop now.

> Being gay is five times as difficult as being straight; if you are a Catholic multiply that by five more; if you are a priest multiply by five more times.

> It is hard to live two lives — one with gay friends, another with everyone else.

> Are you kidding? Even in a place like San Francisco, it is very hard. There are too many expectations, prejudicial stereotypes, not to mention the societal oppression.

> I think it is a great burden that will be lifted from me only at death.

The remaining ten respondents (20%) felt it was easy or easier being gay today.

> It is easier to make sexual contacts today. It is easier to be accepted as being gay today.

> I am so envious of gays today. At least they have an evident option. In my youth I didn't even know there was an option.

Question 32:

DO YOU THINK IT IS EASY BEING A PRIEST TODAY?

The resounding majority of the respondents, forty-seven (94%), felt that being a priest, today is not at all easy. Most of the comments echoed sentiments expressed elsewhere in this survey.

> In many ways the church is an oppressive institution. Other institutions are too, but at least they allow their members to have a personal life where one can find self-expression and support. It seems that the priesthood demands everything from a man and at the same time offers little in the way of support.

> Definitely not! It is much more acceptable to leave the priesthood and it is much less commendable to enter. A priest today needs more personal conviction and strong personal values. The 'system' doesn't carry him like before.

> My ministry is challenging, but the priestly lifestyle is underdeveloped and not very humanly growthful.

Three respondents felt it was relatively easy being a priest today.

> Yes; too easy. There are no concrete challenges or rewards.

> Only if you don't take yourself too seriously. I enjoy the, ministry in its ups and downs.

> It is easier to be a priest today than in the past. I am very grateful that I am living now in a time with much more theological and social openness within the church. The narrow stereotypical expectations of society in general toward the priesthood are declining.

Question 33:

WHAT DO YOU THINK ARE THE MOST IMPORTANT CHANGES THAT HAVE TO BE MADE, BY GAYS OR STRAIGHT SOCIETY OR BOTH, TO IMPROVE GAY LIFE?

To facilitate the respondent in his reply to this question, seven general categories of concern were listed. The respondent was asked to affirm those statements that he felt would bring about the desired effect —the improvement of gay life.

The two categories most often affirmed by the respondents dealt with the need for education. Forty-seven respondents (94%) affirmed the statement: "Educate the people about the true nature of homosexuality." And thirty-seven respondents (74%) affirmed the statement: "Break down religious taboos."

On the other hand, the categories least frequently affirmed by the respondents were those dealing with upholding traditional mores. Only eight respondents (16%) affirmed this statement: "Gay people should behave better in public." And just four respondents (8%) affirmed the statement: "Place less emphasis on sex / adhere to traditional mores." (The reader is reminded that a complete statistical breakdown of the replies to this and all the questions follows at the end of this chapter.)

Question 34:

ARE YOU HAPPY?

The Attitude Inventory concluded with this question. The respondents had one final opportunity to voice their feelings in a general way. The majority of the respondents, thirty-seven (74%), reported that they were "happy" with their lives.

> Now that I have accepted my gayness and have integrated that with my priesthood and my own psychological state, I would definitely answer yes. The only thing that could improve is that I would like to discover a lover.

> As I continue to see myself totally and accept myself for who I am, I work through the pain. I am emerging as a much happier person.

Very happy! I went through hell to get here. I ain't perfect yet, but I am willing to keep working at it.

Yes, I have a network of warm and supportive friends. I enjoy my work enormously. I find life interesting and rewarding. I think that I am deeply blessed (and blessed in being gay).

Six of the respondents (12%) were categorized as "somewhat happy."

Yes basically. However, I am surprised at how much anger and hostility toward the Church I still have in me. I resent the years that I have spent in a kind of 'foster childhood', a lifestyle that encouraged a total lack of responsibility for myself.

The remaining seven respondents (14%) reported they were less than content with their lives. Four respondents were categorized as "somewhat unhappy."

I am a romantic turned realist (or cynic). I am satisfied with myself and my life. Happy — what does that mean?

I could be much happier with a lover.

I don't know. I am not miserable, but there are a few things that keep me from being happy such as celibacy, ignorance of others about my gayness, misunderstandings I have with people in my community. I guess my faith keeps me going through it all.

Three respondents reported being "unhappy."

I am not at all happy. I think this is because of many personal problems, not necessarily because I am gay.

No, I don't. I'm tired of all life's hassles, tired of my private bar life, tired of my closeted existence.

ATTITUDE INVENTORY QUESTIONNAIRE WITH STATISTICAL BREAKDOWN OF REPLIES

1) IN WHAT STATE DO YOU RESIDE?

California	21	Michigan	1
Idaho	3	Minnesota	1
Illinois	4	New Jersey	2
Iowa	1	New York	3
Massachusetts	7	Pennsylvania	5
Washington	2		

2) AT WHAT GRADE LEVEL DID YOU ENTER SEMINARY?

High School	16
College	24
Graduate	10

3) HOW OLD WERE YOU WHEN YOU WERE ORDAINED?

24 — 2	25 — 9	26 — 15
27 — 6	28 — 3	29 — 3
30 — 4	31 — 5	32 — 1
41 — 1	42 — 1	

4) **AT WHAT AGE DID YOU BEGIN TO ADMIT TO YOURSELF YOUR GAY ORIENTATION?**

        10-15 — 10   16-20 — 11   21-25 — 4

        26-30 — 17   31-35 — 6   36-40 — 1

        41-45 — 1

5) **AT WHAT AGE DID YOU BEGIN TO COME OUT TO OTHERS?**

        10-15 — 3   16-20 — 9   21-25 — 8

        26-30 — 18   31-35 — 4   36-40 — 5

        41-45 — 1   46-50 — 2

6) **ARE YOU OUT TO YOUR PARENTS? PROVINCIAL? BISHOP?**

        Parents?   Provincial, Bishop?

        Yes — 14   Yes — 18

        No — 36   No — 36

7) **IF YOU WERE AWARE OF YOUR GAY ORIENTATION IN SEMINARY DID YOU EVER LEAVE OR CONSIDER LEAVING BECAUSE OF THAT?**

    Left or thought of leaving   24

    Never thought of leaving   7

    Were not aware of being gay   19

8) **DID YOU EVER HAVE ANY SAME-SEX EXPERIENCES IN SEMINARY? HOW DID YOU FEEL ABOUT THEM THEN? AND NOW?**

Had same-sex experiences in seminary	28
Positive feelings about them then	2
Negative feelings about them then	26
Positive feelings about them now	27
Negative feelings about them now	1
No same-sex experiences	22

9) **WHAT IS YOUR ATTITUDE TOWARD THE CHURCH'S OFFICIAL POSITION REGARDING HOMOSEXUALITY?**

Strongly disagree	46
Mixed	4

10) **WHAT IS YOUR ATTITUDE TOWARD THE CHURCH'S OFFICIAL POSITION REGARDING MANDATORY CELIBACY FOR PRIESTS?**

Strongly disagree	45
Disagree	4
Agree	1

11) HOW DO YOU UNDERSTAND YOUR COMMITMENT TO CELIBACY?

Total sexual abstinence	11
Forego traditional marriage or gay equivalent	11
Regulate sexuality in terms of general Christian values without precluding sexual expression	13
A relationship to God, gospel values, availability	8
Do not know	7

12) ARE YOU EXPERIENCING ANY GUILT IN RECONCILING THE CHURCH'S POSITION ON HOMOSEXUALITY AND CELIBACY AND YOUR OWN LIFESTYLE? IF NOT HOW ARE YOU PUTTING THESE THINGS TOGETHER?

Guilt free	30
Somewhat guilty	7
Guilty	13

13) HOW WOULD YOU CATEGORIZE THE DIFFERENCE BETWEEN THE CHURCH'S ATTITUDE TOWARD SEXUALITY AND THAT OF THE GAY COMMUNITY?

Church's attitude positive / gay community's negative   1

Church's attitude negative / gay community's positive   18

Both church's attitude and gay community's positive   1

Both church's attitude and gay community's negative   26

No judgment   4

14) HAVE YOU READ ANY OF THE FOLLOWING? IF SO PLEASE RATE THEM ACCORDING TO THEIR HELPFULNESS TO YOU.

(1) = Very helpful
(2) = Helpful
(3) = Not very helpful
(4) = Not at all helpful

	1	2	3	4
The Churxh and the Homosexual	25	17	2	
Another Kind of Love	7	13	9	1
Jonathan Loved David	3	3	3	1
Is the Homosexual My Neighbor	8	6		
The Sexual Celibate	15	14	9	2

15) DO YOU LIVE IN COMMUNITY? ARE THERE ANY OTHER MEMBERS OF YOUR COMMUNITY WHO ARE GAY?

Not living in community	19
Living in community	31
With other gay members	16

16) WOULD YOU PREFER TO LIVE ALONE? WHAT WOULD BE THE ADVANTAGES? DISADVANTAGES?

Would want to live alone	30
Would not want to live alone	20

17) ARE THERE ANY INTIMACY NEEDS THAT YOU EXPERIENCE THAT ARE NOT BEING MET BY YOUR PRIESTLY OR RELIGIOUS LIFESTYLE?

Needs not being met	44
Needs generally being met	6

18) DO YOU ENVY THE FREEDOM OF GAY LAYMEN? HOW WOULD YOU DESCRIBE THIS FREEDOM - POLITICAL, PSYCHOLOGICAL, SEXUAL?

Envious of the freedom	18
Not envious of the freedom	22
Mixed reactions	10

19) DO YOU CONSIDER YOUR CELIBATE LIFESTYLE TO BE A FREE-ING EXPERIENCE - POLITICALLY, PSYCHOLOGICALLY, SEXUALLY, SPIRITUALLY, ETC.?

Celibacy a freeing experience	20
Celibacy not a freeing experience	18
Mixed reactions	12

20) DOES IT CONCERN YOU THAT YOUR FELLOW PRIESTS OR RELI-GIOUS MIGHT COME TO KNOW THAT YOU ARE GAY?

Unequivocal concern	26
Mixed reactions	24

21) HAVE YOU EVER EXPERIENCED HOSTILITY OR OPPRESSION FROM YOUR RELIGIOUS PEERS OR SUPERIORS WHO HAVE COME TO KNOW THAT YOU ARE GAY?

No hostility or oppression	30
Some measure of hostility or oppression	15
Ambiguous	5

22) DOES IT CONCERN YOU THAT A GAY LAY PERSON MIGHT COME TO KNOW THAT YOU ARE A PRIEST?

Unequivocal concern	28
Somewhat concerned	20
Little to no concern	2

23) HAVE YOU EVER EXPERIENCED HOSTILITY OR OPPRESSION FROM YOUR GAY LAY PEERS WHO HAVE COME TO KNOW THAT YOU ARE A PRIEST?

No hostility or oppression	30
Some measure of hostility or oppression	17
Ambiguous	3

24) DO YOU FEAR OPEN ASSOCIATION WITH THE GAY COMMUNITY?

No fear	32
Some degree of fear	18

25) DO YOU FEAR BLACKMAIL?

No — 43   Yes — 7

26) ARE YOU ACTIVE IN THE GAY COMMUNITY, POLITICALLY, MINISTERIALLY, SOCIALLY?

	Yes	No
Politically	31	19
Ministerially	40	10
Socially	39	11

27) DOES YOUR BEING A PRIEST ENHANCE OR DETRACT FROM YOUR SEXUALITY? IN WHAT WAY?

Enhances	18
Detracts	15
Both	17

28) DO YOU EVER. PRETEND TO BE STRAIGHT? WHEN? WHY? HOW DO YOU FEEL ABOUT IT?

Do not pretend	29
Pretend in most situations	12
Pretend sometimes	7
Ambiguous	2

29) DO YOU HAVE A LOVER? DO YOU EXPECT THIS RELATIONSHIP TO BE MONOGAMOUS?

Do have a lover	13
Monogamous	6
Non-monogamous	7

30) IF YOU DON'T HAVE A LOVER WOULD YOU WANT ONE? WHY? WOULD YOU EXPECT THIS RELATIONSHIP TO BE MONOGAMOUS?

Not interested in a lover	12
Interested in a lover	25
Monogamous	13
Non-monogamous	12

31) DO YOU THINK IT IS EASY BEING GAY TODAY?

No — 40   Yes — 10

32) DO YOU THINK IT IS EASY BEING A PRIEST TODAY?

No — 47   Yes — 3

33) WHAT DO YOU THINK ARE THE MOST IMPORTANT CHANGES THAT HAVE TO BE MADE, BY GAYS OR THE STRAIGHT COM-MUNITY OR BOTH, TO IMPROVE GAY LIFE?

a) Educate people about the true nature of homosexuality   47

b) Basic changes would have to take place in the social climate   33

c) Political action should be taken   31

d) Place less emphasis on sex / adhere to traditional mores   4

e) Gay people should endeavor to improve themselves   12

f) Gay people should behave better in public   8

g) Break down religious taboos   37

34) ARE YOU HAPPY?

Happy   37

Somewhat happy   6

Somewhat unhappy   4

Unhappy   3

CHAPTER 5

Summary

The composite picture of the sexual behaviors of this sample of fifty gay priests reveals them to be sexually active. Forty-nine respondents are masturbating at a mean frequency nearly three times that reported by Kinsey in *Sexual Behavior in The Human* Male. (1)

Fourteen respondents report a history of heterosexual coitus. Eight respondents report that this contact occurred after ordination; no one reports an occurrence within the past year.

Forty-eight respondents report a twice-a-week mean frequency of same-sex contact. The remaining two respondents are currently abstaining from same-sex contact. Interestingly enough, this sample has nearly five times the number of respondents reporting 500 or more total partners than Kinsey's sample.

Overall, the respondents report enjoying their sexual activity while experiencing a minimum of sex-related guilt.

It was learned that 50% of the respondents had their first post-pubertal same-sex contact before entering the seminary; another 26% had their first experience during their seminary years.

The majority of the respondents, 62%, self-identified as gay before they were ordained, but only 46% had shared that identity with another person by that same time.

The respondents were almost unanimous in their rejection of official church positions regarding homosexuality and mandatory celibacy for priests. At the same time, nearly half of the respondents still experience some guilt because their lives do not reflect ecclesiastical expectations.

All but six report being unfulfilled in terms of intimacy needs by their priestly or religious lifestyle. Coupled with this is the recurring theme, appearing throughout the responses, of a desire for a lover by the majority of those who are currently without one. Only thirteen respondents report having a lover at this time.

The questions dealing with aspects of the priests' dual identity were particularly revealing of the dissonance in their lives. The amount of discrimination experienced by the respondents for being gay in the church or for being a priest in the gay community is in direct proportion to the degree the priests are "out" to either group. Thus, when the majority of respondents report that they have not experienced hostility or oppression from either the gay community or the church, it is usually because they are still "closeted." The path most frequently taken by the respondents in this regard is not to identify as gay in the church or as a priest in the gay community. This conflict is the source of much personal anguish and disappointment for the respondents.

This study reveals a group of highly motivated men, both professionally and sexually. The respondents seek integration and fulfillment in their personal lives as well as in their work, but they are often frustrated by what they report to be stifling role expectations put upon them by both the church and the gay community. While they are quick to criticize the shortcomings of both the church and the gay community, they report a sense of loyalty to and affection for both. It is as if both communities demand an exclusive commitment, one that would have them disown an integral part of their identity. This dissonance is reinforced by the respondents' refusal to abdicate to either demand.

They are engaged in a process of questioning moral theology as well as reinterpreting traditional expectations of the celibate lifestyle in an effort to minimize the dissonance. Unfortunately, this process has been going on in secret. The fear of disclosure and possible reprisals has made this struggle a lonely one.

Further Research

Further research in this area could follow any number of paths. Two possible modalities are suggested here.

1) **A Longitudinal Study:** Such a study would reveal patterns that develop in the life and sexuality of a gay priest. One major area of interest would be an assessment, over a period of time; of the relationship the gay priest has *vis-à-vis* the Church and *vis-à-vis* the gay community.

   Would the conflict of identity inevitably resolve itself by his withdrawing from one or the other community? What affect would the continuing development of theology and the emergence of the gay liberation movement have upon the gay priest?

   What effect does time have on the gay priest's pattern of sexual partnering? If the movement were toward a lover, would the intimacy of that relationship obviate for him the need for priesthood or religious life?

2) **Comparative Study:** Comparing a group of sexually active gay priests with a group of sexually active heterosexual priests would reveal the unique problems faced by both. One major area of interest would be the difference between patterns of sexual partnering for the heterosexual priest compared to the gay priest.

   Does the social stigma attached to homosexuality produce a more tension-filled environment for the gay priest than his heterosexual counterpart? Is there more pressure to leave the active ministry when the possibility of children is involved? What would be the difference in attitudes voiced by each group in light of their dual loyalties?

FOOTNOTES

Chapter 1

1 Kosnik, et al., 1977, p. 304

2 Boswell, 1980, p. 362

3 Bailey, 1975, p. 83

4 Boswell, 1980, p. 328

5 Curran, 1972, p. 217

6 McNeill, 1976, p. 39

7 Ibid., p. 46

8 Ibid., p. 96

9 Ibid., p. 129

10 Ibid., p. 189

11 Kosnik, 1977, pp. 304-305

12 Mt. 19:12

13 1 Cor. 7:27-28

14 Dehaye, 1967, pp. 369-370

15 Ibid., p. 371

16 Goergen, 1974, p. 225

17 Kosnik, 1977, p. 210

Chapter 3

1 Kinsey, 1948, p. 187.,

2 Gebhard, 1979, p. 188

3 Kinsey, 1948, p. 169

4 Ibid., p. 340

5 Gebhard, 1979, p. 440

6 Ibid., p. 496

7 Ibid., p. 497

8 Ibid., p. 511

9 Ibid., pp. 614-615

10 Ibid., pp. 88-96

11 Ibid., p. 70

12 Ibid., p. 71

13 Ibid., p. 72

14 Ibid., pp. 157-169

15 Ibid., p. 201

16 Ibid., pp. 455-460

17 Ibid., p. 493

18 Ibid., pp. 527-544

19 Ibid., p. 520

20 Ibid., p. 518

21 Ibid., p. 610

22 Ibid., p. 611

Chapter 5

1 Kinsey, 1948, p. 340

BIBLIOGRAPHY

Baily, D.S. *Homosexuality and the Western Christian Tradition.* London: Archon Books, 1975.

Boswell, J. *Christianity, Social Tolerance, and Homosexuality.* Chicago: University of Chicago Press, 1980.

Curran, C. *Catholic Moral Theology in Dialogue.* Notre Dame, IN.: Fides Press, 1972.

Delhaye, P. "History of Celibacy," *The Catholic Encyclopedia*, Vol. 3. New York: McGraw-Hill, 1967.

Gebhard, P.; Johnson, A. *The Kinsey Data: Marginal Tabulations of the 1938 - 1963 Interviews Conducted Ia the Institute for Sex Research.* Philadelphia: W.B. Saunders Co., 1979.

Goergen O.P., D. *The Sexual Celibate.* New York: Seabury Press, 1974.

Horner, T. *Jonathan Loved David, Homosexuality in Biblical Times.* Philadelphia: The Westminster Press, 1978.

Kinsey, A.; Pomeroy, W.; Martin, C. *Sexual Behavior in the Human Male.* Philadelphia: W.B. Saunders Co., 1948.

Kosnik, A.; Carroll, W.; Cunningham, A.; Modras, R.; Schulte, J. *Human Sexuality New Directions in American Catholic Thought*. New York: Paulist Press, 1977.

McNeill S.J., J. *The Church and the Homosexual*. Kansas City: Sheed Andrews & McMeel, 1976.

The New American Bible. New York: Benziger, 1970.

Scanzoni, L., Ramey-Mollenkott, V. *Is the Homosexual My Neighbor? Another Christian View*. San Francisco: Harper & Row, 1978.

Woods O.P., R. Another Kind of Love, Homosexuality and Spirituality. Chicago: Thomas Moore Press, 1977.

ABOUT THE AUTHOR

Richard Wagner, Ph.D., ACS - Psychotherapist, Clinical Sexologist in private practice for over 30 years.

He is the only Catholic priest in the world with a doctorate in Human Sexuality. His practice has included a special outreach to survivors of clergy sex abuse and has had many opportunities to work with clergy offenders. He is available as an advocate for clergy abuse survivors - as a consultant, expert witness and/or therapist.

He is currently working on a follow-up book detailing the sexual molestation he endured at the hands of his Oblate superior while a 14-year-old seminarian in Southern Illinois. How all subsequent religious superiors he told about these incidences did nothing about it. The book will investigate the psychological and emotional trauma of clergy sex abuse and its impact on the psychosexual development of abuse victims.

Richard designs, develops and produces long and short-term seminars and workshops for healing and helping professionals including religious leaders.

He has provided individual therapy and facilitated support groups for gay clergy of numerous denominations.

He's also been involved in many other sex education and sexual enrichment projects. He's been writing an online sex advice column for over 15 years. His column and weekly podcasts can be found at: drdicksexadvice.com. He also contributes to several other websites as a guest columnist.

He is developing a new site, gaycatholicpriests.org, which is a clearinghouse for news and information about gay clergy worldwide. A social media component, where individuals will be able to create profiles, share their stories and find support, will follow.

He often writes and speaks in the public forum on policy issues related to religion, human sexuality, aging and death and dying. He has been a keynote speaker and/or presenter at numerous conventions and symposia.